LIFE CAN BE DIFFERENT: CONCEPTION

Establishing a culture
to develop our collective human spirit,
incorporating the earth plane and spirit world

BY

EMMANUEL VAN DER MEULEN

Life Can Be Different: CONCEPTION
ISBN-13: 978-1-920257-00-2 (First paperback edition)
ISBN-13: 978-1-920257-01-9 (First eBook edition)
ISBN-13: 978-1-920257-02-6 (First audio book downloadable MP3 edition)
ISBN-13: 978-1-920257-03-3 (First audio book CD MP3 edition)
ISBN-13: 978-1-920257-04-0 (First audio book CD set edition)
ISBN-13: 978-1-920257-05-7 (First audio book DVD set edition)

Printed in the United States of America and in the United Kingdom

Published by lifecanbedifferent.com
2007

LIFE CAN BE DIFFERENT: CONCEPTION

Establishing a culture to develop our

collective human spirit, incorporating

the earth plane and spirit world

BY

EMMANUEL VAN DER MEULEN

TABLE OF CONTENTS

DEDICATION

To Sergio Salotto, who supported me
until I saw the beginning of my life's path.

CREDITS

Editing by Arlene W. Robinson (BettyBoopWrites@aol.com)

Read by Marc Cashman (www.cashmancommercials.com)

Images designed by Paula Horn

Tony Parsons: Digital and animated logo design from original illustration (www.tonyparsons.com)

Sam Wall: Digital retouching of illustrations, book, audio book and eBook cover designs, audio book CD labels, audio book inserts (www.samwall.com)

Book design and composition by Kenneth C. Benson, Pegasus Type, Inc. (www.pegtype.com)

ACKNOWLEDGEMENTS

Acknowledgements go to a variety of sources.

The people I acknowledge below, albeit their support for me, should not necessarily be understood or seen as supporting my material, especially in light of the material being contrary to society's standards and norms.

To all people who stood by me or assisted in some way during my much extended growth period and/or who assisted with developing the website, I acknowledge them as follows:

My ex-wife *Truida Zwarts*, and my children, *Pierre van der Meulen*, *Tania van der Meulen* and *Estelle le Roux*, were there in the beginning and provided support when I was lost in my own wilderness.

Sergio Salotto stood by me, and, with his guidance, I got out of my wilderness. I cannot say for sure, but I doubt I would ever have gotten out without his guidance. And don't think for one minute that it was easy or that I made it easy for him. Yet he persevered, and I made it out. My acquaintance with him started out professionally and then we became friends, in fact very good friends. Professionally, he is a life-awareness coach. He was the first person ever whom I considered a genuine person, something I was looking for all my life without knowing it. He is it, the real thing.

Coleen Lotter gave me a few good blows just to shock me back to reality.

Thomas Aagaard Larsen helped program the website. No one else was really up to assisting me with the programming; Thomas came through.

Paula Horn stood by me through thick and thin in my private life and while developing the website, and assisted with usability and functionality testing. She became a very good friend at a time when I doubted that what I had to say would be useful. Paula also designed the illustrations. Because of her intimate understanding of me and what I wanted to say, she was able to capture those things in the illustrations.

LIFE CAN BE DIFFERENT: CONCEPTION

Sue du Randt introduced me to the spirit guides who have been there all along, guiding me along my path.

Organization Representatives

I do freelance computer work, and the company in South Africa where I work has given me great leeway regarding working hours and shorter workweeks, and allowed me to take long breaks to develop the website. It seems that no matter what, the people I report/ed to were always there for me, in particular two people: *Abri de Vries* and *Clyde Oldham*. Clyde also gave me technical assistance from time to time, always in an enthusiastic way.

Spirit Guides and Channels

Theresa Walstra introduced me to *Cynthia*, who I listened to with keen ears as she gave me comforting information from the spirit world and my parents, at a time when I was considering placing my savings on the line to develop the accompanying website by taking off work and thus forfeiting any income. Cynthia, as channeled by Theresa, also trained me to channel. I wasn't really interested in the path she was on, but in a few development circle sittings, I realized I was able to communicate with the spirit world. While not interested in that specifically—I wanted to communicate directly with the spirit guides who were already in my life to create the togetherness I mentioned before—the few developmental lessons with Cynthia channeled by Theresa got me out of the blocks.

White Wolf is channeled by me, enabled originally with the guidance of Sue (living soul) and Cynthia (soul in the spirit world). White Wolf has seemingly been with me for my whole life. It seems we have rubbed off on each other, or he has rubbed off on me. Regardless, this spirit guide is awesome. Possibly all spirit guides are awesome—although I'm not sure whether they aspire to such words as "awesome"—yet this is the main spirit guide of those with which I've had such intimate dealings. He has certainly widened my horizons, and what I like in particular is the way he goes about communicating with me. I can add that he is a no-nonsense soul who provides me with guidance therapy for my own life as well as guidance related to providing a blueprint for inner peace. He also gives me guidance for creating togetherness among independent individual living souls, those who have already passed away, and other souls in the spirit world.

Of late, I have come to recognize different spirit guides with White Wolf, and now refer to them collectively as White Wolf & Co. The following are all seemingly part of the group of behind-the-scenes souls who provide me with guidance.

John, the gatekeeper, appears to me as a Sumo wrestler and provides protection when we (White Wolf & Co. and I) and other souls in the spirit world communicate.

Joan appears to me as a no-nonsense teacher and provides me with planning and expediting guidance.

David appears to me as a flying male fairy and provides me with lightness of being and expediting guidance.

In the following pages, you will meet these spirits by reading their introductions as channeled and written by me. By reading their words, you will understand why their involvement in my life was and is so important, and will also know *how* their messages to you *can* help you on your journey to understanding the statements in the rest of the book.

Content Layout

The following content is laid out in four main sections: *Introduction*, *Conception*, *Spirit Guides* and *Appendices*. These sections are then broken down into group-related material.

The "Introduction" section, which you are reading now, is not the typical introduction. It does introduce the book's intent and potential for inspiration to the reader. Yet you will also meet some interesting individuals that you will meet again, both in the book and the website. For that reason, the Foreword and Preface should not be skipped, or the "About Us" section. The aforementioned parts are channeled from White Wolf & Co. by me. However, the most can be gained by reading all of the Introduction section.

From there, the Conception section follows, and is broken into four parts:

- Core Missing
- Manifesting Without Core
- Why It Is Going Awry
- Standing Up to Regain Core

This section is the crux of the book and website.

The first part, "Core Missing," elaborates that for us to be ourselves, an important part of ourselves will need to be uncovered.

The second part, "Manifesting Without Core," covers what is happening to us as individuals and the collective effect on our species and everything else around us as a consequence of manifesting without our core.

In what follows, "Why It Is Going Awry," the reader observes why the dynamic of us manifesting without core came about, and why we are perpetuating it.

The fourth and final part, "Standing up To Regain Core," looks at what it takes and the difficulties we encounter when we are regaining our core and walking our life down our own path. Thus, this section explains the difficulties that would likely arise when manifesting ourselves.

The "Spirit Guides" section is more of what I channeled from the spirit guides that guide me—White Wolf, Joan, John and David, collectively referred to as White Wolf & Co. Each spirit guide shares their contribution in support of the reader when making the journey of manifesting their self by walking his or her own path. Much can be gained from reading this section in its entirety as the spirit guides provide nuggets of wisdom.

"Afterword: Life can be Different" follows in closing and precedes the Appendices.

The Appendices contain supportive pieces that address specific dynamics described in the rest of the book.

Following the Appendices, you will find "About the Website." This section contains information about the website, lifecanbedifferent. com, like subscription options and where possible updates to material in this book can be found. The Bibliography section follows, which covers books and a movie I found helpful during my own journey. Finally, at the end of the book you will find an expanded table of contents to aid you should you want to return to a certain section of the book.

In summary, the book and accompanying website is laid out to evolve the message to the reader in a way best read from cover to cover. Furthermore, the material is unlikely to go out of date any time soon, and since it is also intended as a reference, the reader would be well served to read and reread any piece or pieces that are of interest or that present obstacles.

PART ONE

INTRODUCTION

About Us

As founder, I developed this book and lifecanbedifferent.com, its accompanying website, to reach anyone in search of their meaning while joining together independent, individual souls, here on Earth and in the spirit world. The intent is to make all readers aware that our species can be turned from where we are headed to a path where we can live with inner peace and in harmony with ourselves, others and anything on this and any other planet. Even more, the book and website can give readers and viewers the opportunity to contribute their individuality to others, both live souls and those in the spirit world. The combined efforts of the group: bidirectional sharing, "training," and exposure of and to one another, are intended to develop the maturity of our collective human spirit, incorporating the earth plane and spirit world.

At first, certain material will be available to viewers of the website, channeled from the spirit guides you will meet in this book and written by me. This will be expanded over time as like-minded souls, both living and in the spirit world, are identified and invited to share further material, directly or channeled, about their experiences and individual specialty.

Almost certainly, very few souls will participate in this togetherness, simply because it seems that few souls, alive or in the spirit world, address causes; most attend only to symptoms. So we will leave addressing symptoms to the masses while our handful of souls reaches out and exposes to all other souls the following vital message: that addressing symptoms cannot yield a permanent change, and as such, those symptoms will reoccur later in the same or similar forms. This group of independent souls can be seen as architects creating a blueprint for the implementation of inner peace within each individual, which would, over time, create peace amongst humankind, even if it takes a million years. The result: a once-and-for-all, no-compromise peace plan, starting and ending with each individual, one at a time, for however long it takes.

Emmanuel

FOREWORD

Why Not Just a Regular Life as We Know It?

Walk With Me! (Spirit Guide: White Wolf)

—The White Wolf Call, Channeled by Emmanuel van der Meulen

This is my journey with you. Today, we will explore why I want to walk with you and possibly without knowing it consciously and explicitly, why you might want to walk with me.

You might be thirsty, and I might have water to quench your thirst. If you are not thirsty, then merely stop your journey with me. You are under no obligation. But for those of you who thirst, I might be able to provide water to you. In this way, we are not obligated to one another, but mere companions on a journey.

You might ask what the thirst is about. Well metaphorically, I'm referring to the thirst of your life: what you might be thirsty for in your life. Perhaps you have lived to the age where you feel your life is not what you like it to be, and have become thirsty for something meaningful.

You might be wondering what that "something meaningful" might be. Walk with me, and you will have the opportunity to see what you thirst for.

The journey we will walk together is slow. There is a reason for this. While we go from here to the next point of the journey, our slowness will allow me to get to know you and you to know me. As we learn about each other, we will also learn to trust each other. Soon, if our walk goes well, you might realize that you are on a journey you always wanted to take.

Here are some things you should know about your journey and mine. For one, our travels will take us into places you have never been before now. If you had visited these places before, we most likely would not be on this journey now.

Also, remember that some of the journey might seem familiar to you. You might even say or think, *Déjà vu*, as you earthlings say, because you're sure you've been somewhere or done something just like this before. Don't let that distract you. There is much more to the journey than that.

On our travels, we will walk and talk. We will also walk and play. Our journey is not, and should not, be only about serious things. Actually, the journey is as light or as heavy as you make it.

The journey will happen at your pace, not anyone else's. No one will hurry you. You might want to hurry yourself. But, there is no need for that. Stay calm and enjoy the journey to your fountain.

You will have doubts along the way. When they occur, please remember that these doubts are nothing more than fear of the unknown. No harm will come to you, no matter what you might think or believe. Belief, by the way, is not real or truth. It is only something you think. This thinking originated with you, or with someone else who passed it along to you. Understanding this will actually help quench your thirst. When you encounter something different on your travels and it causes you to doubt one of your beliefs, that doubt shows that the belief might not serve you.

To help you remember this important point, I will write it again here, as Point 1.

> **Point #1:** When you doubt, it is most likely the result of a belief which is not likely real, but was created by you or by someone else.

Now, what if you reach a point in the journey where you want to stop? Perhaps the path will, at some point, seem too steep or uneven, creating doubts within you, and you will want to stop walking. Perhaps, instead, you just need some time to absorb what you have seen. Or, perhaps it will be the entire journey that, at those times, feels too difficult.

If this happens, you can stop the journey and no harm will come to you. Each part of the journey is separate from the others. So, leaving at any time will in no way harm you. Instead, you will have gained some wisdom for the journey of your life—wisdom you can use from that moment on. And perhaps someday, once you see the benefit of the wisdom you gained on your incomplete journey with me, you might want to return and journey with me again. And that will be 100% okay.

This journey is done in such a way that you should enjoy it. If you do begin to feel worried or strained, please recall Point #1 and see the worry or strain for what it is.

Now that I have told you these things about our journey, let's continue.

Water is our physical body's thirst quencher. What can quench our *life's* thirst?

Let's look at this question for a moment and see if we can find the answer. What do you desire most for your life? Is this what you currently have, or have achieved? Or, is what you want most something you take in, like food or water?

If what you desire isn't any of those things, then what is it? Where will you find it? Will you find it somewhere in a shop? Will you find it in another person? When you do find it . . . have you guessed yet? . . . will you find it in yourself?

Let us make this Point 2:

> **Point #2:** You will find whatever you need to quench your life's thirst within yourself.

Okay, now we know where to look for what we desire most—what will quench our life's thirst. Now that we know where to look, how do we go about looking for it?

Before we try to answer that question, let's look at something else: You and I are on this journey because you have arrived at a place in your life you are certain you do not wish to be. Are there any doubts about that?

I would say this is Point 3:

> **Point #3:** You are on this journey with me because you have gotten to a place in your life where you are certain you don't want to be.

Let's explore further, but remember, this journey is also about fun. The journey does not have to be difficult or painful. It can also be about fun while making the journey to where your life's thirst can be quenched.

Is it possible that you have encountered some of the answer before in your life?

That is possible.

So, when you find what you are thirsting for, will it be something new . . . or will it be something you are partly familiar with?

If this does happen—if we recognize what quenches our thirst—what could you say of it? Is it someone else's creation, or is it yours? Where did it come from? What are its origins? Could it be that you had chosen that as your thirst quencher? If you did, then what made you forget about it? Did you indeed forget about what would quench your life's thirst? Or, is it that you developed your thirst quencher during your life but were not consciously aware of what you were doing—that is, creating your thirst quencher?

So, while you have *survived* until now—as declared in Point #3—could you, at some point in your life, have already developed something to help you find where you want to be instead of where you don't want to be? Something that will quench your life's thirst?

If this is true, your desire to take this journey might well be because you are ready to quench your thirst, and is the reason for you becoming thirsty in the first place. Now to Point 4:

> **Point #4:** Right now, you are likely at a breaking or life-altering point, a crossroad where you have developed a life's thirst while living a life that is not your first choice.

Is this, then, the reason you have become thirsty: because you want to start living *your first-choice life*?

Flying Away (Spirit Guide: Joan)

—What Joan Sees, Channeled by Emmanuel van der Meulen

Zipping away into the unknown is not what we like doing. We prefer to go to places where we have been before—places which are familiar to us.

But a whole world lies waiting for us if we are willing to zip away into the unknown. What we'll find in the unknown is up to us. Each person will find something that interests them. And I'm referring to a specific unknown.

I'd like to introduce you to what is possibly known to some people, but likely unknown to most people. So it's like a paradox; it is unknown to you, but the area itself is not an unknown area.

People who explore here are explorers. I suspect we all like exploring. Think of opening a present, the excitement brought to us by the unknown.

If you are willing, please come and explore with us. To explore is fun and exhilarating. And we can go to a place where we can explore all our lives: where we can be on an exploration journey our whole life. Would that not be fun?

But there's a catch. No one can start this exploration without being willing and, as Emmanuel says, without possessing courage and brutal honesty. If you want to explore in this area and you are not willing to forgo certain things that are currently in your frame of reference, unfortunately, you won't be able to take this exploration journey with us. You see, certain things that might exist in your frame of reference today are inhibitors to you exploring your life to the fullest.

If we take an explorer on an ancient boat, faring the seas wherever the seas and the tides take them . . . say they had some superstition or belief that the world was flat. They wouldn't want to just go in a certain direction for too long, because they would anticipate the end of the sea and would expect to fall over the edge at any time. In short, they lack a firm or definite point of reference. They would be inhibited, and their inhibition would stand in the way of their exploration.

So explorers are usually people who go where others don't go, and therefore they get to places where others haven't been.

With our lives, the same things apply. To explore completely, we need to be able to move aside any superstition or points in our frame of reference that hold us back. If you aren't willing to move these aside, it's best you stop exploring.

I hear you thinking, *Which points of reference would I need to be able to move aside?*

The short answer is: every single one. None of the points of reference will serve you, especially the ones that stop you from moving along with us.

I hear you thinking, *Well, how safe is this journey?* Or perhaps you're thinking, *If you do move aside your frame of reference, might you not endanger yourself?*

Okay, I cannot make any assurances to you other than this: Those before you who had the courage to take this exploration journey, and who were able to move aside their frame of reference, found their lives enriched beyond their wildest dreams or expectations. But anywhere along the journey, when the going gets too tough—where your frame of reference is severely questioned, or, as you earthlings put it, is challenged—if you don't have the courage to move along, you'll find yourself wanting to stop. And stop you may. No harm will come to you if you stop. All that might remain is that you are left with anger or a yearning.

The yearning is fairly self-explanatory; you might yearn to continue, but the courage for it might be lacking. Any anger residue you might experience is likely to be from your frame of reference being questioned or challenged, and you might not have the courage to move that point in your frame of reference aside; because then, your life might have a void that's maybe too big, and you might not want to take such a step. In that case, the anger might be from a conflict between your being expected to move the point aside and your un-willingness to do so.

It seems that you want specific examples of points in your frame of reference that might stop you from moving on. Well, religion is one. Due to your religious beliefs that you'd start questioning while on the exploration journey, you might get to a point where you feel that those beliefs are perhaps not really serving you. And seeing that you were forewarned about any points in your frame of reference that might get in your way and would need to be moved out of the way to move forward, when you consider that you'd have to move your religious beliefs out of the way, you're likely not able to . . . because when you move out of the way what you've believed in for so many years, which was an anchor for you, there will be a void. And with what will you fill that void?

Well, the short answer to you is, if you cannot overcome that crossroads, you won't be in a position to fully explore this journey.

Some people do pursue this exploration journey while holding onto their frame of reference, and in particular this point about religion. Because they most probably cannot see that they could, in fact, fill the void left behind when moving that reference point out of the way. So they walk a path with one foot in exploration territory and the other safely in their frame-of-reference territory, and want to explain their experiences from their religion's frame of reference. But, this is not taking the exploration to the fullest; this is taking the exploration only to the point where it doesn't threaten their frame of reference. To me, it seems like when a baby starts walking. While the baby holds onto things, it's not walking freely— its walking exploration is limited to where it can hold on to external objects.

For this exploration journey, best you let go of everything to truly explore. Holding onto anything would merely result in a second-choice existence, as Emmanuel describes in the chapter, "First-Choice Existence Serves Everyone."

For those of you who have the courage to move aside your frame of reference, enjoy this journey. And be aware that from time to time, certain points in your frame of reference will be questioned or challenged. You have been forewarned, and at any of these questions, you might want to opt out. Or you might even want to continue, but the moment might be too big, and you then might want to stop for whatever time it takes to integrate the newly uncovered information into your frame of reference. The time needed might possibly be a day, a week, a month, or whatever time it takes, and only then will you move farther along the journey. Some of you might not be questioned or challenged so severely, and might still find yourself in a position of wanting to stop or needing to integrate newly uncovered information. To each and every one of you, enjoy your journey.

Bon voyage.

Here We Go Again (Spirit Guide: David)

—How David Works, Channeled by Emmanuel van der Meulen

Hello everyone. Emmanuel asked me to provide a piece for the foreword as an opener to readers—preparing them to take in as much of the material that follows as to make an impact.

I'm the guide, that is, spiritual guide, with Emmanuel, and my task is to guide him to do things, an expediter in a sense. My methods are simple. My head is clear on what I do when guiding him. His head, like that of most earthlings', is not clear. Earthlings' heads are always busy with several thoughts and tasks. Instead, it is much simpler to do things when your heads are quieter.

When your heads are quiet your being is quiet; your concentration is deeper. You are operating from a deeper perspective within yourself. When you are busy and your mind is rushing, you are not giving the same depth of attention as when you are quiet within yourself.

Then there is the aspect of fun. If a task is approached from being a busybody and your mind is racing, you have very little opportunity to have fun with what you are doing. To me, it seems you are then rushing around like a scarecrow and merely chasing away birds. This is like—just touching ground here and there. Where is the fun in that? Why not, instead, soar like a bird, quietly and intentionally soaring in the sky and gliding around without flapping your wings all the time, only flapping them now and then and then keeping them still and navigating in the wind, and in that way taking in the experience of the tasks quietly and intentionally?

Keeping still while in flight, and when necessary, adding some energy by flapping your wings, allows you to thus take the flight in your stride. Work, relax and let the relaxing also do some of the work.

When a bird stops flapping its wings, it doesn't stop in midair or fall to the ground. It flies farther with the momentum of the previously exerted energy. And while it is quietly soaring, it can observe the surrounding area of the flight path and take in some of the pleasantries of the flight path. Move along and rest while not flapping but stay in motion, navigating and swerving in the air and turning slowly or quickly as required to maintain the flight.

Now, when you are reading the material supplied here by Emmanuel and us, the spirit guides guiding his life, remember to stop putting in energy and simply soar with the messages in the material. Open yourself up for the material. But when you get tired from the bombardment of the material, give yourself a break and stay quiet with the material and the messages. Read when you are in a quiet space, read when you have time. After reading, glide with what you have read. Give the material time to settle in; don't rush. Stay in a quiet space for the pieces that you'll be reading in a particular reading session, and stay with them for a while after reading them. You might even want to take some notes after the quiet time to reflect on later. You might even want to contact Emmanuel afterward for support with messages when you cannot see what they mean or how they fit into the main scheme of things or into your life.

Be open to the material, which was carefully selected to provide an insight into your life. The material comes from Emmanuel's personal life. Nothing is secondhand information. Rather, it is from his experiences, painstakingly uncovered in his daily life over many years, and with having spilt many tears as he made the discoveries about himself. What Emmanuel is sharing in the messages and in the material came with a lot of heartache and difficulty.

He recently asked himself about the many hours he has gone through and the obstacles he has overcome to get to the bottom of it all, and he concluded that it was a labor of love for himself that he has painstakingly uncovered his life to himself . . . that is, because of his love for his life, he left no stone unturned to get to the bottom of it all, to uncover his life and the meaning of his life. And it has taken courage and honesty beyond normal day-to-day honesty and courage. We, his spirit guides, watch over him and see what he is doing daily, and are aware that it is not easy for earthlings to be so open and honest, and have so much courage to dig so deep into their lives. We feel for him, but we also see how his life has taken on meaning during this uncovering process.

This is also available to you, each person reading this material. But what you require first is a willingness to look—and the courage to be honest with yourself.

Oh, and it does not end there. It takes even more courage to make the life-altering decision to take the next step. And each step leads to another step. The steps never really end; they just keep on coming and coming, and when you think, *Surely this is the end of it all*, another aspect is opened up. You see, you cannot hide from yourself. You cannot stop halfway. Well, you can, but then, it might be better if you don't start your journey. Only start your journey if you are going to have what it takes to go all the way. And it will take everything you have to go all the way.

And while on this journey, remember the bird when it flies. Take energy to move forward some distance, then soar in the sky with that energy and navigate the wind with your wings while resting. Do not stop your flight when resting. Continue your flight, but conserve your energy. Flap your wings when needed, soar when needed, rest during the soaring.

And when you have had enough for one flight, stop. Rest up fully. Then fly further along on your journey, and continue with this process until it is an automatic process.

Do not tire yourself by wanting to take it all in in one go. Take it slowly and set aside good chunks of time so you can fly, soar and take in the surrounding scenery of your flight path. Observe yourself in flight. See what you experience. Feel the pain that you are experiencing. Take time to make notes about your experiences, because you might want to discuss them with Emmanuel at some later stage.

In the event that you do not take in the material so you can assess your life during the first read, reread it and set aside more time with each reread. Withdraw from the usual activities in which you take part. Give yourself every opportunity to get to the heart of the material. Let it count for you.

Enjoy your flight, your own heartache, your realizations, and your rest. Make a feast of the flight. Take it slowly. Don't rush the material. It is deep material. It is difficult material. Every bit of your life up to the point of reading the material was flight at a frantic pace in another direction all together. Be patient with yourself.

Enjoy your flight.

PREFACE

Is This What You Are Looking For? (Spirit Guide: White Wolf)

—*The White Wolf Call, Channeled by Emmanuel van der Meulen*

In this day and age, we are all looking for something. We feel we'll get it from various things outside of ourselves, like shiny cars or big and grand houses. But my question to you is, do those items have a sustained value, or do they eventually, once you are over the initial excitement, move to the background, having served the initial purpose and become boring?

If this is indeed the case, are we maybe looking in the wrong place for the "something" we are looking for? In the accompanying website, Emmanuel shares many of his experiences related to the point of the "something" we are looking for.

If external things do not give this something to us and we consider looking elsewhere, then where might we look? It is already considered clichéd to look inside; and when we do look inside, what is it we're looking for? How do we know what to look for? I suspect that we all know, once we find it, that this is what we've indeed been looking for.

But if we only know what we are looking for once we find it, do we look everywhere? When do we know we've looked enough, or how far it is still to go? Do we at any time in this journey know where we are on the total road to looking for this something?

When you look at what reincarnation teaches, and the karma that you get involved with during different lives, then it becomes even a greater mystery to get to the point of where you'll find what you're looking for—hell, for even lifetimes' worth of looking.

Might there be another route to getting where you're headed? Let's take a boat on the sea. No destination planned, but it has goods to deliver. It merely floats from one place to another, this day going east, that day going west . . . this month, let's go in circles, and so forth. Without a plan, this boat or ship is just not going to get there. Oh, the chances are that it might, maybe in several lifetimes. It might just incidentally stumble onto its destination to deliver its goods. And just maybe those goods are not needed anymore, or they might be stale or outdated.

Could there be a plan? Emmanuel is an explorer, and he found a plan. He'll share this plan with anyone who is interested. But as you'll see from his experiences, without brute honesty and heaps and heaps of courage, it cannot happen.

So to start your journey off, let me introduce you to what Emmanuel is planning with the accompanying website. Through his own life's experiences, with credit to other people he stumbled upon and searched out on your Earth plane, he has unraveled and uncovered what he refers to as spikes in his experiences—where what your soul is craving for shows you, in the form of daydreams and desires, like a movie script, what you'd rather be experiencing.

But let me add immediately that these spikes are interpreted by your frame of reference that exists at the time when the spikes take place.

In one piece, "Daydreams: Misinterpretation and Undercurrent," Emmanuel shares how he misunderstood such a spike, and for twenty years pursued what he thought the spike was about, when his interpretation was actually based on his frame of reference of the time.

Of course, elsewhere, Emmanuel and I will share with you how our frame of reference is possibly not serving us if we are seeing it, as created, as external to our souls. So once you get a glimpse of how you used to live your life, and how it is so very far divorced from what your soul is interested in, you might stand a chance to direct your ship to your destiny without going all over the place, supposedly even through many lifetimes, to get to your destination. There is also a piece on "Reincarnation and Karma," where you can see for yourself whether you want to or should subscribe to that theory.

In the meantime, while on this journey with Emmanuel and myself, and almost certainly some other souls who are likely to join us here, I wish you a fun journey. Be warned, however, that for the greater part in the beginning of this journey, there will be very little fun. But go in peace and know that, as you earthlings say, it will get worse before it gets better. As you learn to trust yourself and build confidence and see that you are your captain and your ship is your ship, the journey lightens, and the fun begins: albeit slowly at first.

Bon voyage!

Figure 1: Are you the captain of your ship yet?

Inspiration: Emmanuel

Before getting to the next part of the book, I would like to do a more thorough introduction of myself, particularly why and how I came to write this book.

From the treatment I got from my family and other people who had a say in my life, I knew something was wrong. I didn't know what. Then at forty, I fell apart—and started a self-discovery journey. In this book and accompanying website, I share my discoveries and what I uncovered about myself, and also what I see around me.

I see it this way. On arriving here on this planet at birth, I was treated in a certain way. I was perplexed by that treatment. My initial reaction was that something must be wrong with me. Then, in trying to explain it to myself, I had another theory, which was that I must have been adopted.

During my life, I walked around with a deep-seated feeling of something being wrong with me. *Otherwise*, I'd think, *why am I being treated the way I am?* I was born in a blended family of "his children," "my children," and "our children." My parents were in their forties when I was born, and I was the only child in the "our children" category. All in all, there were six children. I was the youngest by thirteen years; my half siblings ranged in age from thirteen to eighteen years older than me.

Looking back, it's not difficult to see what happened and why I felt the way I did about myself. Being so much older, my half siblings all had their lives by the time I came along, but my parents insisted they have responsibilities toward my upbringing. They of course had their own interests, and were in a way forced to attend to me. Why would they want to? After all, I wasn't their responsibility. My parents had their own lives as well, and from what I recall, it wasn't moonlight and roses for them. I remember very many arguments and things being thrown around the house. My father wanted his way and my mother often felt pressured to oblige.

So there I was, in a family where everyone was so into their own lives, they had no time for this newborn who of course needed care and attention. This is where it started for me. This is where I created my Factor-x, which you will find described in the upcoming section, "Factor-x and How It Comes About." The setting and circumstances were perfect.

When I began school, I didn't cope, and this continued throughout my school years. Even today, I don't like learning theoretical stuff. I like practical tasks. Later on in life, I recognized my liking for research.

Anyway, back to school. I struggled with school, especially when it came to learning theory. Again, this fueled my feeling that something must be wrong with me. Throughout my school-going days, I had encounters that confirmed to me that something must be wrong with me.

I got married at a fairly young age, and here it was the same. With what I experienced during my married life of twenty-three years, I had the same deep-seated feeling repeatedly confirmed. I deduced this from the treatment I got from my wife. We had an average or slightly above-average marriage, but there were certain things that just didn't happen. As far as I could gather, I was the cause of it all; something was wrong with me. Again, if it wasn't, why would I be getting the treatment I was getting?

During this time, the only place I felt nothing was wrong with me was with my work. I had developed myself into a computer freelance contractor. Here, I felt I was at home, and of course threw myself into it and had very little actual home life. Besides, I was doing okay at work and not so okay at home, so work became everything for me. And with computer work there's always lots to go around, so when someone throws themselves at it, no one's going to complain.

Then I stumbled at work and created my first big error in judgment. And here it was: I had failed in my work and my wheels came off. Now, everyone could see that something was wrong with me.

It was now finally driven home. At home, my life didn't work out. At work, it was suddenly clear to me that I was not as good as I thought I was. And everything tumbled around me. It was now confirmed, in no uncertain terms, that something was wrong with me.

This might sound like an exaggeration, or that I lived too intensely and oversensitively. Be that as it may, what I share here is a short version of uncovering myself since about the age of forty until today. At the time of this writing, I am fifty-three years old.

At age forty, I cracked up and had nowhere to turn. Even though there were people around me, I was all alone. I had entered a bottomless pit, my own hell here on Earth, and had no idea what was happening and what I was going to do about it. My world as I knew it had ended, and I was lost to myself and to the world, spinning out of control in a world I had created for myself based on wanting to cover up that something was wrong with me.

Unable to cope anymore, I eventually stopped working and took an extended break. Before this break, during this break and after the break, I researched. My liking research really came in handy. I left no stone unturned. I cut all the way to the bone in my self-uncovering escapades. I went for every therapy I could find that I thought would cast light on where I had found myself.

During this time, I found someone who understood me and understood what had happened to me. You first read about him in the book's Acknowledgements. Sergio spent hundreds of hours with me, and thereby gave me an opportunity for me to see myself—the person I had become and the person I really was.

This was a difficult dynamic that had its good and not-so-good aspects. First, I had to deal with me—the person I had become in an attempt to cover up how I felt about myself—and then I had to move that aside so I could see me, the person I really was. That was not very easy. Second, I had one thing going for me: I found out what had happened to me and why I felt the way I felt about myself. Third, what was now required was to break through what I had created—my Factor-x—to see it and me separately. Fourth, I had another thing going for me—I could be brutally honest with myself. Fifth, this process required courage.

In looking back, initially it was courage that was lacking when I uncovered this reality about myself—the courage to move beyond what I had created. This was a big struggle, and even today, courage is the one thing I constantly need to rely on to get me out of a stranglehold that my Factor-x creates.

Where does all this lead to?

Well, as I uncovered myself, I of course assumed that surely other people also created for themselves what I had created. During this time, I relied heavily and often on a particular daydream which I now understood, as you will read about in "Daydreams: Misinterpretation and Undercurrent," again with Sergio's help.

The funny thing is, I lived my life and questioned its meaning often. When my life fell apart, I uncovered my own meaning. As a result, and assuming that there might be other people who, like me, created lives for themselves which they question . . . who, like me, would like to get to the bottom of why they created a life for themselves that they don't like . . . and for those who would like to get beyond what they created . . . this book was written and the accompanying website developed.

All this, I uncovered from a daydream that took me twenty years to unravel and understand. Now that this dream of mine was unraveled and understood and the courage of my convictions was with me, I was able to create a book and accompanying website where anyone participating has a chance to uncover themselves.

The aforementioned was my inspiration to write this book and to develop the accompanying website, to share my experiences, what I uncovered, and what I see around me happening each and every day. I wonder whether my case is an isolated one, or whether it is the norm. Notwithstanding, either way I suspect that, even though they might be questioning the meaning of their lives, very few people would step forward and take on this uncovering journey. It's just too big a step to take, and it takes brutal honesty and great courage to go with our convictions. I'm wondering whether the average person has enough brutal honesty and courage to go beyond the standards and norms dictated by society, and whether others would even see how their Factor-x drives their lives.

Because of the above, I'll give this warning: This book and accompanying website is intended for everyone, but only people who can be brutally honest with themselves and have the courage of their convictions will go with what they see when they uncover themselves. The intimidation of the standards and norms of society and from Factor-x is enormous. Only those with great courage and the ability to be honest with themselves can get beyond that. Again, this brutal honesty with ourselves and the courage of our convictions is required. Anything short of that, and the intimidation will get to us.

Throughout this journey, and the further each of us goes on this journey, the more we'll find ourselves isolated. Keep in mind, this sense of isolation feeds right into our Factor-x. Nevertheless, this is not an impossible journey. When stuck on any aspect, we can check whether our meaning is still present; in all likelihood, it will still be right there.

Have a safe journey, albeit no doubt a rocky one at most times. And remember that you are welcome, at any stage, to visit the website in the likelihood that further information is available, or to contact me when stuck. (Note: Since this is my way of making a living, such contact is subject to a fee, as explained in the website information in the back of this book.)

Notwithstanding anything, my kindest regards,

Emmanuel

PART TWO

CONCEPTION

Core Missing

Whenever we feel something is missing in our lives; when it seems our lives don't have meaning; when we don't know what we'd like to do with our lives: If there were a way to get to the bottom of these feelings, wouldn't you like to know about it? Would you like to uncover why these feelings come about?

Free to Choose (Freedom of Choice)

We talk of freedom of choice.

But has anyone ever sat down and considered what it is that we are supposedly free *from* to make this choice? Do we really ever sit down for a moment to consider what that statement means? Certainly, almost no person reading this will have considered what it is that we are supposedly free from to choose. If anyone has considered what it is that we are supposedly free from, say, for instance, that a minute percentage of people have considered it, what would they likely have come up with?

In reality, and for most, "freedom of choice" is merely a figure of speech and is most probably construed to mean: we can make choices; therefore, we're free.

In fact, let's play devil's advocate and speculate that mostly, we don't give the phrase a second thought because it seems so obvious—we are free to make choices, so what's the big deal? Just let me choose.

However, let's say the phrase's meaning *isn't* "We can choose, therefore we are free," and explore the phrase a bit more.

Freedom of choice implies some choice, and then being free to make that choice. So let's look at choice.

An example: We're asked something by someone, and in fact, we would like to answer one thing. Let's say we would like to answer, "No, I don't want to."

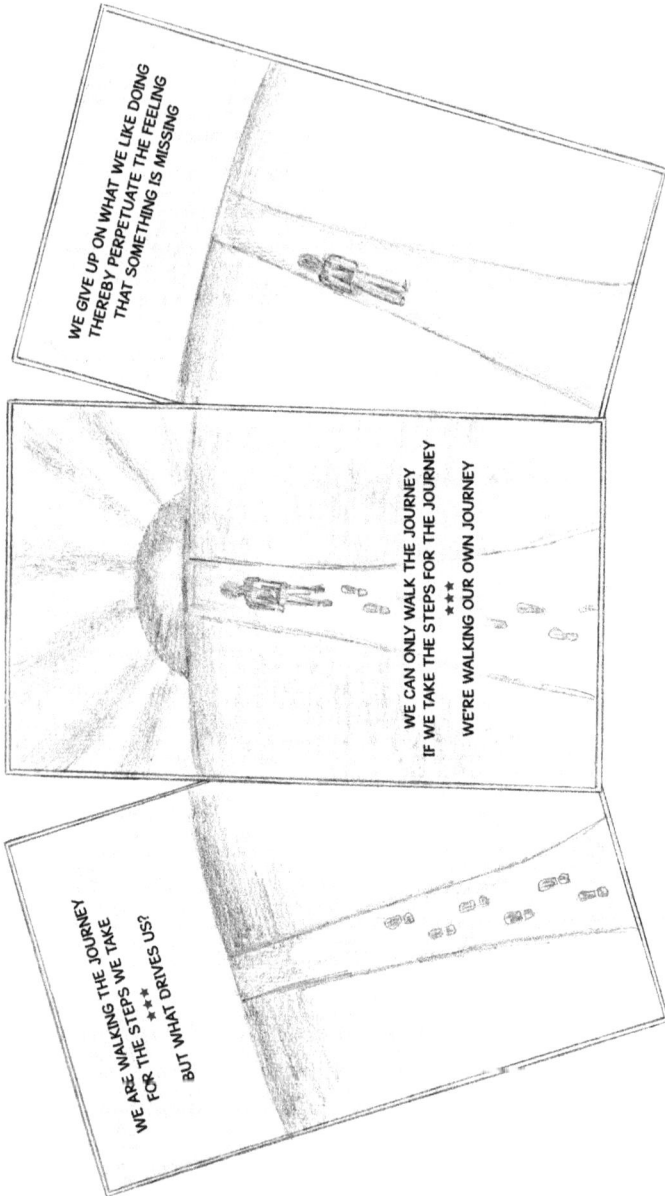

Figure 2: Are we aware of the origin of the feeling that something is missing?

WE GIVE UP ON WHAT WE LIKE DOING
THEREBY PERPETUATE THE FEELING
THAT SOMETHING IS MISSING

WE CAN ONLY WALK THE JOURNEY
IF WE TAKE THE STEPS FOR THE JOURNEY
★★★
WE'RE WALKING OUR OWN JOURNEY

WE ARE WALKING THE JOURNEY
FOR THE STEPS WE TAKE
★★★
BUT WHAT DRIVES US?

Well, how many times do we actually say "Yes"?

If we are honest, there are likely many times when we agree to something when we didn't mean to agree. This is only a small example, but it illustrates that, when we talk of freedom of choice, we don't consider the number of times we say yes when in fact, we wanted to say no. This begs the question: If we replied contrary to what we really wanted to say, then were we indeed free to choose?

Or, let's ask the question another way: Are we only free sometimes, or only when it comes to certain choices?

Another simple example: Let's say we're getting dressed for work one morning. We look at what there is to wear, and perhaps we feel like picking certain pieces of clothing, but then we decide against them.

Let's look at why we said yes when we would have preferred to say no, or why we decided to pick some other clothing after we originally wanted to wear something else.

Bravo if you see this immediately. For those who don't see it immediately, cast yourself back to one of these instances that stands out in your mind. It would be very surprising if such an example does not come up for you. Your example doesn't have to be something important, just an instance where you stated a choice contrary to what you would have preferred. Best not to think—thinking doesn't help. Just observe quietly what example comes up.

If an example does not come up right now, rest assured that, soon, one will occur to you. When this happens, come back here and continue. If all else fails, you may make contact with me via the accompanying website (lifecanbedifferent.com) to explore finding such an instance.

There is also the other side of the coin: that you do not have such an instance. Then we beg the question: you might be free and maybe reading this book merely for informational purposes. Let's continue. At this point, we're assuming you can recall an instance where you chose contrary to what you would have preferred, and will use that as your example.

Now, look at that instance and relive that moment. At first, this might seem difficult or even impossible. However, it is important. In reliving a moment, we encounter what exactly happened retrospectively, at the time. So, look very carefully at what happened to you at that very moment. Look at what you were thinking at that very moment that, as a result, altered your original preference.

Let me introduce something here that you might be experiencing right now. Recalling a past event we agreed to even when we wanted to say no, and seeing exactly what caused that interjection, takes courage, sometimes a very heavy dose of it. Courage is required to be brutally honest with ourselves. So if, at this moment, you don't have the courage to be brutally honest with yourself, simply leave and return here when you recognize that you do have the courage to be brutally honest with yourself. That honesty with yourself is nonnegotiable. Only once you are prepared to take such a big step will you be in a position to see what you would be free from.

Back to the revisited moment. What you see in that revisited moment, that instant where you interjected to keep yourself saying yes when you wanted to say no, is the result of what I term Factor-x. Factor-x will be thoroughly explained next. For now, I'll just say that whenever we choose contrary to what we really want to do, it is highly likely that going against what we'd prefer to do originates in our Factor-x. We all have a Factor-x, and I would be surprised to hear of anyone convinced that they don't.

However, this is not about Factor-x, but about our core that is missing—the fact that when we want to choose something, in any particular moment, about anything, our Factor-x interjects, telling us that we are therefore not free to choose, or that we do not have freedom of choice. Instead, that we are merely giving lip service to the term "freedom of choice," to the point where the phrase already has cliché status with us.

But this goes back farther. What if there was a moment in your past that was a fork in the road for you, and because Factor-x interjected, you took a path contrary to the one you would have preferred to take had your Factor-x *not* come into play? Is it possible that for a day, a week, a month, a year, even decades, that you might have been walking a path to a destination different from where you'd rather be?

If this is indeed the case, you might even be walking around wondering about the meaning of your life.

Might it be, then, that the core is missing in your life? And that if it hadn't been missing—had you not given your life over to Factor-x—your life might have been very different from what it is at the time of this reading? And is that, perhaps, why you are reading this?

If so, now what? Your life up to now might have been on a different path, and as such, you might feel it's been wasted. Or, was it wasted? We can certainly say no, not wasted, but a lot of experience gained. Firsthand experience. And if so, what are you to do with this firsthand experience gained on a path you didn't want to be on in the first place?

Slow down, we'll see.

Factor-x and How It Comes About

In our early childhood, we are influenced by those around us: our parents and immediate family, but also everyone we encounter. This influence continues throughout our lives. Schoolteachers and religion also bring their influence to our lives.

The reality is that those who influence us were influenced by those before them, and those people, yet again, by other people before them. So this influence is handed down from generation to generation, and in this way, we are formed. From time to time, someone brings their own views into the equation and might in some way, large or small, influence our existing influences. But in the main, influence is passed on down the ages and onto us.

In fact, we are all brought up to accept what our caregivers decide for us. The system works like that. Let's look at the saying of "Bend the tree while it is young." That is exactly what happens. Through our various stages of growth, someone imposes their ways onto us which they, in turn, got from somewhere else. So from the time we're born, many other people have had a say in our lives whether we like it or not—and whether their influence works for us or not.

What if we don't want this influence? What if we don't agree with this influence? Or even worse, what about when this influence is brought onto us before we even have the capacity, as babies or toddlers, to state that we are not interested in the influence?

If these influences go against our preferences or against how we feel about the situation, here's what will most likely happen: We'll be made to toe the line in whichever way our imposer (caretaker) deems. Religious influence is one example. Yes, even though almost all religions are advocates of what we refer to as "love," religious influences can be and are imposed on us from a very young age. And mind you, as we grow up, we invariably do exactly the same to others. We have our "ways" (handed down to us, most likely by imposition), and we then hand those ways down to our offspring, again, most likely by imposition. And so the cycle goes on and on and on.

When we are very small, we accept the influences of those around us without question, and we are completely at the mercy of our caretakers. With this drive in our human cycle, what do we experience in this "pressure" situation? We do not know any better, so eventually, with all the pressure we crack: The tree is bent in the ways of someone else—those before us, and before those—in whose immediate care we are. We are oblivious of what is happening, and our caregivers are also oblivious of what they are doing. Nobody really questions the process. In any event, as a two or three year old, there is no thinking of questioning since we are in the hands of our caregivers.

When we crack, we most likely, in that moment, conclude that the pressure we are experiencing must be because something is wrong with us. Meaning that, in our thinking, if something weren't wrong with us, then why would we be experiencing the pressure—why would we be expected to do things we'd prefer not to do? And, if something wasn't wrong with us, why would we be feeling that it—whatever is expected of us—isn't really what we'd like or want to do?

Recall that those doing this to us were exactly in the same boat. And so the cycle continues.

But it goes further. When we crack from the pressure, from that moment on, we live only to prove one thing—that nothing is wrong with us. From that moment, we are lost to ourselves. In that moment, we take on our "Factor-x"—a way to reference that moment and what indeed happens in that moment. So in that moment, Factor-x is born and we are lost to it. And we are likely oblivious about what has indeed happened to us.

Fortunately, we create Factor-x; no one else created it for us. Just as fortunately, Factor-x isn't real.

Why is all this fortunate? If it were real, we wouldn't have any other way forward, other than living to disprove our Factor-x. If someone else created it, then we would be at their mercy. So if we created our Factor-x and it isn't real, then we can undo its creation. And that is what makes it fortunate.

Thus in the same way we created it, we can reverse its creation.

Alas, reversing the creation of Factor-x in a particular moment is easier said than done. We need to *recapture* that moment. We need to *feel* that moment. We need to *accept* that moment. We need to have courage so we can *see* that moment—the courage to be brutally honest with ourselves to see and experience that moment.

But here is another fortunate part of this tragedy. Every moment we endeavor to disprove that something is wrong with us, we have an opportunity to see the following two things: what actually happened when we cracked from being bent while still young, and how and why our Factor-x was born.

With courage and honesty, it isn't difficult to see the influence of this tragedy we created. It is, however, extremely difficult to accept it. Yet without accepting it, there is no moving beyond it. Factor-x holds us hostage. Every person around us, wherever we look, has likely fallen into the hands of their Factor-x. So Factor-x is, in all likelihood, holding almost every soul for ransom.

Factor-x stays with us forever. But it's possible to get out of the grip of what we created—of how we hold ourselves hostage with Factor-x—if we know about it, and if we consciously want to free ourselves.

Be warned, however: To identify Factor-x is one thing, but to break out of its spell is not for the fainthearted.

If we have the honesty to acknowledge our Factor-x and the courage to befriend our Factor-x, we can free ourselves and break the cycle. Even so, that is easier said than done. After reading this book, perhaps you would like to rush out and tell those around you—your direct family or associates—about your discovery. If you do, likely they would frown on you, as if you had a terrible life and upbringing. Unfortunately, but also very fortunately, it works this way. Only people who are ready for this will actually look at what their life is like. And only they will see their Factor-x. Others that haven't looked are oblivious, and when we relate what we've discovered, they'll merely assume we must have had a tough life. They might even feel sorry for us.

So even when we uncover ourselves, those around us are likely not there yet—at the point of questioning and or uncovering themselves. They likely have no idea what has happened to them. So be aware that you will almost certainly stand all on your own in this quest. You won't want to take part in things you used to take part in. You'll uncover your own preferences, most likely very different from your previous ones, and different from those of your social circle as well. This is understandable, since people in our social circles are almost certainly driven by their Factor-x. You, on the other hand, are breaking out of its spell. This can cause a major divide between you and them. Those who know you won't recognize this person you seem to have changed into. Now that you're not taking part in the cycle of passing onto others whatever is dictated to you by your Factor-x, this dynamic might even prevent you from having the courage to recognize your Factor-x and to break out of its influence over you.

So in addition to uncovering yourself—because of your adjusted preferences and different behavior—in all likelihood, you will stand alone. This takes courage—more courage than the average person can easily muster.

Taking Up That Freedom of Choice

Being free to choose is itself based on being free to take up that freedom. No one can do it for us. If we lack freedom to choose, we would not be free to make that choice.

Being free to choose is itself based on being free to take up that freedom. Only we can take up the freedom. No one can give us freedom to choose. Freedom of choice itself exists only as a free choice to set us free. So only if we are free to take up the choice to be free are we able to take up freedom of choice that is available as a free choice. And if someone could give us freedom of choice, then we would not be free and neither would the choice to be free be free.

Briefly, we could be free. Freedom itself is a free choice. We can't be given free choice; if free choice needs to be given to us, then we're not free. Free choice cannot be given, because then it isn't a free choice that can be taken up. It is beautiful—we and it. Yet both need to be free: for freedom of choice to be available to set us free, and for us to take up the free choice to be free.

Let's say you want to be free to explore your freedom of choice. But let's also say that it's possible for someone else to give freedom of choice to you—like a present, or like food, or like something you can purchase at a store. Then, it seems, you sit with a dilemma. If this is the case—if someone else can give freedom of choice to us—then it's not we that took up our freedom of choice out of our own free will. If this is the case, as easily as it came, freedom of choice could be taken away from you again.

Stated clearly, for us to have freedom of choice—to be free to choose—is in itself based on being free to make that choice.

What does this mean to us, this question of whether we are free?

When you read "Free to Choose (Freedom of Choice)," you learned that we say yes when we don't really mean it, and vice versa. This brings another interesting question: Do we mean what we say and do we say what we mean?

Let's take this question a step further. How often do you arrive late for an appointment? Whether a business appointment or just going to the movies, how often are you there in good time? Whether it's you, or I, or anyone else, if we aren't punctual some of the time or even most of the time, without a doubt, we don't mean what we say.

Let's look at why. If we meant what we said when making the appointment or even making plans of our own, like going to the movies, but we arrive late, it's highly likely that it wasn't something important to us. If it was, we'd be there on time or even arrive with time to spare. If our life is so hectic that we got away late, didn't have something to wear, got caught up in traffic, dressed in several outfits before we decided on one . . . the main thing is, we weren't punctual. Thus, the event wasn't important to us. So did we really mean what we said (or planned) when we made the appointment or the plans?

Let's take it another step. If this is indeed the case, then are we living our first-choice lives? When we don't mean what we say or say what we mean, isn't that clear indication that we're living a second-choice life, definitely not a first-choice life?

When we're not living a first-choice life, we're not able to make choices that are important to us. When in such a frame of mind, how would we ever be in a position to become free to take up the choice of freedom of choice: the choice of being free to choose?

Putting it bluntly, if we think for a moment that we have freedom of choice, chances are, we're kidding ourselves and Factor-x is ruling our lives.

You might be thinking, *If this is the case, and if I'm kidding myself, then how can I rid myself of Factor-x?*

Sorry, you can't. Factor-x is with us forever. No matter what, Factor-x is right there at our heels, nibbling away at our peace of mind, interjecting itself with every step of our lives. We are never rid of our Factor-x. We only have one option: To stop fighting our Factor-x and befriend it.

We cannot say, "Surely we should know better." That doesn't work. We can only acknowledge and befriend Factor-x and live with it.

But by *befriending* Factor-x, we might be better able to see it operate in our lives. If we can see that, we stand a chance to acknowledge Factor-x whenever it makes its appearances. We can then say to it with a smile, "I see you!"

What is the result? By taking the power away from your Factor-x in a friendly manner, it mostly melts away, and you have peace of mind. Over time, you would see that your Factor-x isn't so dominating in your life anymore. That it's just there in the shadows. And then, mostly because you no longer fight it, but have acknowledged and accepted it, Factor-x seems to interject less often, or interject with less potency.

Think of two different bodies of water: a smooth, mirror-like pool, and a storm-tossed ocean. Like a pool without ripples, when we then throw the smallest object onto that calm water, the water is severely disrupted and the calm is no more. In the same way, when Factor-x gets hold of us when we least expect it, all hell breaks loose inside us, as if the higher we climb up a ladder, the more it hurts when we fall down. Yet, when we throw a large object into a stormy sea, it will hardly make an impression.

When we aren't at peace with ourselves, equate it to the stormy sea, and compare that to the calm pond of water. If your life is stormy almost all the time, you're probably unaware of not meaning what you say. You make the appointment, but up comes some object and, with a splash, it falls into the already-stormy sea. The result? You get sidetracked, and the meeting or appointment or movie plans are shoved right to the back of the emergency list.

Which is the life you would prefer—one like the calm of the pond, where you are free and have freedom of choice, or the hectic, stormy life like a sea so frenzied and wild, you can only bob around in an attempt to survive it?

This is where the ability to see our Factor-x operating is so helpful. If you see your Factor-x operating and can see these objects tossed in, you can exercise your freedom of choice and decide what is tossed in or not.

But here it comes . . . that is also easier said than done. Rest assured, should you exercise that freedom of choice, you might then go down other forks in the path that you are possibly unprepared for or reluctant to take. And guess what you would likely find around the next corner? Lo and behold—Factor-x, full blown, biting at your heels or chewing on your ears about such an alternate path and its consequences. Mind you, Factor-x is a great salesman that will go far to convince you to take another path even though you know you'd prefer not to.

But this is a simplistic analogy of a very important step in our lives. As discussed further in the later section, "Doing What I Want or Like, and Doing What I Like Doing," this shows the difference between when we're really and truly ourselves and mistakenly *thinking* we're ourselves when all that has happened is that we've become an arrogant person. Why arrogant? Because instead of having uncovered ourselves and taking up our freedom of choice, we're thinking we possess "new tricks." When we're in the arrogant league, we don't see that we are. But we're not free at all, and we feel it. The arrogance is driven by Factor-x being utterly in control of our lives. When we're arrogant, we're in fact *out of control*, because Factor-x is in control. And when Factor-x controls us, we rarely have peace of mind.

It is critical for us to uncover ourselves. In that lies our peace of mind, our inner peace, and the ability to truly be ourselves. But to be yourself, you are in the fortunate position I mentioned—you can achieve that for yourself by getting together the courage to take up your freedom of choice, irrespective of what the consequences are of that choice and every subsequent one. Once done, once you've taken up your freedom of choice and thus are free to choose, every subsequent choice becomes easier and almost automatic, even though intentional.

\(\psi \)

Manifesting Without Core

We Are Walking the Journey For the Steps We Take

—Emmanuel van der Meulen (with White Wolf & Co.),
September 2005

While we are oblivious to our inner mechanics and unaware of what drives us, we likely unconsciously manifest ourselves based on a figment of our imagination.
This usually occurs while we are still in search of meaning and attempting to fill an apparent emptiness.

Treating Symptoms and Addressing the Cause

Do we realize how much of what we do in our day-to-day lives is
about treating symptoms (incidents and events) rather than causes?
It seems that most of us aren't aware that causes even exist, or that if
we only treat symptoms, the symptoms will reoccur over and over, as
they likely have for years gone by and will for years to come.

However, the only way to stop an incident from reoccurring is to
look for the cause and then address the cause. In that way, and only
in that way, do we stand a chance to stop unwanted incidents from
reoccurring.

Let's take an example. It might happen that there is a war in prog-
ress, and you are a healthcare provider who attends to people injured
in the war. No matter what your intentions are, no matter what your
healthcare credentials are, merely by treating those people who are
injured, you can only treat symptoms to the best of your ability.

You might say, "The cause of the problem isn't that I have patients
to attend to, but the *war itself.*"

But that isn't so, either—the war is also just another symptom.
Why not look further and see why there is a war? If you do, you'll
likely find that the warring parties and those starting the war would

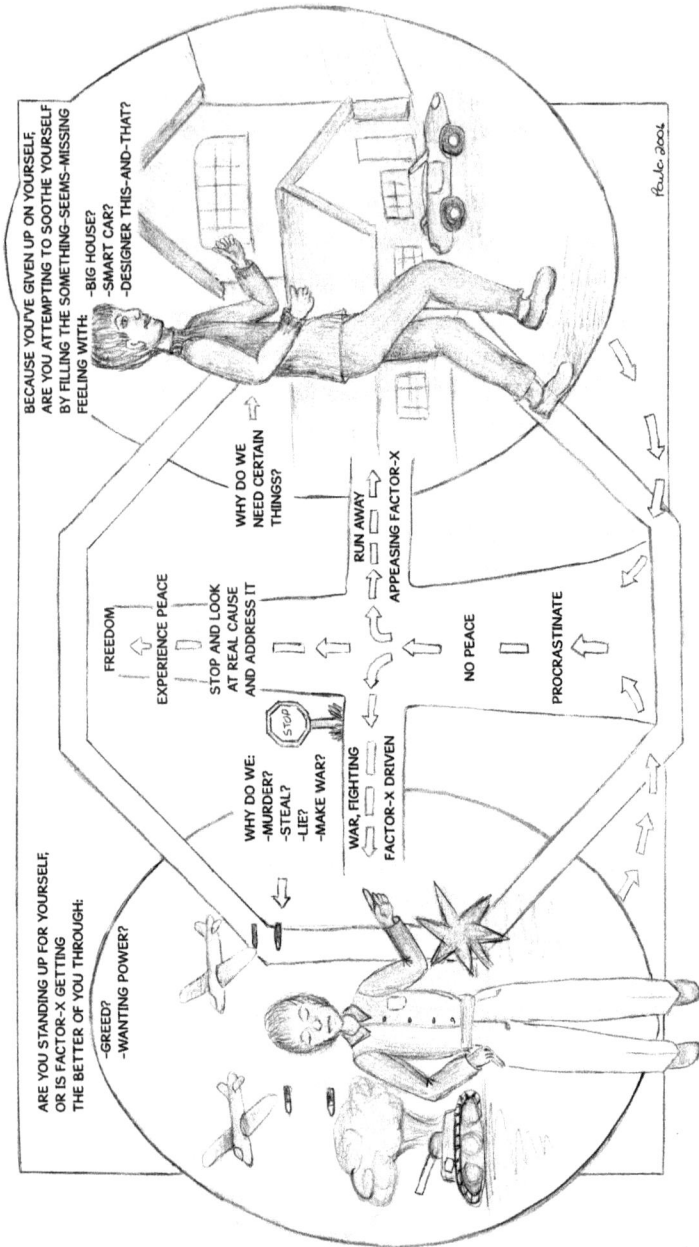

Figure 3: The outcome when we manifest while something is missing

give what sound like very good reasons why it was necessary to start the war.

But all those reasons are merely more symptoms.

Looking further, why is it that people go to war? Why is it that people and individuals are in positions to create wars? Why do those individuals choose to go to war?

Let's look from another side of yet-another coin. When a child doesn't want to listen to a parent, the child is chastised, perhaps commanded to obey. On how many occasions does the parent chastise the child based only on what other people might say in relation to the parent's parenting capabilities? That just possibly, the parent is chastising the child because the parent wants to be seen in a particular way by others, i.e., that the parent has control of their child.

So is it possible that is why people who are in positions to decide on war are doing it—because they want to be seen in a certain way by others?

There is also another angle on this topic: going to war for the sake of money that can directly or indirectly be made from going to war. The person then making the decision, again, is doing it to be seen in a certain way by those wanting to make money from the war. It might even be that the person doesn't want to be seen as weak. Again, it has to do with the individual wanting to be seen in a certain way by others. To take it even further, possibly not now wanting to be seen as a weakling in the eyes of the person's god.

However, on whatever basis a person says they're making a decision to go to war, it's highly likely that their basis is merely another symptom.

This doesn't apply only to dramatic decisions like starting a war. It might even be something small, like saying yes when we'd rather say no, and vice versa. Not saying or doing what we'd prefer to say or do is also only a symptom—also one we don't recognize as being linked to an underlying cause—and likely to be driven by the person's individual Factor-x.

And so this will continue until we as a species, here on the Earth and the souls in the spirit world, recognize that for every unwanted aspect of our lives, we might merely be treating the symptom, and that while we only treat the symptoms, the unwanted aspect will re-occur over and over.

Let's look at symptom-treating in itself. You might ask the question, "But shouldn't symptoms be treated? Should those patients who are hurt in the war be left to their own devices and most probably retain permanent damage?"

Of course we would treat those patients hurt in the war. But we could, at the same time, create a culture separate from direct involvement with the war that addresses causes only. This isn't something that could be achieved en masse. No, it can only be achieved by individuals who recognize this distinction and live their own lives of addressing causes only. Over time, and it might take many, many years for this to gain the necessary momentum, the distinction of symptoms and causes would be conveyed to enough people that a critical mass would tip the scales and then slowly, but surely, people would recognize this distinction and live their lives accordingly.

And as this happens, and in many, many years from now, even maybe a million years from now, things would change. People would live differently from how we live today—on the Earth plane as well as in the spirit world, people would live their meaning as opposed to treating symptoms. We can only partly imagine how differently people would behave, or the differences in our daily lives, during the transitional stages. It would certainly not be the same as today. Yes, there will be similarities but the essence will most likely be so different.

One example I envision: Today when people do undesirable things, they (and we) probably don't know why they exhibit that behavior. From what is available in the media, it certainly seems we don't know why. During and after this transitional phase, we would know why people do such things to themselves and others.

During the transitional phase, we're likely to want to stay far away from people not living their own meaning—but, the moment such a person comes forward and states that they see their ways and don't want to have that life anymore, we would jump at the opportunity to support their journey to uncover their meaning.

In all likelihood, there would be compassion and guidance from those who have seen the light to others still living with unwanted behavior. Poverty is likely to diminish, perhaps disappear all together. Anything and everything available on this planet is likely to be made available to everyone at no charge. Yes, at no charge, because it's likely that the need for money would eventually disappear. Also likely is that people would live their daily lives doing the things that are important to them, not only doing things based on treating symptoms or earning money. We would like the things we do. We can also suppose that the existence of Factor-x would be exposed wide open, and that people would have the tools to see why they do unwanted things to themselves and others.

As we earthling souls grew in this way and developed our spirits, so the spirit-world souls would develop, and so the cycle of spiritual maturation would continue. Spirit-world souls would also be exposed to their own Factor-x, to the extent that their guidance to earthling souls would grow and mature to the point where, when we had unwanted behavior, they would guide us in seeing where and how and why that unwanted behavior originated. Over time and with the continued exposure of Factor-x, here on the Earth and in the spirit world, souls would develop on a grand scale. Albeit one soul at a time, we would all attain inner peace and peace of mind.

You might be tempted to say, "So what if we're treating symptoms and never treat the cause? This behavior doesn't affect me."

However, as you will see in the section titled, "One," we're all affected by another's unwanted behavior. For now, consider this: When one individual lives a second-choice life, does another individual who is living a first-choice life stay unaffected by the other's behavior?

Responsibility: Do We Recognize Our Responsibility?

Are we part of the human race? Do we contribute toward the human race? Are we merely here on Earth and do what we are told, or do we have a say in what goes on around us and what goes on with the human race?

When we see and experience something that doesn't serve us, and it's clear to us that it probably serves no one else, do we merely leave it alone because we feel, *Well, what can I do about it?* Or perhaps do we ask, *Who am I to want to do anything about it?* Do we recognize that we are part of our society, and that we have an equal say in what goes on around us?

We can expect that few people recognize that we are part of the society that governs our lives, and that we don't have an equal say in society, almost certainly because we aren't brought up to recognize these things. It might also be that we'd like to participate, but feel we aren't capable of adding value to the system. It might also be that we aren't given a chance to participate, perhaps because such participation is usually reserved for those with funds. Can we be sure our leader represent everyone, or only those that put them in the position? Or, do they represent earning even more funds from the position?

The question is, really, are we being represented? If not, then who has our interest at heart? Who can have our interests at heart if not ourselves? And, if we get into a position where we can represent ourselves, then what about those we don't represent? Is "Who governs who?" a catch-22? Or should we govern ourselves?

Most likely, no single answer to this question fits all.

Maybe the answer lies elsewhere. Maybe the first thing required is that we recognize that no one really represents us like we would.

If we want to represent ourselves, then *why* would we want to do it?

Could it be that it is necessary for us to realize that we alone are responsible for our lives? When we live first-choice lives, we are certainly responsible for our lives. But we can also ask, "What about others' interference in our lives?" Are we an island? We are certainly not. Although we might be tempted to isolate ourselves, it's almost impossible, even with endless resources. Even if we could isolate ourselves, we aren't separate from other earthling souls, and not even separate from souls in the spirit world.

However, when we take up being responsible for our lives and therefore stand up for ourselves, we are most likely going to take part in representing ourselves in one way or another. Looking at it from another perspective, when we're not responsible for ourselves, we're living second-choice existences.

Once we take up responsibility for our lives and live first-choice existences, only then do we stand a chance to represent ourselves. And it starts with us, not with anyone or anywhere else. Once we live our first-choice existence, we start seeing how much of our lives are in the hands of others who don't have theirs or ours or any other person's best interests at heart. Once we live our first-choice existence, we automatically have each and every person's—in fact, every soul's—best interests at heart. At this time, this might sound like a contradiction; however, once we get to this point with our lives, as you'll read about in the section titled "Taking Up That Freedom of Choice," then we automatically serve ourselves and others. What is vital to understand is that with second-choice existences, no one is served, not even ourselves.

Responsibility: Looking Only to Blame—Even Ourselves

Being responsible for our lives has nothing to do with blame. Placing any blame anywhere, even on ourselves, abdicates responsibility.

Here is how it works. (Note: The emotion of anger is used here merely as an example. The discussion also applies to other emotional states, such as anxiety, feeling down and the like.) Assuming we get angry at what someone does, or at what someone did, or at what someone didn't do, looking at who is to blame doesn't give the possibility of getting to the cause of the anger. Instead, the cause of the anger is overlooked because there is someone to blame. That someone could even be us. So, by placing blame anywhere, the real cause of the anger is overlooked.

Placing blame doesn't only apply to anger. Whenever we find we're looking to blame something or someone, bear in mind that blame isn't about being responsible, but merely abdicating responsibility, and we are back into living a second-choice existence.

When looking at anger, for example, what relates to a first-choice existence is when we look at *why* we're getting angry. Why is the anger set off? In an upcoming section titled "Reliving the Moment to Uncover Its Importance," you'll learn the importance of slowing down or breaking down the moment when we get angry, to determine what in us results in our anger and then wanting to place blame. And then, in that slowed-down moment, looking very carefully at what lies underneath the anger. It is highly likely that in that moment before the anger sets in, our Factor-x kicked in.

A warning: Blaming is not about being responsible, and it doesn't help at all to blame Factor-x. This, again, is abdicating responsibility. Instead, what should be accepted is that, once again, Factor-x is at the bottom of the anger, so resulted in the anger: thus, where the anger originated. Being responsible is accepting this as the origin of the anger, and knowing that Factor-x doesn't serve us—and recognizing that we would prefer to eradicate Factor-x's influence in our lives. That is being responsible—not placing blame at any doorstep. While placing blame, we are unable to look at what really happened and miss a great opportunity to look at the cause of the anger.

By the way, the more we address things in our lives in this way, the more we see what drives our lives. While this is extremely difficult at first, and could be for many years, at some point, looking at the cause of things become easier when being responsible takes on a dimension that overshadows everything else in our lives. When we go forward looking for the cause of anything that disturbs our inner peace (our peace of mind), our responsibility for our lives grows.

There is always the trap of blame. We could be in a situation where we lose peace of mind, where we recognize something has thrown us into disarray, that we are deeply troubled, and we then find ourselves saying, "But I should know better," and, "Surely this shouldn't be happening to me."

Again, the blame is there, and it ruins it for us. What is needed every single time, without fail, is to look at what lies underneath us getting angry—the anger's underlying cause. Saying we should know better places blame on ourselves—again, abdicating responsibility. And again, this doesn't serve us. This is a very easy trap to fall into, so be warned. Being responsible and not blaming is the only way forward in a first-choice existence.

Humankind Follows: What Drives Leaders?

As a very trusting species, we humans follow very easily. In our upbringing, we are discouraged from questioning and are also expected to comply at all times. And it seems that we just never shake off our automatic compliance. We see proof of this happening in our own lives, and what we experience emotionally, when we even think of questioning anything or anyone—and not just questioning for the sake of questioning.

Do we ever stop for a moment and check how we really feel about the things that we do? Do we notice that we take for granted that the way things are and work is how they are *supposed* to be and work?

So if we hardly question anything or anyone, it goes without saying that we likely are followers.

As one example, recapture a moment when our "No" wasn't no, and our "Yes" wasn't yes, and recall what happened. See how our Factor-x kicked in and took control. The reason you might have said yes when you meant to say no is because we are not brought up to question—only to follow. Following is enforced on us.

It would be at least a step in the right direction if we could rely on our caretakers or caregivers, or those in positions to guide us, or the people who are our leaders: *if* they have their own and our best interests at heart.

But, what drives *them*?

And can we rely on them?

This is not about knocking anyone, but rather, about seeing things as they are.

Parents

Let's look at our parents: our caregivers, our immediate "leaders" or role models. Did they empower us through their guidance so we could take care of ourselves . . . so we can manifest our first-choice existences? Or did they enforce their own will and lives on us, in many cases with force? How many parents and caregivers give guidance and support to those who are in their care? Or is it merely a case of: they are in charge, and with force, they will rule our lives?

Companies

Next, let's look at companies. Businesses are interested in making money; in fact, that's their primary objective. They do almost whatever it takes to achieve their primary objective. Some companies will look after their staff, but is that because they really care, or because they know that while they do certain things, their staff will comply? Most likely, they don't do it because it's their first choice. It most likely has more to do with appeasing their staff. Some companies possibly contribute to their communities, again not as a first choice, but almost certainly to appease the community so they can continue in their ways. Are these leaders living first-choice existences?

Religion

Let's look at religious leaders and their various God-roles. Are those leaders even aware that their religion is based on minimizing their followers? Are they aware that their religion grows their followers' Factor-x? Have you ever stopped to consider what lies at the core of religions?

Please don't think this is about knocking religion. Rather, I'm asking you to take a careful look at what lies at the core of God, or by whatever name that role is referred to by our religions and us as individuals. Religion, or the god–role, has only one thing at its core—that it invokes our Factor-x. It only survives because it fires up our Factor-x. If we are brave enough, we can stop for a moment and look realistically at the core of the teachings of various religions and role of their deity. As seen in an upcoming section, "Forms of Crutches," religions and their god–role in our lives are merely a crutch used by us, because we follow and accept, oblivious to the role that our Factor-x plays in driving us to this crutch.

Leaders

Let's stop for a moment and imagine the lives of our leaders. Do they not, just maybe, also have a Factor-x driving them? Is this, perhaps, where their hunger for power comes from? Is this, perhaps, where their greed comes from? We very likely rely on other people to lead us. In the event that they themselves are driven by their Factor-x, then in a sense, our lives are twice removed from us: first, removed by our own lives, seeing that we're most likely living a second-choice existence; second, removed by those we follow, who are most likely also living second-choice existences.

Extreme

Now, let's take this eventuality to its utmost extreme. If we are indeed living second-choice existences, and if our caretakers and leaders are indeed also living second-choice existences, is it any wonder that we, as a species, have created our lives the way they are? This situation doesn't serve anyone. As examples, there are many people who starve, yet we have money to make war. Some of our children don't have food or warm clothing, yet their parents might be drinking with the rent money or with the money for the little food their children might have had.

Okay, Because We Have . . .

Then there are those of us who have whatever resources we need or possibly have even more resources than we need. These people might be thinking that whatever drives our leaders isn't really for us—we don't need to follow, we're okay. We have, and therefore we're okay.

Is this really the case? Can those of us who have just enough resources, or possibly have a little more than we need, or even have a great deal more than we need—can we really say we don't feel something is missing in our lives? Why is it that, even when we have more resources than we need, we might still have that feeling of something being missing? Is it maybe, just maybe, possible that those of us who have some or enough resources are living second-choice existences because Factor-x doesn't allow even us to do just the things that are important to us? Instead, is it likely that those of us that have some, or more-than-enough resources, spend our lives just to be in a position to have stuff, things—thus, merely an existence? To have . . . to survive . . . to cope, as opposed to living what is really in our hearts— our first-choice existences?

Are we really living when our lives are about having resources because the consequences of *not* having resources are just too much or too difficult to contemplate?

Serving What We Create

Coming back to us following and what drives our leaders: It's highly likely that we cannot even imagine or contemplate what our lives would be like if we live first-choice lives. If we could even imagine a first-choice life, we might not be so willing to abdicate our life choices to our supposed leaders. We possibly wouldn't even have the leadership structures that exist today—when leaders aren't driven by their Factor-x, they are thus true leaders living their lives as first-choice existences—we might have a society where each person is served by what we create—as opposed to as it stands today, where we serve what we create.

Everyone Sharing in Everything That Is Available

When we actually see what we are doing to ourselves and to others—our leaders included, our parents included—we'll almost certainly stop dead in our tracks. We'd probably start taking very good care of ourselves and everyone and everything. And everyone would start sharing equally in all that exists. Most probably, we would no longer overexploit our resources. Everyone would most likely take good care of everything they have, or are in charge of, or are responsible for, or in their care. When we eventually see what we're doing to ourselves and everyone and everything around us, it's likely these things would happen because we are living first-choice lives, and would almost certainly do things—automatically—so that everyone would win and no one would lose. Yet instead, it seems that we operate as products of our circumstances.

Circumstances Okay: We Are of High Spirit, It Seems Our Life Has Meaning

Okay, now we come to this very interesting aspect in everyday life. You find yourself high of spirit, light-hearted, and life is great. This feeling that things are just great has persisted for a week, or a month, or even for the last number of years, perhaps even decades.

From this feeling you experience, you feel that your life has meaning.

But is this really the case? Maybe you're feeling this way just because things have been going your way. Especially if you've been working hard at ensuring things go your way, your life actually seems to have meaning.

But is this really about meaning? Or, is it about being in the euphoria of things going your way?

Let's look at this another way. If things *stopped* going your way, what would your life then be like? What if you lost something that was important to your ongoing elation? Something like . . .

… the high-powered job
… the glamour of your job
… the honeymoon phase of your new relationship
… the massive profits you're making in business or the stock market
… the great house you purchased
… the continuous training your company sends you on or other perks
… the great things you can buy at whim because you have the funds
… the admiration you receive from your peers, boss, subordinates

… your well-known beauty or physical attractiveness
… your acclaimed stylishness
… your adeptness and success in sports
… your winning many awards and accolades

Say that one or more of these things ends for whatever reason. What then? Well, we can be sure that if a person loses any one of these things, almost any high will most likely end. It's also likely that the meaning these things brought to our life might come into question.

But what are we to make of it?

And is this really about meaning? Or, is it about us being in the euphoria of things going our way?

Let's consider that when we lose something, just maybe the elation and joy we felt about gaining it initially wasn't about meaning, but just about the euphoria.

What, then, is meaning?

Whenever we find true meaning, it most certainly won't come from something outside ourselves. Any meaning we find in life isn't derived from what we do. Whenever we do things, they either work or they don't work. When they do work, we get a high. When they don't work, we have a low. And as mentioned, it's highly likely that the euphoria we feel when things do work out comes from the high of things going our way.

Yet, this is all external stimuli. And external stimulus is not about meaning. It is when we look internally and *uncover* our meaning that we bring our meaning to what we do. *That* is meaning. *That* is a fulfilled life. That is also usually when we are creating. Not necessarily creating as in artifacts we create when doing activities like carpentry, sewing, painting, sculpting and so forth. These things aren't excluded, but aren't necessarily about manifesting our meaning. Rather, manifesting our meaning is about our life . . . about what we create with our life . . . our first-choice existence.

When we're living a first-choice existence, when things don't go our way, they just don't go our way, and we recognize that eventuality. When things do go our way, we recognize it's just that—things went right. Neither of these outcomes conjures up any meaning in itself. They are merely a by-product of our activities. It might make us feel great when things go our way, and we might feel heavy-spirited, even awful when things turn out different from what we would have preferred. But these by-products don't define us. When things don't work out, we'll merely dust ourselves off and look for other avenues, or even drop that particular endeavor, knowing that not achieving something doesn't mean we're failures, and it doesn't define us; it's just something that didn't work out. When our endeavor does work out, then it's just that—something that worked out, and that, in itself, doesn't define us. Because something worked out doesn't mean we're better than another person; it doesn't mean we're greater than others in any way; again, that something worked out doesn't define us. It's merely a by-product of an activity we undertook that worked out.

Aha! But with things that either work out or don't work out, we seem to insist that it must mean more than that. And why is that? Is it because we don't live our meaning, but instead derive meaning from the outcome of our activities?

Once we uncover our meaning, we will notice we do things for different reasons—definitely not because what we do defines us, but perhaps just because it's something that we do. And that "something" we do might just work out or might not work out, nothing more, nothing less!

Circumstances Change: We Plunge, and Our Life Seems to Have No Meaning

It might be that for several days, weeks, months, years or even decades, everything in your life has worked out well. In your younger years you also have lots of energy, and with our species' natural longing to fit into society, you worked hard at making your life work. Even if you didn't consciously work at making your life work, when you started your adult life, there were so many new things that occupied your time, you might not even have realized that the things you were busy with just incidentally worked out for you. Even while still in school, you might have been good at academics or a sport—or possibly good at academics *and* sports—so things worked out very nicely.

(There are of course students who do not like academics or sports who usually struggle at school. They might not yet know where their interests are. And there are those students who have interests elsewhere that might not be catered to. However, here, we're exploring where students excel in academics or sports or both.)

So imagine that year after year, or possibly even decades have gone by with everything just falling into place and working out exactly for you. Well, almost exactly. From time to time, things might not work out. But with some effort, you got yourself back on a track and maneuvered things until they worked out.

No doubt, everyone reading this can empathize with the above scenario. As we all experience, when things work out for us, we're on top of the world. We feel we can conquer everything. And, we experience that when things turn out slightly differently than we expected, it doesn't feel that good. We might even feel down. And then we find something or do something to get us out of what brings us down so we can stay on top. After all, being on top certainly is a good feeling. And by comparison, being down doesn't feel great at all. In fact, we'll do almost anything to avoid feeling down.

So far, we've looked at the smaller "down periods." But what about when something happens and we're down for an extended period, say, a month or even a year? What if we have an experience and are down for, say, five to ten years, and it turns out that we cannot see why we're down, but no matter what we do, we stay down?

What, then, if we're down for extended periods? As we all experience, a down period that only lasts for an hour or a day feels terrible. So what about feeling down for months, or a year, or even longer? Could anyone who hasn't experienced that even know what it feels like? Most probably not.

During these periods, we feel as if our life has no meaning, and we might become desperate to find something that'll get us out of "the down" just so we can feel alive again.

But perhaps we cannot get out of feeling down, so we stay down.

There are certainly people who seem to make things work out all the time. Their lives always seem to go well, and they probably don't know what it's like to have an extended down period. Of course, this is highly unlikely, and outside observers don't know everything about these people's lives. But it's still possible these people have never experienced an extended down period.

Either way, if our circumstances result in a feeling that our life has meaning, and then those circumstances turn to ones where we feel our life no longer has meaning, it begs the questions: Did our life have meaning to begin with? Had we actually been deriving "meaning" from our circumstances working out, and then lost our "meaning" when our circumstances didn't work out?

Is this indeed meaning, when the supposed meaning is influenced by circumstances?

Looking very carefully at meaning and circumstances, note that circumstances are things outside us. Yet our meaning isn't something that exists outside of us, but inside us.

So when things work out, and it feels that our lives have meaning, is that indeed the case?

Is it also possible that, even if our life works out during our whole lifetime, that our life perhaps isn't based on us living our meaning?

Product of Our Circumstances

As described elsewhere, whether our circumstances work out for us or don't work out, even when we live first-choice lives, it's almost certain that our emotions will still oscillate from euphoria to feeling down, even severely down.

When this happens to you, look carefully, if you dare, at what is happening in your life, and you'll see the following from your experiences: Whether up or down, we merely field the circumstances continuously thrown at us. Is it then fair to say that we're merely products of our circumstances? Are we, then, anything more than a product of the circumstances? Is this, then, anything more than a second-choice existence? When we live our lives with the belief that our circumstances define us, we tend to feed from or feed the circumstances, and our lives are invariably ineffectual. And then the question goes begging—do our lives indeed have meaning?

On the other hand, when we live first-choice lives and we manifest our meaning, then when circumstances are thrown at us, we merely roll with them. They don't define us, and we don't feed from or feed the circumstances.

Imagine living our whole life not being aware of this dynamic, and simply struggling from one circumstance to another to attempt to cope with what life throws at us. It seems such a waste, doesn't it? Especially since every person has wonderful meaning, albeit unrecognized. We could even equate our lives as equal to that of the sun or any marvelous natural creation, since we are, after all, natural creations.

There are also those of us who experience great circumstances. These people probably never struggle, or when they do, their struggle might be so short-lived or their resources so inexhaustible, adversity doesn't affect them. And because they have so few struggles and/or so many resources, they are unaware their life is most probably not a first-choice existence. What a tragedy!

People living first-choice existences don't usually have an abundance of resources, however. For them, it's usually a struggle to persist and make a stand. Having great ideas, like spreading this dynamic—of choosing to live a first or second-choice life or by living as products of our circumstances—is usually accompanied by a lack of resources to establish that message and get it to the world. Once we see that and want to break out—to no longer live in a fight with our Factor-x but *work alongside* our Factor-x—it can be difficult to spread the dynamic, because we also usually find that we have limited resources to "reestablish" ourselves and manifest our first-choice existences.

Luckily, having the resources or lack of resources doesn't define us, and doesn't need to stop us from living a first-choice life. Yet this definitely isn't a matter for the fainthearted. Ironically, this dynamic, being dependant on resources, also keeps us on track as being products of our circumstances.

The question is: Are we *willing* to break out—to uncover ourselves and live our first-choice lives?

Humankind Oblivious to Its Behavior

Every day, wherever we go, whatever we read, and whomever we encounter, it's the same things over and over. Humankind behaves in certain, specific ways, and we seem to be oblivious to our behavior.

Some of the Many Examples

State leaders summon their country to go to war. Governments, corporation managers, religious leaders, parents . . . just about everyone lies, is corrupt, and/or hurts other people or the environment in many ways. People in certain situations are requested to be open and honest, and you'll often hear or read of someone insisting that they were open and honest . . . in a particular case. People state that we need integrity for this or that. Yet we still have white-collar criminals, murderers, rapists, thieves, abusers, and this list can go on forever, to the point where it would become boring to write or to read.

The point is, we live in this world, we create and manifest more and more of this nonserving behavior every single moment, and it is indeed evident in our behavior. But it seems no one asks, "Why are we in this state?" or "How did we get here?" Are we then not in a state of hurting and abusing ourselves and others and everything else that exists on this planet, and either being oblivious to or in denial about it?

It is the purpose of this book and website to expose to humankind what it's doing to itself and everything around it, and why.

There Are No More Places to Hide

Starting with this book and with the accompanying website, in particular, thanks to the far-reaching ability of the Internet, these dynamics will be exposed in such a way that no literate person will ever again be able to say, "I didn't know what and why we're doing what we're doing to ourselves and to everything and everyone else."

When looking at documentaries, or the writings of different religions, or to whoever we want to listen to who has a theory on humankind's behavior, you'll notice that these sources rarely take their information to an easy and logically understandable place: making the information easy enough for anyone to see and understand. The numerous theories that exist are elaborate, all encompassing . . . *and likely based on guesswork.* To the average reader, none of it makes any sense. Even to the better-than-average reader, at least some of what these sources proclaim seems illogical. Take reincarnation for example, which you'll read more about in the sections titled, "Is This What You Are Looking For? (Spirit Guide: White Wolf)" and "Reincarnation and Karma." And often, you'll find that the writings of many different religions and organizations that look to cast clarity on why humankind does what it does are also . . . long, muddled, and boring.

You might be asking yourself, *What makes what's covered in this book and on the accompanying website any different?*

This is easy to answer. Everything we want to know about our lives and ourselves is already inside us, just waiting to be uncovered. We don't need to look anywhere else to find the answers. We merely need to observe our own behavior and see why we feel the way we feel and why we do whatever we do. You see, our wisdom lives inside of us. If we are brave enough to live our lives with integrity, we manifest ourselves. That automatically results in our being in harmony with ourselves, and with everyone and everything else. That is a first-choice existence: us in our natural, not nurtured form.

We seem to live our lives according to what everyone else decides or prescribes for us. No one says to us, "Stop, observe and decide for yourselves." No, quite the opposite, we are threatened: "If you don't do this or that, then this or that will happen to you."

Instead of threats and admonitions, are we guided by example by our caregivers? By our leaders? By our role models? Do we ever consider this? Why don't we stop and consider why we're being prescribed to—and why decisions are being made for us and we accept them without any consideration on our part.

How conducive are such threats to serving us? Not conducive at all. But we don't stop to question any of it.

So why don't we ask questions like these:

"Hey, why aren't we always open and honest?"

"Why do we live without integrity?"

"Why do companies need to be made aware of the need to comply with corporate governance?"

"Why is it so difficult to live openly and honestly or with integrity?"

"Why do we have fronts, and why do we put up fronts with others?"

"Why do we play certain roles?"

"Why do we go to war?"

"Why do we abuse ourselves?"

"Why do we abuse one another?"

"Why do we do the things we do to our children?"

This list could go on forever—and also become boring—but these should give you a list of the many questions we don't ask, but perhaps should.

It's likely that few people exist who are willing to look and listen, and then take one slow-but-assertive step at a time to live beyond what we are exposed to everyday. This book and website are designed to help this brave minority accomplish exactly those things, and offers that help in a clear and simple manner. In fact, they exist only for that purpose—to bring to the attention of anyone willing to look and listen to what goes on inside them, thereby exposing a simplified view of why we do what we do.

But the question remains: Why are we oblivious of what goes on around us, and even our own behavior?

Circumstantial Honesty

It seems that we are honest . . . when the need arises. Not honest as a matter of course, but only on specific and certain occasions.

How many people will steal something just because they are absolutely certain no one's watching?

How many people won't ever steal, even if they know with a hundred percent certainty that no one's watching?

Why are our openness and honesty circumstantial? Do we even recognize this dynamic? Do we take it for granted that it's seemingly our nature to be dishonest, and therefore we don't have the option to be open and honest?

Is the dynamic of being open and honest just there for certain people to live or to be?

In sports, we cheat as long as we're not caught. In relationships, we cheat as long as we're not caught. Is it the same with taxes? How many of us stick to speed limits?

Why is it that we're only honest when we absolutely have to be honest?

How much time is spent in courts to prove this or that, irrespective of whether this or that is, in fact, reflecting actual facts? "Good" lawyers and advocates and attorneys and solicitors will get someone off on a charge, not because of being honest and open about the real facts, but because they are seemingly good at their job.

When it serves us, will we lie?

But does this state of affairs serve anyone? On the surface, this might seem the case. But does lying really serve anyone? It's highly unlikely that dishonesty serves anyone. Perhaps in the short term, we might think it helped to be dishonest, or to be dishonest "just this once." Yet humankind as a species gets more and more "broken" as the openness and honesty is removed from its fabric.

But does anyone stand up and state, "This is enough!"?

Why is that?

Large corporations, government . . . in just about any situation requiring leadership roles, there are corrupt officials. These officials bend their honesty this way and that way to suit them. In this case as well, does anyone stand up to say, "This is enough!"?

We play around with openness and honesty as if they're commodities unrelated to our own fabric. Nevertheless, over time, we'll get farther and farther separated from our souls, eventually living only as survival machines that employ every technique we can muster up to survive the onslaught. It's as though we don't recognize that we, almost each individual, in our everyday lives, create and feed the onslaught of not being open and honest.

But when we stop and look at what drives the onslaught, what are we most likely to find? Likely, what drives the onslaught is nothing more and nothing less than our Factor-x.

This runaway train we're on, which results in us being economical with our openness and honesty, can only be stopped by us, by each individual—for our own sake and for no other reason. Where lays the responsibility for stopping it? If we don't see that it starts with each one of us, one at a time, then we need to look again.

The runaway train can't be stopped by the masses. We might say, "Why should we stop if it's unlikely that anyone else will stop?" Or, "If this is done one at a time, then it will take forever."

The reality is, dishonesty cannot be stopped en masse. It cannot be stopped in any other way than one individual at a time. Yes, it most probably would be several lifetimes later before it stops totally. But it starts with us, and now. It's up to us, one individual at a time, to withdraw from perpetuating the state of affairs. Each one of us, when we turn our lives from a second to a first-choice existence, contributes to stopping the runaway train of dishonesty. Only then do we become part of the solution. Until then, we're merely part of perpetuating the runaway train of dishonesty. Only when individuals take up their first-choice existences do they become unconditionally open and honest. When we are open and honest with ourselves, our inner peace starts. Only with such actions do we stand a chance to stop the runaway train of dishonesty. As seen previously how Factor-x drives us and when observing whether we are indeed free to choose, if we are not free to choose, we're likely to struggle with being open and honest, even with ourselves.

Spirit Manifesting Physically

When we are born, we aren't aware of our spirituality. Our parents were in exactly the same boat. Our soul, which is part of us and part of our spirituality, is nowhere to be seen. Nowhere in our life, as seen from humankind's behavior, would anyone even say we have a soul, or that we are spiritual beings.

Continuously throughout our life, our soul attempts to make us aware that it's there. Throughout our life, we more or less ignore our souls.

As a result, what we manifest with our life is certainly not us. When we look at Factor-x, as seen in "Factor-x and How It Comes About," we see that we're likely only manifesting disproving the existence of our Factor-x. (Therefore, in essence, we're likely nowhere to be found in our own lives.)

This anomaly of manifesting Factor-x as opposed to manifesting our own souls is handed down from our parents, from their parents, and so forth. This will continue until individuals see it for themselves and take back their own lives and start manifesting their own souls. This isn't something that can be achieved by one person on behalf of another person. Nor can it be achieved en masse.

We might wonder when or how we can recognize our souls. Well, it's relatively easy to recognize our souls, but it's not so easy to stop manifesting our Factor-x, which should first be stopped to allow us to manifest our souls.

Our behavior is merely an extension of either our Factor-x or our soul. Whenever we do or say one thing, but would have rather said or done another, these are instances of our soul being suppressed. Unfortunately, letting our souls out is easier said than done.

In looking at symptoms and causes, as you read about in "Treating Symptoms and Addressing the Cause," we see that we might be traveling down a road of merely looking at the symptom, not looking at underlying causes at all. So by attending only to symptoms, we don't stand a chance of getting to our soul. Instead, we're continuously in a struggle to look for the best of the worst options.

To really address the cause is to have the courage to address Factor-x. By doing so, we will thereby uncover ourselves, thus uncovering our souls as the core of our lives. Only once this is done can our souls be uncovered fully. Like with a baby learning to walk who has fallen, it's a matter of having the courage to get up and attempt it again. After a while, as with learning to walk, it becomes easier to see what our souls prefer, moment by moment. Unfortunately, this isn't possible without courage and brutal honesty with ourselves.

This isn't about changing the world; it's about individuals seeing their ways and consciously giving recognition to their souls. By doing this, one at a time, humankind has a chance to stop its current self-destructive path.

But in saying "humankind," I don't mean this is about another person. It is about us, starting with each individual being on a self-destructive path. It's about carrying this forward to our environment and everyone around us, including where children exist: perpetuating the anomaly to them, and they in turn transferring these things to their environment, and to their children, when they become adults. This reference to humankind is, in fact, a reference to each individual making up humankind. So be assured this isn't about someone else; it's about each individual. It is about us.

When looking at what humankind in general is doing and what individuals are specifically doing, it begs the question. *What are humankind's intentions through each individual?*

Guessing about it, quite possibly, we aren't even aware of our souls, or that we're part of a collective human spirit, incorporating the earth plane and spirit world. Likely, individuals don't even see themselves as spirit beings, or that they have souls that are being smothered. This reference to "soul" isn't about something external, this is referring to ourselves—as in, we are smothering ourselves. Are we living our lives feeling that we are being smothered? If so, that smothering is being done by us to ourselves.

Most likely, an individual isn't even aware of his or her role in the bigger scheme of things—that individuals make up humankind. We contribute to humankind whether we know it, understand it, or agree with it. In doing nothing and continuing to manifest our Factor-x, we contribute to humankind's destruction.

You might be asking, "Who am I?" or "What can I do?" When we uncover our souls and see our roles in humankind and in the spirit world, then our contribution is about turning humankind around, away from its own destruction . . . one individual at a time . . . automatically . . . just by being ourselves. We don't have to do anything specific or special. Our own manifestation is specific and special—simply by our manifestation, we'll automatically contribute to humankind's wellbeing.

Is it safe to say, then, based on our current behavior, it's clear we're not manifesting our souls: that we don't see ourselves as spirit beings manifesting physically here on Earth as earthlings? That what we're doing instead is manifesting our Factor-x, thereby smothering ourselves? Once we recognize this, it is possible to start uncovering ourselves.

Recognizing Spirit After Trauma

Several books have been written, and we might have seen movies or documentaries, about people whose lives dramatically changed after they had traumatic experiences. There are also people who get to a certain age and start questioning their lives and make drastic changes. And you might very well have had traumatic experiences, or even started questioning your life. Perhaps one of these reasons is why you feel the thirst and are reading this book. Or, perhaps you haven't yet worked through a traumatic experience. If you've not yet had any of these experiences, it's likely that, at some point in your life, you will find yourself in one of these situations—either the survivor or a near survivor of a harrowing experience, or a person still grappling with a traumatic experience. Or, you might be a person who has reached a point in your life where you don't feel satisfied.

When we are placed in harsh conditions, for us to survive, we are required to dig deep: We are required to work very hard to save ourselves. If we are lucky, we might even dig deep enough to see our souls. In those books and movies I just mentioned, the changes that happened most likely occurred when the person uncovered their soul and then allowed their soul to guide their lives starting from the traumatic incident.

Yet, if we never have such a life-changing experience, what are we to do if we thirst for a change in our lives?

We can do nothing, and simply live our second-choice existence. Or, we could be brutally honest with ourselves to find out if the life we created is indeed the life we like, or if we are merely caught up in the flow of circumstances that make up our lives. In other words, we can decide to *stop and look at our second-choice existences*, or we can *admit that we cannot or do not have the courage to stop and look at our lives*.

The choice can be difficult, because it takes courage to make needed changes in our lives. Courage is needed because those adjustments might take more pain and work than we are willing to put forth. Yet if we decide to do nothing, all that remains is the *second-choice* existence, with no chance of ever living our *first-choice* existence.

This latter choice—to do nothing—might be okay for some people, but not okay for others. People who have had difficult and traumatic experiences, and even near death experiences—those who had no choice—often say they feel as if they got a second chance with their lives.

The question is, why wait for a trauma that might never happen? Why not just look at your life right now instead?

In some cases, people recalling their traumatic experience say they saw flashes of their lives. This might have happened to you. Whether or not it has, have you ever considered why this occurs? Why these people see their lives flash by? Why they invariably make life-altering changes? Why they say it seems, to them, that they now have a second chance at their lives?

Could it be that they saw what their lives had come to? Could it be that what they saw, they didn't like? Could it be that they saw their *second-choice existences* flash by?

If we look really closely at our lives in an open and honest way, *without* waiting for a traumatic experience to "force" us to, might we see the same existence as what people who've endured traumatic experiences see?

Not Recognizing Our Flight to Crutches

While living second-choice existences, it is possible we feel smothered, and that our lives, therefore, are likely not pleasant at all? If circumstances go as expected, then of course we are elated. But when circumstances don't go as expected, then our lives are most probably not that great. And yes, this isn't a pleasant state of affairs for us.

How do we counter it when we're not feeling great?

Do we even recognize our patterns?

What are our patterns when things don't go according to plan?

Do we even recognize that we have patterns when things don't go according to plan?

Apart from us feeling terrible, possibly even about ourselves, and wanting to then do things to bring fun into our lives—things to make us feel better: these things, mind you, again are outside of ourselves, so this strategy merely treats the symptoms. And as said before, we are likely oblivious to our patterns and that we even do these things.

Oh, but wait. We might even search for things to keep us feeling good, just so we never get to the part where we feel bad. Either way, there is a dynamic of escaping built into our lives, just so we don't feel the pain of when things don't work out for us.

What are typical things we run to when we're down and want to feel good, or things we do to avoid being quiet, to prevent the pain from setting in?

Look at the different things we do to keep us busy. Are these things serving us, or only keeping us from dealing with the source of the problem? Whenever we do things to keep us busy or to keep us from feeling pain, are we using these things as crutches because it seems easier than addressing the cause of why we're feeling terrible or why we're feeling pain? How many times have we said or thought the following? *Oh, I could never be on my own*, or, *I want to have fun with my life*, or, *I don't like spending quiet time on my own.*

What are these activities, other than possible crutches to suppress the loneliness we feel? Were we to stop for a moment and experience what we feel, then we might stand a chance to know ourselves better and better. And in so doing, we might have the chance to see whether we run away from reality into a life of living with crutches to suppress what we're really experiencing.

How much of this is going on in our lives? What could be the cause of this dynamic? Is it pointing to the fact that, quite possibly, we're living second-choice existences, and the pain of doing so is so great, we run to crutches to suppress it?

But does it really help to suppress it? Is this dynamic of running for crutches symptomatic of the real cause: We're living second-choice existences and thereby smothering ourselves—and to get away, we run to crutches?

Have you ever considered why, when we sit still for more than a moment, why it starts to become so difficult to remain still? Ever wonder why we keep ourselves busy continuously? Ever considered why we have unwanted habits we can't shake off?

Could relying on these crutches be related to us living second-choice existences? That when we become quiet, or wish to shake off unwanted habits, it overwhelms us, and as a result, we employ crutch-like mechanisms to suppress our real feelings? And that we do this because we possibly think our life has no meaning or is just a meaningless struggle, the result of us not living our first-choice existences?

What are the chances that we employ crutches as a survival mechanism—to avoid the pain we inflict on ourselves by not addressing the dynamic of us living our lives to disprove our Factor-x and thus not living our meaning?

The question begs asking again—do the crutches help?

Forms of Crutches

There are oh, so many forms of crutches. Let's look at various crutches and attempt to see them for what they are.

- *Drugs, Smoking and Alcohol:* Drugs, smoking and alcohol are easily recognizable as crutches.

Now, are we brave enough to recognize the others?

- *Religions, churches and the god-role:* Controversial as it might seem, can religions and the inherent god-role that we follow and aspire to live by also be crutches? Very likely. When things are going well with us, we might not be as keen to follow our religion. But when things don't go well, we are quite possibly there like a shot. What does this tell us?

- *Money:* We have crutches like money. Without it, we feel we are nothing, as if the money defines us. Is this, then, not a crutch?
- *Parents, and Having Children:* How many children are born so the woman can stay at home so as not to be part of making a living? How many men keep their wives or partners pregnant and at home for their own crutch? Oh, and about women that don't insist on participating in earning an income to contribute toward household expenses: Could it be that this particular crutch cuts both ways—for the woman, so she doesn't need to contribute to the household earnings, and for the man so he can have a kept woman?

  How many children are born as a crutch to either or both of their parents? Or, perhaps their birth provides some particular value to the lives of the parents. Are these really reasons to have children? In this situation, the parents aren't really having the child for the child's sake, but for the particular value the child brings to either parent or possibly both parents. Could this be just another form of a crutch?
- *Relationship Expenses:* When we're single and dating, and long after the courting stage, men are expected to pay for everything, and women rarely offer to contribute. This dynamic seems to cut even further. Men keep woman barefoot and in the kitchen; women expect men to pay for them: And vice versa. Could this dynamic be anything different from a crutch?

  My suggestion to anyone who finds themselves in this position, whether they are kept by their partner or spouse, or provide full support to a partner or spouse, is to look carefully at why we expect this of our partner or spouse.

  Let's also look at this in another way. When we don't display this behavior, what happens to the party who expects this behavior? When this expected behavior plays out as expected we feel okay; otherwise, we don't. Again, are these possibly crutches we've devised because we're living second-choice existences?
- *Wanting Better Things:* Look carefully at the saying of "living up to the Joneses." Why would we do this? Could it be that we believe we'll feel good about ourselves when we consider ourselves

like or even better than the Joneses? In reality, we're saying that when we have what the Joneses have (or even more), then we can be "proud" of ourselves. Or until then, we're possibly not as good as the Joneses are. Or words to that effect.

Or perhaps we have a need to show we're even better than they are. If this is the case, doesn't this imply that, right now, we feel inferior to them? That until we have or achieve "this or that," we really feel inferior? Again, this shows that we deem things outside ourselves as defining us. Is this not a crutch?

What about when we want certain things like shiny cars, a particular person as a partner, a house in a particular suburb, particular accessories, a particular style of clothing, a particular mobile phone . . . this list is probably without end. But do we ever stop and look at why these particular things are so important to us? Could it be that these items and things give us meaning, albeit briefly?

Have you ever considered why we do the various things we do? Yes, it will take courage to look and to see. We might look and not see. Yet the idea, of course, is to look and to see why we do the things we do.

- *Mr. Nice Guy or Ms. Nice Gal:* When we want to be Mr. Nice Guy or Ms. Nice Gal, what lies behind this? Are we not being like this to portray us in a certain light? Why is this? Is it possible that if we do this, we then consider ourselves superior? Is this not a crutch?

- *Abuse:* When we abuse a child, a spouse, a partner, or anyone or anything, is it possible that doing this provides us with a feeling of superiority? Is this, then, not a crutch?

- *Relationships-and-People Dependencies:* We have the tendency of habitually going into relationships. Or, to feel depressed or lost when not in a relationship. So when we're not in a relationship, we get into a variety of activities to go looking for someone to be in a relationship with, hoping to bounce right into another relationship after having broken up a previous relationship.

Then there is the condition of latching onto other people for company. We have the notion of surrounding ourselves, in lesser or greater degree, with people to have company. In effect, so we won't be alone.

Do we build great friendships and relationships based on the need for company?

Do we make periodic visits to others, not necessarily enjoying the visit, but preferring the visit to being alone, thinking that being with someone, anyone, is better than being by ourselves, even though when we're with them, we're not necessarily enjoying ourselves? Do we do this because being alone is just too unbearable?

When we have this behavior—to be in relationships, whether as partner or friend or family member—and these are based on not wanting to be on our own, then are we not *using* the other person? And this cuts both ways: in which case, are both parties using the other? That begs the question: Are those genuine relationships, or friendships, or family bonds? If we were living our meaning, and were independent people secure in ourselves, would we then still have these dependencies? Would we then still have these friendships, or relationships, or family bonds, and would we still be taking part in such activities?

Looking at it from another angle: If we were living our meaning, would we still have such dependencies and almost-ritualistic behaviors? If not, aren't these activities crutches?

• *Distractions:* When alone, do we have a tendency to have the television or radio on in the background? Consider this in your own life. Do you ever just spend time on your own, just yourself without distractions? Are you forever keeping busy to fill time? Are you in a constant process of distracting yourself in various ways—perhaps some of those ways just mentioned? Do you ever consider why we employ these likely distractions? Is it possibly because we find some security in such distractions: for example, because we don't want to feel cut off from the world? Conversely, if we felt secure within ourselves, would we need those distractions to keep us from feeling cut off from the world? While we are creating such distractions, are we really giving ourselves an opportunity to get to know ourselves; to uncover ourselves; to uncover what we'd really like to be doing with our life? Are these distractions anything more than our mechanism to cover up an emptiness?

- *Not Seeing the Actual Person:* Factor-x gets us into things we aren't even aware of. You'll likely be surprised to see the variants of Factor-x's manifestations.

  A specific, person-to-person example is when we do things with and associate with others for no reason other than to appease our Factor-x. Thus, instead of seeing the person for himself or herself—the actual person, the real person—we see them in relation to whether they appease our Factor-x.

  Do you, perhaps, spend time with people because they appease your Factor-x in some way; are you really there because that's where you want to be? Do you, perhaps, measure people according to whether they appease your Factor-x—if they appease your Factor-x you like them, otherwise, you don't? Do you ever see the real person you're spending time with?

  Oh, and then there's the fact that we continue doing things with others just because we can't say no. In this situation as well, we're there not because we really want to be, but because of the consequences: possibly losing the friendship or relationship. And for most of us, that's too disastrous to contemplate.

  You might not even be aware you behave in this way—that you only associate with people in relation to whether they satisfy your Factor-x or that you see and recognize this behavior in yourself. Now, if I don't see my behavior, do I actually stand a chance to see myself or the other person? This dynamic is likely also the same for the other person. Thus, we likely don't see each other: the real people we are. Instead, we likely only see each other from a stance of what our Factor-x perceives.

- *Keeping Busy as Opposed to Living with Purpose:* How much time do we spend merely keeping busy? Is keeping busy rewarding? Is keeping busy a healthy way to live life? Is keeping busy meaningful? While keeping busy, we likely feel something is missing. So why do we *keep busy* as opposed to *living with purpose?*

When we're young and innocent and playful, without a worry or a care, we go about things peacefully, playfully. Soon our caregivers start reining us in, as they were reined in themselves as children. Sometime after this "restricting process" begins, we give up fighting for ourselves and we create our Factor-x. Since we're only children, even if we were aware of what's happening to us, it would be virtually impossible for us to get our supposed caregivers to see that we'd like to just get on with our own thing. Even if they weren't bigger and stronger than we are, they supposedly have all the good reasons in the world for tempering us.

But it seems no one ever stops and sees what we're doing to our young ones. Eventually, the child we are just gives in. The fight and struggle is just too much, and we take on our Factor-x. Once this happens, everything changes. From that moment, we don't care about anything other than disproving that we have a Factor-x. After taking on Factor-x, our lives are no longer about us. And as we grow into older children, teenagers, young adults, and then grownups, we never shake this way of living just to disprove our Factor-x. Instead of going for what we like doing with our lives, we likely don't, because we've been ingrained with the knowledge that if we do the things we like doing, we're going to be reprimanded, possibly even punished. Our actions remain that of children, not maturing at all. The pattern has been interwoven into our lives that we dare not do what is important to us, the things we like doing. We're stuck in the past, keeping busy to merely pass time. We have likely given up on ourselves, to the point where it takes material like this book to get us to stop and look at what we're doing to ourselves, individually and as a species.

Looking at all these behaviors and attitudes carefully, aren't all of them possibly crutches? Isn't it time for us to see our behavior and get to the point of saying, "No more"? Isn't it time to break out and stop merely filling time? Isn't it time for us to uncover ourselves and stand up for what we like doing? Isn't it time for us as a species to manifest ourselves, starting with each individual? Isn't it time for us to live our first-choice life? Isn't it time to *stop* keeping busy, to *stop* thoughtlessly engaging in behaviors and thought processes that don't benefit us (or anyone else)? Isn't it time to *stop* leaning on crutches so we can live our lives fully?

Letting Go of Crutches

You might have been dependant on a crutch, or even several crutches, for your whole life, or maybe for a shorter period. It might be that you really didn't know any better, and as a result held onto things because you thought that was how your life should be. And now, by reading this material, you might see that these past behaviors were only a crutch or crutches you used because you lacked your own strength.

So now, when you consider giving up a crutch or breaking away from a crutch, it seems that doing so might cause your whole world to crumble, and you don't have the courage to let go. Or you might be thinking that you'll find something to put in the place of a crutch: a substitute. Is this not exchanging one crutch for another?

Let's take a smoker; once they stop smoking, they might start eating sweets. Is this behavior not merely exchanging one crutch for another?

When the craving or need arises for lighting a cigarette, my suggestion to the smoker is to instead look for what created the craving, and address that instead of exchanging one crutch for another. (For further help in determining why the need arises, read "Reliving the Moment to Uncover Its Importance" later in this book.)

What applies to smoking applies to other crutches as well. Say a Christian (or a person of whatever religion) wants to get out of using their religion as a crutch. Bearing in mind that this person's life might have revolved around the religion, including its worship rituals, such a person might not know what to do next. The point is, we don't need to do anything next in the sense of replacing one crutch with another. The mere fact that we might be considering *What next?*

is most likely about identifying something to put in the place of the crutch. Whatever we take up in the place of a crutch, it's likely to be just another crutch. In such a case, the person might just decide to leave things be and stay with the existing crutch.

The only way past this is to recognize that we have crutches, look at the reason why a crutch became necessary, and identify what transpires in us when considering dropping the crutch. Yes, it's likely that giving up the crutch will result in a void. It's also highly likely to be difficult to give up a crutch. The remnant void is likely just too painful to contemplate, and if we gave up the crutch, we'd likely want to return to it, or to find another crutch to fill the void left by giving it up. However, the most important thing is to recognize that the crutch exists, that it might have been a lifelong habit, and that we most probably have deep-rooted scars due to needing the crutch. But again, it's important to look at why we needed the crutch in the first place.

Or, we can *look at the moment when we usually take flight to a crutch*.

When we drop such crutches . . . and we don't run for the crutch when the first difficulty or opportunity arises that usually drives us to a crutch, even if panic sets in . . . if we instead quiet ourselves . . . then, when all the frenzy subsides, and we look at what else is there in our lives at that moment . . . what else comes up in our feelings in that moment . . . what daydreams we might have in that moment . . . even look at what else we'd rather be doing at that time: *in that moment when we usually take flight to a crutch*, we can recognize the void created by letting go of a crutch, and the difficulty that might result from that void.

Be aware. Recognize the temptation to look for a replacement crutch to fill the void left by letting go of a current crutch. Recognize the anxiety that might arise from letting go of the crutch. Recognize that others might not accept us when we let go of the crutch. Recognize peer and family pressures, especially with religions or dogmas and their like. Recognize the pressures we put on ourselves related to feeling we'd be ostracized when we let go of a crutch. Recognize the temptations of wanting to replace a crutch with something else, or even the related inertia when thinking about letting go of a crutch. Recognize that letting go of lifelong crutches is a daunting experience.

Recognizing that it isn't easy to let go of a crutch, you might be thinking, *Why should we let go of the crutches at all?*

This comes back to the first and second-choice existences. When looking carefully at the dynamics of crutches, crutches fill a void. They're about giving us security, and they're external things supposedly giving us what already exists within each of us. Yet crutches also keep us from getting to know ourselves. Crutches keep us from experiencing ourselves. Crutches cover up the fact that there are voids in our lives. Crutches hold us back from uncovering our meaning. Crutches hold us back from discovering what it is we'd prefer to do with our lives. Crutches hold us back and hold us in the clutches of our Factor-x.

To let go of a crutch is not where it starts. It starts at recognizing that crutches exist in our lives. It starts at recognizing the need for the crutch in our lives. It starts at why there is a need for the crutch in our lives. Now, we're getting somewhere: to the bottom of where the need for the crutch arises.

It's highly likely that the need for the crutch originates in line with our Factor-x: that the void that exists in our lives is likely a result of our creation of our Factor-x. Factor-x leaves a void in our life that needs filling. We fill it with crutches.

Is Factor-x something real, or is it a fabrication by us? Say Factor-x is a fabrication by us, and therefore Factor-x has no substance. If this is true, then the void also doesn't exist. But is a crutch needed to fix (support) something that isn't broken or empty?

Yes, we attempt that with our crutches. But do we succeed? Not likely. Instead, crutches take up the space in our lives that exists due to our voids, so we never get to see or address the voids. Therefore, we never get to know ourselves and what our lives are really about. Acknowledging the role of our Factor-x is an important step in learning to identify and address our crutches. So in fact, our dependency on crutches has quite the opposite effect by hiding our first-choice existence from us.

Crutch Now Reality

You might ask yourself: Could a crutch be something I actually want? Could it be that once I've healed myself from Factor-x's influence, what served as a crutch is now something I'll want to keep?

Say that we might have been using someone as a crutch in a mostly Factor-x–driven friendship or relationship. Once we're healed, if we see we like the person for who they are rather than because of the influence of our Factor-x, can we now continue to have a healthy friendship or relationship with the person?

Yes, we can. Let's look at a house, car, job, friend or partner. Let's say we once extracted value or self-worth from our upmarket house or fancy car or glamorous job, or from a fabulous friend or partner— or even that we were using a friend or partner as a crutch against loneliness or feelings of inadequacy. And let's say we've shaken our behavior at the root cause of extracting self-worth and other values imposed by Factor-x. Now, once we've seen our behavior and addressed the cause—where it originates with our Factor-x—then certainly we'd likely keep those possessions, retain our friendship, stay in our job, or remain with our partner. In this case, there's no need to toss out our possessions, break up a friendship, or leave our partner.

Thus, there are some crutches we'd probably not want to get rid of after waking up to our Factor-x–driven ways. But there might be other crutches we won't want to retain after seeing our ways and then freeing ourselves; the abuse of ourselves or others is an example of a crutch we would definitely shed. But, there is a danger in the dynamic of retaining a crutch after seeing our ways and our dependency on it. We could easily kid ourselves into thinking and justifying to ourselves that we have indeed shaken the need for the crutch while we still unknowingly extract self-worth from it.

It's not farfetched that what was previously a crutch, once the value extracted from it isn't necessary for our self-worth anymore, is then seen for what it is: a house is merely a roof over our head; a car is just transport; a friend is simply someone to share common interests with; a partner is purely someone to share our life with, and so forth. No reason likely exists to toss those out. Yet the above might not be the case: When we get over our need for the crutch and we see we don't want a possession—say the possession doesn't suit us anymore, or we recognize we just don't get along with someone we previously saw as a friend or partner—then in all likelihood, we'd get rid of the possession or break off the friendship or break up with our partner.

So after freeing yourself, if you find yourself wanting to retain the thing or person you once used as a crutch, be careful; doing so might mean you haven't shaken the need yet. Also, in looking back at a crutch-based relationship, it's likely it wasn't a real friendship or partnership with that person to begin with.

Hope

Do we ever do things just because we like doing them? Where we don't expect them to work? Where we have no hope that they'll work? Where we just do them for the sake of doing them, just because it's something we like doing?

Invariably, the answer is no. We almost certainly never do anything without hope. When a child plays, the child isn't concerned about the outcome. When we grow up, we become almost obsessed with wanting an outcome of some sort. We won't do anything without hoping for an outcome.

Let's look at this in another way. Let's say we take a journey. Of course we want to get to our destination. When we set out to make something, of course we want to end up with that item. When we set out to write a book, of course we want to end up with a book. So it's clear that these types of outcomes aren't what are meant here.

Say we want to write that book, and of course we'll end up with a book. But perhaps we want to write a book whether it sells or not. Will we still write the book?

A book is only one example. If there is anything that we'd like to do just because it is important to us, and there are absolutely no guarantees of the outcome, will we actually still do that particular thing?

Oh, and this isn't about a fun thing to do; it's about something important, like writing a book. Or perhaps something bigger: going into an undertaking based on a dream, and possibly even putting everything we have into it irrespective of whether it'll work out or not. There are movies with this theme, where the actor stops a particular career to pursue a dream, and puts everything on the line just because that's what they'd like doing—again, irrespective of the outcome. Yet this occurs in everyday life. In our jobs or with whatever we do, we might hope that what we do gets recognized, as opposed to doing something because it's important to us irrespective of whether that deed is recognized or not.

When slowing down our minds so we can look carefully at what goes on, how much of what we do is about *hope this* or *hope that*, as though almost always hoping for a particular outcome is part of the equation?

Or, turning the topic the other way: How much of what's going on in our lives is about things that are important, and not reliant on *some hope this way* or *some hope that way*? Can we ever say we're doing something important to us—and taking it further, that we'll do it even without any guarantees of the outcome? That notwithstanding the outcome, we'll do it anyway, even when it's likely the outcome will be a flop?

Consider this. How much of what we do is based on hope of a particular outcome, rather than doing it just because it's important?

There is another side to this. Assume that we're entirely outcome based; therefore, we do things merely because we hope to achieve some outcome. However, when we have almost a guarantee that we won't create the desired outcome, would we then still pursue the particular activity? If we can say yes, can we then see in a new light what we're doing, and recognize that when we're doing something important to us, we'll do it irrespective of the outcome? And if we'd rather not pursue a particular activity because its outcome isn't guaranteed, can we then deduce that just maybe the activity isn't important to us?

Could we also say that when an activity is important, we'll do it whether we create the desired outcome or not, and that we're doing it just because it's important to us? If so, and when we're not driven by the outcome when pursuing an activity, *hope* doesn't come into the picture at all.

False Sense of Security

Let's look at some of our behavior and explore what it provides us.

- *Crutches*

  When we look at crutches as mentioned previously in "Forms of Crutches," are they anything other than something for us to lean on: something that provides us with some form of security? If we were secure in ourselves, would we look externally for security? Then is it fair to say that crutches provide us with a false sense of security?

- *Hoping and Wishing*

  A few questions.

  > … How much of what we do is done hoping and wishing for a certain result?
  > … How much of what we do is to fill a certain need or particular needs?
  > … How many of these hopes are realized—how many of them materialize to give us security in our lives?
  > … When we look carefully at each of these situations where we do things, then hope and wish for a particular result, did we do them to provide us with some form of security?
  > … If we were really okay with ourselves, then would we want to do or have any of those things that provide us with supposed security?

  Maybe not.

  Even so, consider how much of what we do in our everyday lives that might fall into this category: doing things for the security doing them supposedly provides us, perhaps much more than we realize or would like to admit. If this is the case, then just maybe we aren't okay within ourselves.

Let's consider the following behavior.

- *Favoritism, Status and Wealth:* Say we do something for someone else, perhaps to be in that person's good graces. Then to be in that person's good graces gives us something—most likely, some security.

  Let's look at another example. Say we accumulate wealth so we can consider ourselves as "having arrived" or to have status. Is this newly found status, or "having arrived," not a form of making us feel secure? And again, if this is the case, then if we were already secure within ourselves, would we have pursued accumulating wealth?

- *Association:* Say we associate with a certain person because we feel that person understands us, and without that person, we wouldn't have anyone else to associate with who understands us. Through this association, we feel secure within ourselves. Again, if we were already secure within ourselves, would we then have this association?

- *Holding onto Things:* Like associating with certain people, or our expensive house, luxurious car, or "status job." Not just because we need those for what they are—for example, the car is for transportation—but for the security they provide us.

- *Superstition:* By doing things in a certain way, or wearing a certain item, or like sportsman who have certain rituals, superstition is likely to provide security.

- *Wanting to Please:* We might want to please a particular person or people in general, or even God, as a way of keeping us entrenched in their favor, or because this behavior makes others dependant on us. Again, we're likely doing it for the security it provides.

- *Brands, Image and Religion:* We derive external security from having money, a particular partner, a certain job, specific clothing brands or jewelry; projecting a certain image, residing in a certain neighborhood, being part of a certain group, going to a certain school, belonging to a religion or a particular religious group, having membership in a certain organization, being married, having children, shopping at certain places.

- *Status, Figure and Titles:* In England we have a queen. How much of that is about status and image? In England, people are honored by decorating them with honorary titles. How much of that is also about status and image? And again, that status and image likely provides those receiving the honorary title with security. But if those people were already secure within themselves, would they be looking for security outside themselves?

- *Wanting Things Done for Us by Spouse, Partner or Children:* When we expect our spouses, partners or children (if we have them) to do things for us, aside from the daily "share the load" chores we'd rather not do ourselves—and we sulk or morally blackmail them if they don't do what we want them to do, do we do this because we feel we deserve it, or to feel powerful or wanted? If we do this, are we not manipulating them to do things for us, thereby enforcing our importance on them? Is the importance we derive not giving us a false sense of security? If we already felt our inner security and power, would we then need to derive it externally by forcing our importance on spouses, partners or children?

- *Looking for Signs:* When we find ourselves in a position of making decisions, especially those that aren't easy and straightforward: Do we look for signs, whether minor or major, to help us make the decision . . . to bring meaning so we can make the decision? If we were living our meaning, if we were secure in ourselves, wouldn't we likely make the decision by ourselves? If we did, irrespective of how it turned out, we would stand by it. After all, it was our decision.

- *Being Spiteful:* Sometimes we feel like being spiteful, or we're treated in a spiteful way. Is this anything other than the person being spiteful, being in a position of power at that time for some reason, and then exerting that power by being spiteful? The momentary-power position likely gives us (or them) a sense of security. If that were the case, and it is likely the case—if we're already experiencing our own inner security and our own inner power, then would there be any need to be spiteful? Does being spiteful then not give us a false sense of security?

- *Working Well Under Pressures of Deadlines:* Why do we like working under pressure to meet deadlines? Those of us who struggle to make decisions likely struggle because we could be wrong, and if we're wrong, that would put us in the spotlight—and this is, of course, food for our Factor-x. As a result, we usually refrain from making decisions. Under the pressures of deadlines, when something goes wrong, we can blame the deadline. Under a pressing deadline, we feel it's okay to make decisions and to be assertive. If problems arise, we can blame the deadline. However, if we were already strong and secure within ourselves, wouldn't we work without deadlines and enjoy what we're doing much, much more? And we might even stay away from tasks where deadlines are the order of the day.

- *Promises:* Do we make promises from time to time? First, as you will read about later in "Expectations: Frustration, Anger and Irritation," promises are about expectations. Second, promises give some form of relief, and that relief, in turn, gives us a feeling, however fleeting, that we're secure from the threat of consequences for which we made the promise. But it seems that it's the same as before—if we were already secure within ourselves, the promise, which also sets us up for expectations, would possibly not be necessary.

These are merely some examples. The list could probably wrap the Earth—even be boring in its extent.

Consider this statement: *Well, if I'm doing all these things for the security they provide me, and in the event I find my own security—which when found, I'd find within myself—then surely doing things like associating with certain people or things or having superstitions provides a false sense of security.*

Again, if we were secure within ourselves, would we seek security externally? If we were secure within ourselves, would we want to be doing or having these things for the supposed security they provide us? Highly unlikely.

The bigger questions are:

How much of our lives consist of relying on a false sense of security?

Even more important, are we even aware that this pattern exists in our lives?

Also, if we lived from our own inner security, then how different would our lives be?

Taking it even further, when humankind realizes this and we—each individual making up humankind—start living our lives from our own inner security, then how much different will our lives be? How different would the things be that you undertake in your life? How different would your behavior be? How different would your experiences be? How different would *humankind's* behavior be?

When we do things that are unrelated to gaining a false sense of security, we'd most probably be doing very different things with our lives. It is most probably unimaginable what our lives would be like.

The main thing is to become aware that you likely have and live this pattern of looking for security in many things outside of your-self. Yet when you do find security, you will find that it already exists within you, albeit dormant—in a sort of winter sleep—for all this time, possibly even for your whole life.

Why are these activities that provide us with security necessary? Most probably because they add some value to our lives. However, the question remains, do they really add value? Or is this value merely based on some perception not based on reality?

Whatever you or I do to provide us with external security, when we lose it, we're likely to feel devastation. Our lives could even fall apart. As a result, we'd feel lost. We'd struggle to find our feet. We might even become suicidal.

When our pillar/s of strength wobbles for whatever reason, and a particular activity or activities which we lean on for security changes or disappears, or when we cannot rely on our pillar/s of strength anymore, it's likely that our lives become threatened and possibly even become meaningless.

Should this happen to you, is this not clear indication that these things didn't really serve you? That they instead provided you with a false sense of security, which you wouldn't have needed if you uncovered your own inner security?

Integrity

How many times do we say what we mean, or even mean what we say? How much of our lives consist of doing what is important? How often do we do things that are important to us? Do we *ever* do things that are important to us? Are we even aware of the things that we do that are important to us?

Consider this: If you're only doing things that are important to you, moment for moment, wouldn't you then mean what you say and say what you mean? If you find that you don't say what you mean or mean what you say, is it possible that you don't do things that are important to you?

And along with "say what I mean" and "mean what I say," we can also include "do what I say" and "say what I'll do."

And when we don't "say and do" what we mean, or don't mean what we "say and do," do we then have integrity?

And when we are *not* "saying and doing" things that are important to us, do we then have integrity?

If the above is the case for you, then whose life are you living? What drives your life?

The above are tongue twisters, but when looking carefully at them, and they apply in our lives, then just maybe we aren't living our lives with integrity.

That being the case, how many people on this Planet Earth are in this same boat of not living their integrity?

Is it any wonder, then, that we do what we do to ourselves and others, and to the planet itself? And is it any wonder that humankind is likely on a self-destructive path? Oh, and by the way, this self-destructive path starts in our own lives. So if it's indeed the case, then isn't each of us also likely on this path?

When reading, watching or listening to the news, it is easy to observe many examples where people display their lack of integrity. Presidents, politicians and governments declare war on other nations. Spouses abuse their partners, either physically or emotionally. Parents abuse their children, either physically or emotionally. We get robbed. Men and women and children are being raped. We dare not leave anything unattended or unlocked. Our children cannot walk to school. We have political and business leaders who don't practice good corporate governance or are outright corrupt. We have military and police who are corrupt or commit crimes. Adults and children starve and suffer malnutrition. There are people who have enough and even more than enough, yet there are people who do not have the essentials. Adults and children use drugs. Women get pregnant without realizing they have a guidance and caretaking responsibility toward their children. We ruin our environment; we strip it bare to appease our greed.

The system we created and feed every single day serves nobody. Some people cope and others don't cope within this skewed system. Those who cannot cope are left out to dry. Nobody seems aware that the beggars and homeless and criminals are merely people who didn't cope in the system we all created and continuously feed. Likely, this is because nobody seems to question the system. Those who have achieved within the system frown upon those that don't cope, and blame them for not coping. They even look upon those who don't cope as weaklings.

That we're oblivious to the system we're an integral part of doesn't serve anyone. We are oblivious to the knowledge that we have a say in the system. Those who have "made it" won't stop for a moment to say, "Hey, let's fix the system so that everyone can have a fair chance with their lives."

But that's just as well, because one person can't make it right for another person. It is best for each of us to see our ways, and then adjust things for ourselves. Over time, as we adjust our lives, those around us stand a better chance, and perhaps a million years of one individual at a time making their own adjustment will enable each person to walk over the line to live their integrity.

But while we live without our integrity, the things that happen around us, and sometimes to us, will continue until we self-destruct—all because we almost certainly lack integrity.

Demystifying What/Who We Are

Every so often, we hear people saying, "This is what I am" or "This is who I am."

But is this really the case, or is it merely that those people are saying; "This is what I *think* I am" or "This is who I *think* I am"?

And when people say they are: murderers, or doctors, or drug lords, or preachers or lonely people, or angry people, or prostitutes, or Christians, or reincarnated, or jealous people, or Jewish, or clever, or stupid, or models, or artists, or musicians, or religious, or strict, or kind, or loving, or sexy, or good, or bad . . . what are they referring to?

We openly state, by example, that our car defines us—say we have a "super" car, or the best super car that exists, or even several super cars—we're saying that the car says who we are. We even say that we could never say in words what the car says about us. What exactly is meant when our car is required to provide meaning, or to prove meaning, or to show meaning, or to define us? Why is the car needed to define us? Why is the car needed to make the statement for us on our behalf?

When we say the aforementioned things about ourselves, are we, in some cases, merely referring to some behavioral trait we have? In other cases, are we not merely referring to personality attributes? In still other cases, are we not merely referring to our need to please, impress or conform to some crutch-like organization that we are members of or that we subscribe to?

It seems likely we don't know what we're really saying when we say, "This is what I am" or "This is who I am." For good measure, sometimes something else is added to the statement: ". . . and I can do nothing about it."

Whenever you hear these statements, or even say them yourself, why not take a moment to reflect on it and explore where the statement comes from or why the statement is being made? And while exploring it, why not reflect upon and explore your essence?

Look at a rose or a tree. It's highly unlikely that they need to say what or who they are. It is clear to see and experience their beauty, and to stand in wonderment of their existence. Why not so with the human species? Why is it necessary for us to say what or who we are?

When we prepare a cob of corn for dinner, do we ever consider its wonderment, and that we recognize this without it needing to say anything about itself? Do we ever consider its role in our lives? Do we ever think what the cob of corn gets in return for its role in our lives? It is highly unlikely that we give the life of a cob of corn a second thought.

Are *you and I* anything more than a seemingly insignificant cob of corn? Why is it that we most likely think we're different from a cob of corn in the sense of being "worth more"? As the cob of corn is part of a cycle, are we not similarly part of a cycle?

Could it be that we have these thoughts or such an understanding of ourselves because being "equal" to a cob of corn is just too much to grasp or understand or accept?

This can also be turned around.

Let's look at the sun. It is mighty and plays a mighty role in many, many lives. Are we any different from it? Or say, the majestic Table Mountain, which is near the lowest tip of Africa where I live. Are we any different from that place, in that we're also capable of playing a role in another person's life to the extent of the cob, the sun, or Table Mountain?

You might frown on this and feel it's certainly not possible—that your life, or any human's life, can't be that significant or that mighty—but is it indeed possible that our lives are exactly like that?

And, cutting it another way: Is the reason we can't accept this because we, unlike the ear of corn, the sun, or the mountain, expect something in return; we expect a reward or acknowledgement for living our lives?

And in the event that we do expect something in return or expect acknowledgement, then what does that mean? Might it mean that with the reward or the acknowledgement, we feel worthy, and therefore that's why we do what we do—the converse being that unless rewarded or acknowledged, we feel unworthy?

To grasp this dynamic, you'd need to let go of everything you've been taught and everything you believe in. Otherwise, it wouldn't be possible to see the relationship between being rewarded, being acknowledged, and feeling worthy.

Let's take businesspeople. They wouldn't be in business if it weren't for the reward or the acknowledgement provided indirectly by the financial reward. How far is that removed from what a cob of corn, the sun or Table Mountain provides to us *without* wanting reward or acknowledgement?

Quite possibly, you might feel that surely you aren't comparable with a cob of corn, the sun or Table Mountain. But are we indeed not—or is it merely a *perception* that we are different?

Is it at all possible to have the courage to remove ourselves far enough from our current "perceived reality" to speculate that our species could indeed flourish if we were able to put ourselves in the same light as the rest of nature and lose our desire for rewards or acknowledgement for simply living our lives?

If we can't, then perhaps it begs the question: Why can't we live our lives without wanting reward or acknowledgement?

What does reward or acknowledgement mean to you? Do you, perhaps, derive self-worth from being rewarded or acknowledged?

Or is it that when you or I obtain certain rewards or acknowledgements, we invariably want more and more, and more, and more? Is it possible that no amount of reward or acknowledgement we want, or get, satisfies us? When we look at this dynamic very carefully, we might notice that we can never find anything outside of ourselves that could fill a void that exists inside us.

Why is it that nothing outside of ourselves can possibly define us? Is it possible that everything you and I require to be ourselves and to flourish is already there inside of us, just waiting to be uncovered? Babies don't need the things we perceive we need. Is it possible that we, the caretakers of children, force from their lives their states of not needing to be rewarded and not needing to be acknowledged? Thus, if we were to guide them and support them for their own sake, so they, and all of us from the time when we were children ourselves, might grow up without needing to be rewarded and not needing acknowledgement—that is, accepting that we are merely ourselves for our own sake?

So then, is our present system of needing rewards and acknowledgements conducive to our well-being? And when we say, "This is who I am" or "This is what I am," are we really only speaking of a *perception* we have of ourselves?

And is it possible that you and I, and most of the people walking Planet Earth, actually haven't yet seen, or encountered, or uncovered "what or who" we really are?

Respect

Can we have respect for anyone or anything else if we don't have self-respect? You can easily see whether people have self-respect by how they treat other people or other things, and importantly, how they treat themselves.

Yes, having respect starts with us. When you have respect for yourself, automatically through your own integrity and your own self-respect, you cannot help but have respect for anyone or anything else. If it isn't evident that someone has respect for other things or other people, you will surely find that they lack self-respect.

Here are just some examples. A lack of self-respect manifests in:

… abuse of ourselves and others, mentally and physically

… abuse of the environment

… manipulation of others

… arrogant behavior

… expecting from others what we might not be willing to do ourselves

When people abuse the environment or in fact abuse anything, can such people possibly have self-respect?

We treat ourselves and others and things with the respect we have for ourselves. So, if anywhere in our behavior there is some form of disrespect (big or small or minute), is it then likely we don't have respect for ourselves?

Regarding respect, as with everything else, it clearly begins with us: with you and me. Not "them," or "the government," or "that group of people," but with ourselves.

Forgiveness

Part of our makeup is to forgive someone for what they have done.

Let's take a careful look at the dynamics of forgiveness. For us to forgive someone, that someone must have done something wrong—some action or statement of theirs was adjudged as being wrong. But, in whose eyes is that determined?

To understand that certain behavior is wrong, that behavior must be compared to something else, some other set of behaviors considered as right. Who decides against what such behavior is compared? Each person makes that determination. By knowing against what a certain behavior can be compared, we're in a position to measure the behavior. After measuring the behavior, we are in a position to judge the behavior as right or wrong.

Another side of the coin: If the person perpetrating the wrong behavior knew the behavior was wrong, would they then have acted in that way? If they had known it was wrong and still behaved wrongly, then surely they were out of control. If they were out of control, then surely they weren't being themselves.

But does the dynamic end here?

Yet another side of the coin (although admittedly, by adding another side to it, I've created a rather unusual coin!): Have we maybe *created* a set of rules, a moral standing against which we measure ourselves and others? Then because of these rules, we are able to adjudge that someone has done something right or wrong, and with wrong behavior, we can therefore forgive that person.

Say the rules and moral standing on which we base such required behavior are flawed. Say, due to our evolution, now we have old and nonserving rules. We likely still expect people to abide by these old rules, and when they don't abide, they are judged as doing wrong. What if those rules are flawed, and thus don't serve us? Regardless, a ritual still exists whereby people supposedly have done something wrong, and those who are affected are expected to forgive those wrongdoers.

Let's take it a step further. Let's look at an event as harsh as murder. Did the person committing the murder really see what they were doing when murdering? Because if they were aware of what they were doing, wouldn't they have stopped themselves from murdering? If they didn't stop themselves, then surely they were out of control. Thus, they were likely not themselves. Thus, Factor-x was likely driving their behavior.

There are three aspects around the idea or concept of forgiveness:

One: Some behavior is wrong
Two: Some behavior is judged
Three: A yardstick is required to judge the behavior

To judge behavior requires behavior being weighed against something. When measured favorably, behavior is judged as right. When measured unfavorably, behavior is judged as wrong. Creating the yardstick against which behavior is measured is critical. Let's consider these questions about that need: Who creates the yardstick? How is that yardstick formulated? Did everyone have a say in creating the yardstick? Who does the measuring? If the yardstick or the judger is flawed, then is judging of the person not flawed?

Why not look at this in a very different way? Most important: Why do we judge?

Let's start at a different point all together. Let's say there are absolutely no rules and no moral standing. In other words, we're starting with a clean slate. And importantly, nothing anyone ever does is wrong. No judging, no rules, no moral standing: each person behaves in whatever way they behave.

Starting from this stance, there must have been a reason why rules and moral standing were instituted to measure a person's behavior. That means certain people in any given group, at some point, had an inkling of what behavior we and other people should have. Those who had this inkling saw that others didn't have their idea of proper behavior. Thus, those in the first group created the rules and moral standing for the other group.

Well, the first group certainly didn't create these rules for themselves. Why would they? If they already knew how to behave, why create rules for themselves? So, these rules must have been created for those who *didn't* know how to behave.

Here is the first dilemma: One group of people has created a set of rules or a moral standing for another group to follow.

The second dilemma, which is likely the important one, is: *Why did this group of people feel it necessary to create those rules or the moral standing for the other group?* Could it be that when we make rules for others, it is so we can manipulate others, or feel superior to them or emotionally secure? We can forgive another when they break those rules or moral standing. Yet why is it necessary for one person to forgive another? Is it, perhaps, so those doing the forgiving can feel emotionally secure or even superior? That if they *don't* forgive those doing wrong against them, they likely become driven or frantic and can't live normally? In this latter case, the person struggles with the deed done against them, and with those having done the deed against them, and they don't really cope. So, to bring closure for themselves, they forgive the other person.

Let's look at this carefully. For the person who has been wronged to feel better, they forgive the other person. So who, then, are they doing the forgiving for? What does this have to do with the other person, or their behavior? For whose sake are they forgiving the other person?

So, what are we actually doing when we forgive another? Is this ritual of judging and forgiving likely about our own lack of emotional security? Possibly it is, because we're driven by Factor-x.

When we're manipulating others with our rules and moral standing, it is understood, and we don't need to elaborate much on it, except to ask ourselves this question: Why would we *want* to manipulate another person? What do we derive from such manipulation?

And then, when the behavior is measured against such manipulative rules and moral standing and adjudged as wrong, we derive further value from the forgiveness. Again, if we are emotionally secure, why would we want to manipulate another person?

As we're creating rules and moral standing from a feeling of superiority, why would we want to enforce that feeling on another person? What do we derive from enforcing our superiority, or from forgiving another person whose behavior we have judged as wrong? Again, if we didn't have the need to project our seeming superiority, would we create rules or moral standing for others to follow?

Let's look at yet another side of the coin—yes, we're now creating an interesting four-sided coin! And like that unique currency, this might not be an easy dynamic to grasp: How about that *nothing* is necessarily right or wrong?

Let's momentarily remove Factor-x from the equation if we dare—Factor-x requires measuring to vindicate itself. Rather, here is the dynamic I want you to consider: *Behavior just is, like things just are.* Yet we likely place some value *on* behavior so we can extract some value *from* behavior. Whereas, just possibly, behavior and things just are the way they are, and that no value exists in any behavior or thing—and that we, the humans making up humankind, place value upon and extract value from behavior to measure ourselves and others, and thereby judge ourselves and others as being right, wrong, okay or cool and the like.

But if we were okay within ourselves, would we need this external mechanism or dynamic of creating rules and moral standing and the ensuing forgiving?

This begs the question: Is forgiveness about the person we are forgiving, or about appeasing ourselves? And if we were okay within ourselves, would we really need to appease ourselves?

Yet another side of this already-unique coin is something we likely haven't considered, yet it's likely the most important: Is creating rules or a moral standing treating the symptom or addressing the cause of the unwanted misbehavior? By creating rules and a moral standing, we are prescriptive in our approach: one individual or group over another individual or group. Why don't we instead take a guidance stance? Why don't we ask: *Why don't these people already know how to behave?* Why don't we look at the *cause* of the unwanted behavior?

By addressing the cause, people have the chance to see for themselves why they do what they do, and this knowledge empowers them to uncover themselves, and thereby heal themselves. Then, we're addressing the cause. Then, the value we extract from the symptomatic ritual of right and wrong behavior, and the subsequent forgiveness, isn't required anymore. Even better, when addressing the cause, it's not an individual or group being prescriptive over another, but empowering each person to heal themselves.

Recognizing Our Contribution to a Crippling Society

Every day, we see and experience the hardships of our society. Are you affected by the hardships? Are you part of creating the hardships?

You'll likely answer no to each of these questions. If not to both questions, you'll certainly say no to the question of, "Are you part of creating the hardships?"

I'd like to show you how I see it.

In the section titled "One," White Wolf elaborates on our connectedness—that is, the connectedness of souls within humankind; within the spirit world; and between both humankind and the spirit world. He shares with us this point from our spiritual perspective: At the core, we're all part of a species, and thus are indeed interconnected and affected by the behavior of individuals within the species, whether we know the individuals or not. He also conveys that within our species, we function according to a system of our own creation, created and evolved over time by individuals making up our species—and specifically, that the system isn't created to include everyone. Rather, the system only includes individuals that can make it—survive—within the system. Thus, when individuals can't make it within the system, there's just no place for them, making the system itself ill-devised and ineffectual.

My question to you is, "Is it thus not time to adjust the system to make a place for everyone?"

I'm certain most of you don't see mine and White Wolf's view as accurate, or how it affects all of us in our everyday lives and how we perpetuate this ill-devised and ineffectual system every day of our lives. In fact, I'm certain you don't see the connection—our interconnectedness. I'm certain you feel that if individuals can't "hack it" within the system, that's their problem. Why should those who make it within the system concern themselves with those who can't? Maybe you even feel like I used to: "Maybe those individuals who can't hack it are just lazy."

If you feel this way, it's likely because you don't see how we are all interconnected—even those not catered to by the system. Also, you likely don't see how you and I are affected by those individuals excluded from the ill-devised and ineffective system, or the effect we have on them.

Well, here is the connection.

Do we have clogged up and even gridlocked traffic? Do we encounter "road hogs"? Do we make use of service providers who provide less-than-average services? Do we sit in jobs where we have very little say—even where there is discrimination of some sort? Do we feel safe when we go out at night? Do we lock our houses and our cars? Do we have burglar bars and alarms to protect our property? Do we feel safe about our children walking to school? Do we have bullies at school terrorizing our children? Do we have terrorists terrorizing our society?

This is another list that could wrap Planet Earth. But even though White Wolf and I indicate the connectedness and ensuing effects the system has on us and on each individual—and certainly daily—my guess is, you likely still don't see the connection. Even more, you likely don't see how you and I perpetuate the state of affairs. Notwithstanding, it is indeed easy to see—but only for those who have the courage to see what is conveyed via this material.

For instance, our system is based on money. That means everyone must have money, preferably enough for sustenance plus more. So if we're one of the fortunate ones who can roll our skills into a job or career or business where we can earn an income—and the more the better—we're able to fend for ourselves financially.

But stop and look for a moment. What if you *weren't* able to do this, like those among us unable to fend for themselves financially? What if you or these individuals had other skills—possibly even distinct skills—but were unable to roll them into a form to earn an income? What if they don't get or are unable to create a break for themselves for some very logical reason—say, not being able to work with money, or some other arbitrary reason—and thus fail. Then, they are invariably lost within the system and end up doing whatever they can to make ends meet. Either that, or not make it at all, and end up in the slums or living off the streets.

But in almost all cases we—you and I, as well as those who don't make it in the system—are likely *not* doing what we'd like to be doing with our lives. And quite possibly, we've even lost interest in what we're doing. Some might even be sidetracked into crime from sheer desperation, and become criminals to at least have a meal or to feed their Factor-x with the seeming power such criminal deeds provide.

Aforementioned is an oversimplification of one of the flaws in our system: the creation of and need for money. And as seen in another section, "Forms of Crutches," because Factor-x likely drives us, we have different crutches we lean on to cope within this ill-conceived and inadequate system—which comprises our entrenched way of perpetuating and proliferating the system.

Let's look at why this happens.

First, you and I take part in our system, and possibly without questioning it. Or, if you *are* questioning it, it might be merely questioning, without constructively doing anything about it.

Second, we're seemingly so overwhelmed by surviving in our system, our lives consist merely of straining ourselves to cope within it. So, we never really get to a point where we take a breather and sit back and look at our lives to see whether we indeed like what we've created for ourselves within the system—or whether we even like our system.

Third, you likely aren't consciously aware of your own contribution and your interconnectedness. And you might feel that as long as you aren't *directly* adversely affected, why bother to adjust the system? In any event, with your Factor-x likely flourishing in your life, you might even say, "Well, what can I do about it?"

I say, you only need to stop and look at how our daily lives contribute to perpetuating and proliferating the current system—a system that doesn't serve you or anyone else. That acknowledgment to yourself is the only start required, with each individual, one at a time, to make a difference. You don't have to *do* anything first, except just acknowledge that you indeed see the dynamics at play. That's all that is required as a start. Once that first step is taken—the acknowledgment that the system doesn't serve us because it is ill-devised and ineffectual—the rest will follow virtually automatically: a scary experience, certainly, but one that can be dealt with one slow but intentional step at a time.

WHY IT IS GOING AWRY

We are seemingly oblivious to the fact that our natural life is different from our perceptions of it. In fact, the more we uncover our own lives, the more we see that we base our very existence on being unaware of truth: truth about what drives us, truth about what we want with our lives, and truth about things that don't make sense. In short, we are seemingly oblivious to the undercurrents in our lives. Thus, we don't live up to our potential—our natural lives.

Our Factor-x Patterned Lives

When we stop long enough to look at our lives, we almost always find that we've carved out lives that aren't really working for us. During our lives, as a matter of course, we usually stop and look when there are big decisions or changes in the usual pattern of our day-to-day lives. One example of such a change is when we leave school and either start working or pursuing advanced studies. Another example is when we reach the stage where our children have grown up and leave home. Suddenly we find we have more time on our hands. Other examples of these big transitions are when we have near-death or traumatic experiences. If we choose, we could also stop at any time to take stock of our lives.

How we get to the point of stopping and looking at our lives isn't what's important. What's important is that we stop, and that when we look, we're brutally honest with ourselves. If we are, we'll invariably see that we have a life that doesn't work for us, and possibly hasn't worked for us for many years, especially if we're older when we stop and look at our lives. That our life isn't working might be because of many different things.

... Perhaps we've spent months or years studying a craft or academic path that doesn't really interest us.

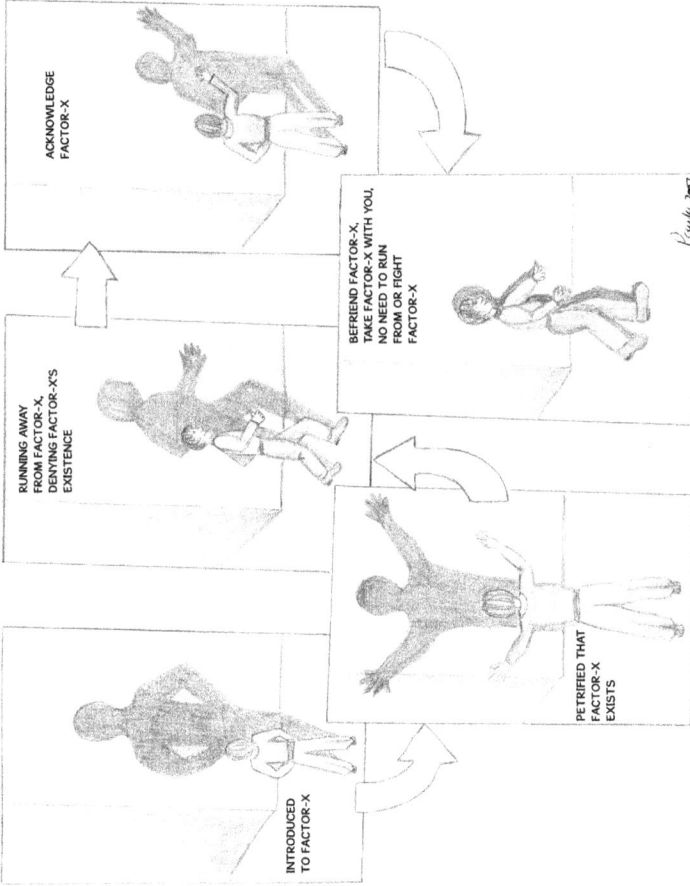

Figure 4: Exposing why things are the way they are

INTRODUCED TO FACTOR-X

PETRIFIED THAT FACTOR-X EXISTS

RUNNING AWAY FROM FACTOR-X, DENYING FACTOR-X'S EXISTENCE

ACKNOWLEDGE FACTOR-X

BEFRIEND FACTOR-X, TAKE FACTOR-X WITH YOU, NO NEED TO RUN FROM OR FIGHT FACTOR-X

... We might be married to or in a relationship with someone who doesn't suit us, or we don't suit them.

... We might be working long hours and have no life outside work.

... We might be living a life our parents wanted for us, not one we chose.

... We might have notched up huge amounts of debt for whatever reason.

... We might have turned out to be cheats, or thieves, or drug abusers, or promiscuous.

... We might have a life of continuously fighting with those we meet in our daily lives.

... We might not be on speaking terms with our parents or close family, even though we want to speak with them.

... Our lives might just not work for a reason we can't even begin to figure out.

... And the list could quite possibly wrap around Planet Earth several times.

The point is, if you stop long enough and look carefully at your life, you might see that your life turned out different from what you'd have preferred. In fact, almost anyone who stops and looks will have the same realization.

And why is this? Have we been on a roller coaster ride with our lives, for a short period or possibly for our whole lives, even at the point that we already have grandchildren?

If our lives to this point developed in a direction that wasn't what we envisaged, why did this happen? Is it possible that Factor-x crept in and we gave our lives away to it? Could it be that we didn't exercise our freedom of choice? Were we not free to steer our lives in the direction of our choice? Has our life ended up as a second-choice existence?

When you stop long enough to look brutally honestly at your life, has it turned out to follow particular patterns dictated by your Factor-x? Have you lived a life of proving that you aren't what you feel you are when your Factor-x kicks in? If you feel you are living a second-choice life, is the influence of your Factor-x why you ended up with a life that isn't your first-choice existence? That rather than living a first-choice existence, you ended up with a life of following a quest or a pattern of continuously wanting to disprove your Factor-x?

Here is the no-brainer. All this time, it's highly likely that you were oblivious of the existence of either Factor-x or this pattern governing your life. If this is the case, then you likely haven't lived your life as a free, independent individual, but governed by the existence of your Factor-x: meaning that you molded your life from your desire to disprove the feelings created by your Factor-x.

Consider this: that most of us, for as long as we've been alive, haven't been ourselves, but rather caught up in a pattern of disproving something.

Consider further: Whenever we have inner conflict or get strained, is it possible that those inner struggles result from this pattern: where on one side we just want to be ourselves as free, independent individuals, and on the other side we're in total conflict and compromise ourselves by having to disprove these feelings created by our Factor-x? How is that for a realization?

And to crown it all, all this time, we were probably oblivious to the dynamic taking place, and to why it was taking place!

Fortunately—yes, you and I are very fortunate indeed—Factor-x was created as a figment of our imagination, albeit from a very real feeling underlying that imagination: so real, we didn't realize that it's devoid of any truth or substance.

Why fortunately? Because we "created" our Factor-x, so we can "uncreate" it and take back our lives.

This is easier said than done, of course. It takes brutal honesty and courage, beyond what we usually are accustomed to and need. But yes, it's possible to take back our lives and live as free individuals. As a result, we break out of our patterned lives.

Be forewarned. This pattern and Factor-x are devious, and seek any and every opportunity to reenter our lives. But when we become friends with it, thus not fighting Factor-x, its power is diminished and we can live almost entirely free of Factor-x's unwanted interference.

Looking Past Factor-x, Not Willing to Go Wherever It Takes You

Whenever we see the effects of Factor-x and we see why it hinders us to move forward, the possibility exists that when we want to move forward, we won't know where that next step will take us. This might create major anxiety, and might possibly prevent us from taking the route indicated by the next step in breaking out of our Factor-x–patterned lives. As a result, when faced with the unknown, taking the route into the unknown is a struggle. And invariably, we'll stay put: stay with the status quo.

Factor-x has this effect on us. Whenever we encounter a path where we can't see what the way forward will bring—and there usually seems to be no guarantees—we tend to stay put, whether staying put serves us and those around us. The unknown, related to moving away from Factor-x, is usually just too much to handle.

Scary as this unknown might seem, when we don't take that route into the unknown, how will we ever see where it leads us? Besides, failing to move forward contradicts our enjoyment and excitement of exploring the unknown.

Recall when you were a child and received something you weren't familiar with, or when you went on holiday to a place you'd never been, perhaps a different country or city or town. During these times, you were excited about the unknown. Now, this excitement likely won't happen if you're up against the unknown, and especially when Factor-x is staring you in the face. This is a very different reality, and you're likely to think the following: *I'm making a mistake.* This certainly takes away the fun and excitement of the unknown.

It doesn't have to be this way.

It takes courage and brutal honesty to see what holds us back—what holds us at status quo. But once you see that you're struggling, and why you're struggling to move forward on an unknown path, you're already part of the way there. When you realize why you're unable to move forward and are brutally honest with yourself, you're able to see past Factor-x. When you have the courage to see and accept that you want to go in a particular direction, and then have the willingness to go wherever it takes you, that liberates you from Factor-x.

Again, this is easier said than done. To move into the unknown and reach the point of letting go of Factor-x isn't that straightforward. It might take more courage than you have at that time, or that you've ever needed before. Some steps might be easy, some slightly more difficult, and then there most likely is a big step—a step so big, every time you attempt to get past it, it just absorbs you to the extent that it seems impossible for you to move forward.

The big one, the difficult one in terms of standing at a crossroads and wanting to move forward, brings new meaning to the words, "having the courage of one's convictions." Not for the fainthearted at all. So, with this big step, you might not succeed the first time, or the tenth time, or the hundredth time: That's just how big "a big one" might be.

But don't despair. It isn't impossible. If your intentions are there, and you see it, even if only vaguely at first, rest assured by the umpteenth time, it becomes clearer, and by the umpteenth time plus one, it's likely you'll take the step past the big one . . . the big crossroads . . . the big, scary unknown. And if you take that step when finding yourself at a big crossroads, your life is likely to be very different than before.

And again, be aware that, while you might understand conceptually how your Factor-x influences your life, and you might have every intention of breaking out of that pattern, when confronted with the unknown, you might throw the whole idea out. You might even reject the existence of your Factor-x. That's how scary the unknown is likely to be. Yet if we do reject this knowledge, we'll be back to square one with our lives: back to where Factor-x governs our every move— our very existence—and we remain in our second-choice existence.

To break out of the pattern when the path into the unknown is too big for us, all you and I can do is to be aware of the dynamics taking place and acknowledge them. To fight it will not help. Our best ploy is to accept it. Accept that it's possibly just too big for us—at the time. Perhaps at a later stage, you might have the courage to overcome it. Perhaps at that umpteenth time plus one, you will have the courage to take that route—the scary step into the unknown and away from Factor-x. When you do, you'll be one more step away from living your second-choice life and one step closer to your first-choice life.

Just Prior to Conception: Our Intentions Are Surely That of a Spirit Being

Assuming we are spirit beings, taking up life of the physical being when our parents conceive us, and that we already possess all the loving attributes to turn out as considerate, upstanding and well-mannered people . . .

Well, we all know this is absolutely the exception to the rule. Not long after we're born, we start playing up to ourselves and other people. Ever consider why that might be?

Why is it that shortly after we're born, say around the toddler stage, we lose that *sweetness*? In some cases, even long before that age, we lose our sweetness?

So when a spiritual being brings life to the physical being, somewhere along the line, at a relatively early age, the "ingredients" brought by the spiritual being are seemingly lost. Could it be that the physical world's attitude and behavior is so overwhelming and intimidating, the baby or child just can't cope? That even though the spiritual ingredients are present, the physical being just isn't equipped for what they're exposed to here on the Earth plane?

It's definitely not a conducive state of affairs when our world cannot take care of its own, or that we as a species are so harsh we force the *sweetness* from our children.

Getting back to assuming that the spirit being takes up life as the physical being, let's take that one step further. If the spiritual ingredients we're born with are indeed that of pure loving and giving and accepting and sweetness, and each one of us has the inherent capability to be just that: perfectly loving, accepting and sweet human beings . . . then why aren't we?

Let's look at this a bit further. So now we have a spiritual being and a physical being making up a human being, and the spiritual being provides attributes like loving, accepting and sweetness, among others. Now, let's look at where we find the things we usually look for outside ourselves. Happiness, for example. As previously discussed, when we eventually find genuine happiness, it's found within. In fact, if we find any of the things we usually look for outside of ourselves, they're usually right there inside of us, just waiting to be uncovered.

Then is it safe to say that the previously mentioned assumptions are maybe more than assumptions?

And is it then fair to say about these humane attributes already inside us, that somehow we lose the fact that they exist inside us? Could it be that if they're inside us when we're conceived, and that when we go looking for them, we find them inside us—that somewhere along the line during our lives, they got lost?

Why is it that our humaneness gets lost along the way? Is it possible that the behaviors and attitudes of our species aren't conducive to recognizing and growing our spiritual ingredients? That it's in fact the opposite; we just frighten our spiritual ingredients away—smothering them—removing them from our lives as we go?

This being the case, wouldn't it be great, as individuals and as a species, to be able to get back our humaneness?

If your answer to this question is yes, this is great. However, it's highly unlikely that we can reclaim our humaneness unless we stop and look at why our spiritual ingredients were lost in the first place.

Before we pursue getting our humaneness back, if the previous assumptions are indeed so, could we make another assumption: that your life and mine would have been all together different if we had manifested our spiritual ingredients? Almost certainly, had we not lost our humaneness and weren't constantly looking for, say, happiness, we would instead be living our happiness. We can almost certainly take it a step further and state that all of humankind would have been very different from the state in which it currently finds itself.

Why did we lose our humaneness?

Reading the other sections of this book and the website will help you to answer this important question. Here are some thoughts that will help you in this process.

When looking at our lives, and when we recapture any moment, we recognize that we're most likely the product of our circumstances.

If we take these two vital steps, we realize that, at a very young age, we took on our Factor-x. Once we understand these things, we can then recognize that we believe we're to blame for what's happening to us, and so our lives then became a quest to disprove our Factor-x instead of just living our lives and manifesting ourselves.

Is it any wonder that we lost our humaneness, and that we were most likely oblivious of this state of affairs?

But now, *you* have the beginnings of the understanding and knowledge to change that for yourself.

Pushing Back Our Spirit Being As If It's a Second-Rate Citizen

In our quest to prove that nothing is wrong with us, instead of living our lives as intended, we push back our spiritual beings as though they are second-rate citizens.

As you have learned so far about Factor-x, as a young child, once we get to the point where the mounting pressure of the environment—through our caregivers, parents, and society—cracks us, we most likely feel that something must be wrong with us, hence other people's behavior towards us. From that point, we set out to disprove that anything's wrong with us; from that moment on, we become second-rate citizens in our own bodies and lives. From then on, nothing else matters. Instinctively, it then becomes our life's goal to disprove how and what we feel about ourselves; all we want is to disprove the existence of our Factor-x. This of course stays with us for the duration of our lives, even if we get beyond our Factor-x, by way of impacting on our lives in varying degrees afterward.

Yet even if you feel something's missing, that your life doesn't have meaning, or you wonder about the meaning of your life or life in general, you might never stop, even for a moment, to try to find the source of these feelings and thoughts. For most of us in this situation, we want to remedy things by following what we see around us: from the behavior of humankind in general. We follow the media, and get into designer this and designer that. We want better cars and houses and so on. All this to disprove that something's wrong with us. And this seems to be all we can do about our troubled feelings, because the real "us" was pushed back from a very young age because of our quest to disprove our Factor-x. All because our souls have been pushed to the background.

Our souls were pushed to the background. This is most likely why we feel our lives have no meaning, or that something's missing from our lives. This is the origin of our inner conflict. Our soul, our spirit, is saying one thing to us, and our quest to disprove our Factor-x is saying another thing to us, hence the inner conflict.

Why else do you think governments would have massive budgets for, say, their defense forces? Why else would they pay billions for a vehicle of destruction even when many of their people are starving?

This writing isn't about starving children, even though that dynamic is also a symptom of Factor-x woven into the fabric of our society. This isn't about someone or some government setting things right either, but about ourselves: about one-by-one recognizing what we're doing to ourselves and why. The point is, if we weren't so busy living to disprove our Factor-x, we would see what we've created, what we've done to ourselves, and what society is doing to itself.

That's what this writing is about: that we stop and look at our own lives and set it straight, or more accurately, that we recognize that we pushed back our spiritual beings in our own lives, and that unbeknownst to us, they're being held hostage as second-rate citizens. None of this, unfortunately (or perhaps fortunately), applies to "mass fixing." It doesn't and can't work that way. It needs to start with each individual to see the dynamic of what we've done to ourselves and are still doing to ourselves moment by moment.

It isn't impossible, but it's probably unimaginable for you, right now, to see beyond the current point in your life: to envision what your life might be like once you recognize your spiritual being, your soul, and give it a chance to come forward from where it's being kept hostage within you. Yet in a way, you do get to see it moment for moment. Sometimes in minute ways, other times through lovely daydreams. It's always there, just beneath the surface, wanting to be a part of your life, away from this quest we're all on to disprove our Factor-x. It's present in our inner conflicts, and it creates our daydreams: those lovely moments we escape to when things aren't going so well.

So although we can't quite imagine our lives when our spiritual beings are again in the forefront, we get a taste of it each day, albeit mostly only in its struggle to be part of our everyday lives.

Oh, and by the way, our spiritual beings aren't something different from us; they're a direct part of our lives that, generally speaking, we're unaware of. Notwithstanding our spiritual beings, our souls are part and parcel of our lives, irrespective of whether we agree that our lives include spiritual beings or souls, and whether we accept this dynamic. Rather than something different or separate or invasive, our spiritual beings or souls are part of us, if mostly unknown and seemingly unfamiliar.

Inner Conflict

Almost every day, we experience inner conflict. When things go all right, our conflict is less. When things don't work out, our conflict is greater.

This conflict is inevitable between our spiritual being and our soul wanting us to do things in a certain way (or not do them), and our quest to disprove our Factor-x. Therein lies the origins of our inner conflict between us wanting to disprove our Factor-x and the wishes of our spiritual being: our soul. Keep in mind that these are components of one and the same person; we aren't separate from our spiritual being or our souls, and we aren't separate from our Factor-x. They are all one. So in essence, we are in conflict with ourselves.

At the heart of it, we have the inner conflict because we aren't free beings. We created our Factor-x from a perception, so it isn't real. Yet due to this figment of our imagination, we aren't free beings, but controlled by our belief that our Factor-x is indeed a true reflection of us.

Herein lies a further irony. Due to our wanting to believe that our Factor-x is indeed true, we ascribe many things, situations and circumstances to it. In this way, we continuously feed, grow, and perpetuate our Factor-x.

But imagine this, if you dare. Imagine that you didn't have this dynamic taking place inside you. Imagine how different your life might be if you *weren't* dealing with this dynamic daily, almost moment for moment. Imagine if you *hadn't* made such a life-altering decision as a very young child. Imagine how it might have been had you lived your entire life as a free spirit.

It's fairly impossible for any of us to imagine how our lives might have been. But perhaps with the attempt, just maybe you and I can see that our lives might have been different, even drastically different, had we not been in this dilemma with our spiritual being and Factor-x.

It's very likely that our lives would be on very different paths today. It might be that every one of us walking this planet might have been on very different paths today, had we not created our Factor-x.

> … It's highly likely that the people here on Earth might not have been carrying so much anger and destruction around inside of us.
>
> … It's also highly likely there would be no social outcasts.
>
> … It's highly likely that we wouldn't have abuse of one another, or abuse in families, or war between countries or communities.
>
> … It's highly likely that we wouldn't have affected other species the way we do today. We wouldn't damage nature. We wouldn't destroy our natural environment.
>
> … We wouldn't turn everything into moneymaking opportunities.
>
> … It's highly likely that if this inner conflict didn't exist within us, Planet Earth would have been a different place for everyone and everything.

Keep in mind that the origin of all this destruction, all this conflict, is our lack of inner peace. That lack comes from our Factor-x being in conflict with our spiritual being, our soul. And in turn, we're all on a quest to disprove our Factor-x. Keep in mind that our Factor-x is based on a perception—a perception based on a figment of our imagination.

So all the destruction around us, and of which we are all a part, is caused by a figment of our imagination.

The origin of destruction and abuse—any form of destruction and abuse—is a person or persons in the process of their quest to disprove the existence of their Factor-x.

That inner conflict we live with daily is the first encounter we have in our lives that something is out of place. What's out of place is our belief that our Factor-x is indeed fact.

Luckily for us, it isn't fact, but merely a figment of our imagination.

Unfortunately for us, this is easier said than to overcome. To take back our lives from being dictated to by our Factor-x isn't for the fainthearted. It takes great amounts of courage and brutal honesty. Fortunately, no one can force it on us and no one can take it away from us; it's truly fortunate that each of us is the only one that created this figment of the imagination. And since we created it, we can abolish it—fortunately, each person can create or reverse their Factor-x on their own.

This being the origin of our inner conflict, keep in mind that we might be following a path that's mostly or even entirely about our Factor-x, and that we might have been on that path for several weeks, months, years or even decades. So it might not be of any use to want to only unravel the moment of conflict. That moment might be related to a moment in the past, which might have resulted in a life-changing decision on a path based on our quest to disprove the existence of our Factor-x.

So, wanting to fix it "in the moment" might not be what's required, but instead attending to the origin. When addressing symptoms, the symptom merely returns, sometimes in different forms, but it'll most likely return.

The only way to address the cause is to go to the origin and have the brutal honesty to see things for what they are, see why things are the way they are, and then address the cause. It doesn't help to look shallowly at the inner conflict; it requires going all the way back to the origin and addressing it in relation to why it started in the first place.

No One Is to Blame: Blame Doesn't Set Us Free

We can blame as much as we like. We can even blame ourselves. However, no matter how much we blame, it doesn't help. Blame doesn't set us free.

When we blame, we don't look at the facts. When we don't look at the facts, we miss the point all together. When this happens, there is no accountability. Accountability isn't blame at all. Being responsible and being accountable isn't about giving blame or taking blame. When we're accountable, we state that the decision or action was done because that's what we intended to do.

An example, if an exaggerated one: We can easily state, "This or that gave me no choice, so I stole the money . . . or I killed the person." Yet we always have choice. Perhaps we didn't want to steal. Perhaps we didn't want to kill. (In fact, we can be 100% certain that no one living a first-choice existence would steal or want to hurt another human being.)

So when we do the deed and say, "Well, I had no choice," that's not true. When we state after the event that we did this or that, and for this or that reason, then we're being responsible and taking accountability for our deeds.

There's also the other side of the coin. What if we look at why we wanted to do the deed in the first place? Why do we not look before doing the deed at the reason we're thinking about or contemplating doing it? Why don't we slow down and just look at what we want to do and why? Beforehand, we can see whether that action is indeed what we want to be doing. Are we at peace with it? Do we have inner conflict or inner peace with it?

When there is inner conflict about these questions, we're surely contemplating something that goes against our spiritual being, against our soul, against what we like doing. When this is the case, then we're most likely not accountable and not being responsible, even if afterward we blame ourselves or another party or some obscure reason for doing the deed.

It isn't just about doing something; the inner conflict also pertains to things we don't do. Perhaps your spiritual being or soul is prodding you in a certain direction, to do something in particular, but you're fighting it. That's also going against the actions your spiritual being or soul would like to do. That will also create inner conflict.

Keeping this in mind, it's imperative that you and I get to understand ourselves profoundly, to know ourselves much, much better than we likely think we know ourselves. That's why we need to be brutally honest with ourselves. That's why we need absolute courage to see what's really happening inside ourselves.

The process of uncovering ourselves—going beyond blame and even beyond stating after the event that we're responsible or that we're accountable—takes brutal honesty and openness with ourselves. It also takes heaps of courage. Most of us don't have this honesty and courage, yet without it, we're lost to our Factor-x and to blaming others or even ourselves.

Blaming is one or more steps short of the core reasons why we're doing or not doing certain deeds or thinking or not thinking certain thoughts. When we live first-choice existences, we take that one or more steps further, to where we know the origin of everything we do and think, or don't do or don't think. When we live from that space, we're truly responsible for our thoughts and actions. We're then also truly accountable for our thoughts and actions.

When we live with this integrity, we're automatically responsible and accountable. There is no blame; we don't blame any other person, persons or things, and we don't even blame ourselves.

We Are Not Free, So We Don't Exercise Our Freedom of Choice

Being free of our Factor-x is truly being free. Otherwise we aren't free; we're merely making some arbitrary choice or taking some arbitrary option, usually based on what's dictated to us by our comfort zone and/or our Factor-x.

Let's look at this in more depth.

To exercise your freedom of choice, you first need to be free. We talk of freedom, we use language saying things that all boil down to the statement: "I'll do whatever I want."

But when we're doing whatever we want, are we doing this because we are free? Most likely, we're not. Being free is about doing the things we like doing. When we're doing things we enjoy or look forward to, we would never do anything to the detriment of ourselves or any other person, or anything else on the planet.

For instance, let's look at breaking up a relationship. You could say, "If that person doesn't want to break up with me, surely that's to the detriment of the other person."

Perhaps not. If we stay in a relationship due to our Factor-x dictating that we'll be lonely without the other person, or that we might not meet another person like the person we're breaking up with, then if we stay, it isn't because we're free. Also, if we're contemplating ending the relationship, we might feel animosity or irritation toward that person. Because we're staying there without really wanting to be there, we might be miserable, or making the other person's life a misery. That situation is to the detriment of both people. That serves no one. Best we get out and be at peace. And eventually, even if the breakup is difficult, our ex-partner might realize they are better off without the relationship.

This is merely an example to illustrate the point that it's best to look under the surface when contemplating if a decision we make would truly be detrimental to another. Besides, when we're miserable, we propagate that in our daily lives, so everyone who encounters us when miserable experiences that from our behavior. So in the example, not only would ending the relationship serve us, it would serve our partner and those we encounter in our daily lives.

Being free isn't something that just comes to us, or just happens to us. It's about consciously deciding that being free is what we want in our lives. If it is any other way, then it isn't about being free. If anyone can give freedom to us, or if we just happened to be free, then whoever gave it to us, or however it just happened to us, it can just as well be taken away from us.

Being free is available to everyone, fortunately. But it's something that's available only if we consciously decide we want to be free. Not having made a conscious choice invalidates any claim we might have on being free or exercising our freedom of choice. Only when we take on that choice, irrespective of whether our Factor-x prevents us or creates massive conflict within us, do we set ourselves free and can we exercise our freedom of choice. Only then are we free to choose.

When this does occur, then we're opening our physical lives up to our spiritual being and soul. As a result, we live our integrity by design, and automatically serve ourselves and everything and everyone. We're then automatically responsible and accountable before, during and after any action.

But until then, we aren't free, we're not exercising our freedom of choice, and we aren't free to choose. In fact, we're not even being ourselves, but a product of the environment and of our imaginary Factor-x.

Perpetuating Our Feeling That Something Is Missing

Deep inside us, we likely feel an emptiness or a hole: something missing. What we're likely doing, unbeknownst to us, is ensuring that this feeling of something missing stays with us.

Let me elaborate. Each time we get to a point where we want to do something (or the converse, to not do something), instead of going with it, a little voice in us says, "Oh, but what about this or what about that?" What we then likely do is not go with what we like doing. We even question whether what we're stopping ourselves from doing as a result of the little inner voice—likely Factor-x's voice—is indeed something we even like doing in the first place. And the bigger the threat to our Factor-x, the easier we'll give up.

In this way, we then deny ourselves something we like doing. And in this way we perpetuate the emptiness, the feeling that something is missing, the emotional hole.

What is that "something" that seems missing? Well, with Factor-x always close on our heels until we recognize how it's spoiling things for us, we invariably take a path which, in our view, is about disproving Factor-x's existence and not the one we'd like to take: doing something we like doing. So something always feels missing. What is missing is that we're forever giving up on ourselves. Thus, what we like doing is what's missing from our lives. Thus, *we* are missing from our lives, because we give up on ourselves.

And as aforementioned, in the way we ensure the survival of Factor-x, we perpetuate Factor-x.

Instead, what is required is that we stop and recognize this pattern, and break out of its spell even though it feels risky and scary—this is indeed liberating. And over time, even if afraid, as we see Factor-x clearer and see its traits, and recognize when it attempts to spoil things for us, we take Factor-x along on our journey but do things we like doing instead of denying ourselves. Thus, we take Factor-x along with us by seeing it, but even though it's there tugging at us, we continue with what we like doing. By going for what we like doing, we overcome what creates, ensures and guarantees the something-is-missing feeling. By doing this, we'll slowly, ever so slowly, remove the hole, the emptiness, the feeling that something is missing.

This is worth repeating: What's missing is that we're forever giving up on ourselves. What we like doing is what's missing from our lives. Thus *we* are missing from our lives, because we give up on ourselves. With us living by such a pattern, it cannot feel different; it can only feel that something is missing. Invariably, with our Factor-x–driven pattern, we take a route, a path, an option that treats the symptom. And as seen elsewhere in "Treating Symptoms and Addressing the Cause," this pattern reoccurs until we take action by addressing the cause. Only this breaks us out of the cycle of perpetuating Factor-x. Only such actions liberate us.

For example: Say we're living our lives mostly wanting to do the right thing. Say we meet someone, we meet their parents, and we get married. We settle into setting up house. We have children. In the meantime, we settle into our job. We might first have a few jobs just to see where our interests are, but eventually we settle. So now, we have the perfect setting. And as in the movies, maybe we even have the brookie lace front porch, even the picket fence. And, yes, in some cases pets. And during this time, what we do is to ensure that this perfect picture isn't disturbed. We might have wanted something else, or to do more with our lives. We might not know what yet. But this perfect picture gets all our attention.

And at some point, we are likely to question whether this is really what our life is about. Perhaps we'll ask this question during times like the following ones.

> ... Perhaps, as the person who does the cooking, we don't feel like cooking on occasion (or many times).
> ... If we are the person who maintains the garden, we might not feel like doing the garden on occasion (or many times).
> ... Perhaps there is ritualistic visiting back and forth by friends or family that we don't want to be part of on occasion (or many times).
> ... If we are the main breadwinner, we might not feel like working for the next few months.
> ... Or perhaps, on occasion, maybe we just want to spend a quiet evening in our own thoughts in the dark.

There might be several more examples we could add, but the main thing is, each time we do those things because we're afraid to break up the perfect setting, that's an occasion where we guarantee that our Factor-x survives.

The aforementioned examples are light in tone, befitting a seemingly healthy family life, part of the perfect picture. But imagine, in other lives where such a perfect picture doesn't exist, how people give up on what they like doing.

> ... There might be abuse, where the abused person would like to get out, but is too afraid of being lonely, so they stay and take the abuse. Or it might be the reverse situation, where the abuser wants to stop, but can't because of feeling inferior, and thus continues to abuse to feel the power they lack.
> ... Certain families have constraints on family members. One of those might be not allowing a family member to go out with someone outside their religion. What if you meet someone

you like, but the person is outside your family religion? Or, say in your culture, your family arranges your partner. What if that goes against your preference, which is to choose your own partner?

… Then there is just plain old Factor-x influencing our every decision. Say we lead what might constitute a fairly regular life, one where we have monthly commitments we struggle to meet, yet we do. We live with the usual expectations. And we have dreams. Only thing is, we dare not go for our dreams. Perhaps we don't know how. Maybe we feel we don't deserve to. Maybe we're just plain afraid of the consequences.

Whether it is minor or major, each time we give up on what we like doing, we perpetuate the feeling that something is missing, the feeling of emptiness, the hole we're desperately wanting to fill. Only by stopping and not giving up on ourselves, by starting and doing the things we like doing, irrespective of whether our Factor-x interferes with that seemingly innocent quiet voice in our mind's ears, do we heal ourselves. It is indeed a courageous set of acts to stop and to reverse the process, to go for what we like doing in spite of the fear of ending up alone, either through our own actions or by being ostracized by others, even those close to us.

The hole, the emptiness or feeling that something is missing, comes about through our running away from the cause—by our treating the symptom. Thus, we anchor ourselves to treating the symptom. Thus, we anchor ourselves to other things or other people. But what is required is that we address the cause: to be responsible, to be committed to our lives, and most importantly, to anchor us to ourselves.

A sure way to heal ourselves is to see this pattern in our lives, to acknowledge the existence of the pattern. When we feel threatened emotionally, we invariably address what threatens us as a likely symptom, so we don't fix the hole or emptiness. Instead of running away, rather address the cause of what threatens us emotionally: sink into the threatening feeling, sink into the emotion, sink into the pain, feel the emotion, feel the pain, feel the fear, stop running or fighting, sink into it, feel it—irrespective of the pain, the fear, or how much it hurts. Irrespective of what transpires.

This happened in my own life. Sometime back, I wanted to stop work to have time to work on a milestone: developing a part of the accompanying website for this book. It was the first time I ever consciously and explicitly took time off for something that was important to me, while still taking care of myself financially. Being freelance, it meant that for the time I didn't work, I wouldn't earn any income. So I would need to delve into my hard-earned savings and possibly go into the red with my overdraft and credit card. This was a frightening prospect. I worked through it, saw how my Factor-x was interjecting, how it wanted me to instead just continue working and earning. Though haunted by the fear of ending up living in a cardboard box, I recognized this as my Factor-x, and stopped working and took time off for my project for the time I planned. Had I not been aware of the dynamic at play, I could just as easily have not taken that time for myself: time to do what I like doing.

What is of extreme importance, so I'll repeat it here, is that when our Factor-x interjects, we usually run in the opposite direction of what we like doing. But if we sink into the feeling Factor-x brings— the anxiety, the desperation—when we sink into it without running from it, we give ourselves the chance to feel it, full-blown, and to overcome it so we can pursue the things we like doing. If we don't sink into it, we're likely to just run from it, and thus maintain the emptiness, the hole, the feeling that something is missing.

In this way, not running away but sinking into it, we provide ourselves with the opportunity to anchor ourselves to ourselves, as opposed to giving up on ourselves. This also breeds confidence. Each subsequent time we recognize that, the last time around, the consequences *didn't* swallow us, we likely have more courage, albeit possibly just a minute amount more, for the next time. But that will suffice. As we do this more and more, our experience grows. Our confidence grows. We mature. And we experience more and more of our inner power. The more we have the courage to continue to anchor ourselves to ourselves as opposed to things and people, the more our confidence grows. We have less need for crutches, until eventually we're able to walk away from crutches all together and stand on our own two feet, doing the things we like doing. And so the hole, the emptiness, the feeling that something is missing is eradicated, one slow but intentional step at a time.

STANDING UP TO REGAIN CORE

**We Can Only Walk the Journey If We
Take the Steps For the Journey**

*—Emmanuel van der Meulen (with White Wolf & Co.),
September 2005*

Once we uncover our core and recognize ourselves, our own value and our meaning—and if we are sincere, honest and have the courage of our convictions—it is possible for us to regain our core. Notwithstanding, we'll encounter various difficulties during the ensuing journey.

Recognize Ourselves First

Invariably, we look for value and meaning in things outside of us. When we have this or that, like a shiny, fast car or a certain hairstyle and so forth, then we'll be happy or feel great about ourselves, or have confidence, or like ourselves, or have status, and . . .

This list can go on forever.

However, we cannot find self-value in anything outside ourselves. In fact, when we find any of these things, like happiness, confidence, and feeling secure, it will always be something that exists inside ourselves and has existed inside us forever.

Here is another approach that might serve you far better than looking outside yourself.

Why not look carefully at which fundamental values lie at the heart of your daydreams?

When you wish for something, why not look carefully at which fundamental values lie at the heart of your wishes?

When you have inner conflicts, why not look carefully at which fundamental values lie at the heart of your inner conflicts?

Figure 5: Breaking out of the standards and norms and Factor-x

Why *don't* we stop regularly and look carefully at which fundamental values lie at the heart of what we'd like our life to be like? Why don't we find our meaning first and then manifest that, as opposed to finding meaning from things outside ourselves?

Do we ever stop, never mind stopping regularly, to look carefully at what we want with our lives? When we look carefully at our lives, can we say, without any doubts, that our lives are meaningful?

Do we live our lives in a way that we experience inner peace, never mind now and then, but often, or almost always?

Are you content within yourself, and if so, is this the case only from time to time, almost never, or almost all the time?

Is it time to not just stop and look, but look carefully to see what you're experiencing in your day-to-day life, moment by moment?

Do you have the courage to be brutally honest with yourself?

In the event that we see what we experience and realize that it isn't really what we want with our lives, do we have the courage to make the necessary life-changing decisions? When we recognize any of the above, or connect with some of the other material discussed here, does it ring true that our life hasn't amounted to what we would have preferred? If so, is it fair to say that a life-changing decision is necessary?

Is it fair to say that as you're reading right now, you're experiencing all sorts of anxiety? When you look carefully at this anxiety, do you see the connection between what you'd like to do and what your thoughts are at this moment, and that it relates to your Factor-x?

If we're brutally honest with ourselves, we're likely to see that we might be experiencing anxiety. Recognizing our experiences for what they are is a step in the direction of setting ourselves free. The next step is to see how that anxiety translates into having or not having the courage to take the next step, beyond the anxiety brought about by our Factor-x. Perhaps we don't have the courage for that step. But at the least, do we have the courage to see that we're experiencing the anxiety, and that we lack the courage in the moment to take that next step: the step toward what we'd really like with our lives?

Any of the following experiences is all about getting a glimpse of ourselves:

... anxiety when contemplating change
... recognizing what we've created with our lives
... seeing where we stand with ourselves
... seeing that we have a life that we'd rather not have the way it is
... seeing clearly (or maybe not so clearly) that we'd like to change it
... seeing we have the courage (or not) to accept these observations about ourselves

The more we stop and look at what we experience—and accept our observations of ourselves—the more we'll get to know ourselves.

And perhaps we'll recognize that we do have the courage to take some smaller steps. And the more we do it, the more we'll develop the courage to do it again. But, and this is a big but: The smaller steps build our courage, and the more we practice taking smaller steps, the easier it becomes as our courage and confidence grows.

But here is the "but": There is one big step, one we almost certainly won't have the courage to take.

For now, just be aware that there is a big step on the path to our first-choice existence. Fighting it or denying it won't make it any easier to take that step. Yet if we resist the idea of it, we might never take the bigger or biggest step or steps, and as a result, always live a second-choice existence. The main thing is to acknowledge our experiences for what they are. Meaning that: perhaps we realize that we're anxious; perhaps we see the next step but lack the courage to take it; perhaps we accept that we lack the courage to be brutally honest or to even see the next step—or at least acknowledge those experiences and observations. Yet refusing to acknowledge our reality doesn't help. On the contrary, acknowledging our present state is a good start, and one from which we can grow. And acknowledging what we observe about ourselves, and accepting whatever we observe, in itself is a step toward liberating ourselves.

And if we stand up to our Factor-x and get beyond it without fighting it or denying it, we stand a chance of getting to live our first-choice existence.

Always keep in mind that until we stand first in our lives—and this includes not allowing our Factor-x to drive our lives—we'll have a second-choice existence. Only by stopping, observing, seeing and accepting what we want in the moment—that which we see when stopping to observe ourselves—do we recognize ourselves. Only then do we stand a chance of putting ourselves first.

Recognize Our Own Value

What we can do, and usually do, is look for meaning outside ourselves. But, we can uncover our meaning inside ourselves. Then, instead of doing things to find meaning, we can do things that include our meaning. When we do the things we like doing, we manifest our meaning through those things.

Well then, you might ask, "How do I uncover my meaning?" If you recognize yourself first, it isn't impossible to uncover your meaning.

When you do uncover your meaning, what are you likely to find? Invariably, you'll find the things you usually look for externally: security, inner peace, wisdom, clarity, maturity, contentment, meaning, fun, and many other human ingredients. This list isn't complete, but is indicative of inner values you'll uncover.

And if you uncover your meaning, you won't then do something for the clarity it will give you, but because of the clarity you possess that you can bring to whatever you do. As you uncover more of these values inside yourself, using the necessary courage to get past your Factor-x that will attempt to hold you back, you'll uncover further values. As you uncover your own values, you'll also notice how those values grow and lead you to uncover further values. This will provide you with strength and confidence to uncover yourself even further; like a perpetual cycle. Oh, but only if you have the courage to be brutally honest.

A warning: You'll also have many doubts; from time to time, you'll doubt yourself, because in uncovering yourself more and more, you'll fit less and less into what society has created and what society you're a part of. Over time, you'll see things very differently from how you used to see them and how other people see them. You'll see things for what they are, because you aren't looking for value in things outside yourself anymore. Your value system will be very different from what you encounter around you on a daily basis, even moment by moment.

Your preferences will change. Things you used to do will lose their appeal, and you'll have courage for things you didn't have courage for previously.

Taking this route won't necessarily make your life easier, because it will be so diametrically different from your previous supposed preferences and what society expects and dictates. One change, though, is that your life will have meaning. At the same time, you'll see more and more how society searches for meaning. Your behavior will change. You'll notice that in situations where you would have reacted in a certain way, now you'll respond in some other way: not just to be different, but because the situation and your actions will have different meaning for you.

You might even lose interest in your job, likely because whatever goals or influences drove you before are likely to wane away.

You'll likely uncover new interests, and might recognize things from your daydreams that now come to fruition.

Every now and then, you might get to a point where you struggle big time. This is likely to be because you're resisting a next step down the path of your new journey. This will happen because Factor-x is always there; all you have at your disposal is to befriend your Factor-x, thereby defusing its power over you. So, the bigger the struggle, the more your Factor-x influences you to reject or resist taking the next step. Yet you won't have peace until you exercise your freedom and take the step.

You might even get out of long-term relationships or a marriage, because you now see what has kept you in them, and that it isn't really serving your partners or you to stay in them.

You might even end friendships, because when you look closely at a friendship with your meaning present, you might see that the friendship is merely a crutch or a false sense of security, or perhaps was never a friendship at all.

Whatever happens and however difficult it might seem at times, you can always remember to look at one thing, and to ask yourself these questions:

With whatever you're experiencing at the time during tough times, does your life in general have meaning?

Does what you're struggling with have meaning?

Is what you're struggling with an attempt to bring meaning to your life? Is what you're struggling with an attempt to shake off an external stimuli that previously gave you meaning, and now you see that it doesn't?

What you'll notice is that as your life revolves around living your meaning, the search for meaning—doing things to bring happiness and so forth—tends to lose its appeal.

And when in a difficult situation or needing to make difficult decisions, you can look at it this way: with your life having meaning, the difficulty seems worth it. Invariably, when you get over the difficulty, you'll come out the other end even more at peace. Unless, of course, your Factor-x got the better of you. Then, you don't get to the other end but stay in a circle, repeating the same or similar things, thus merely treating symptoms.

When the dust settles to a certain degree with each difficulty, you're likely to see your life differently. And it's likely that you'll want to share your own findings in your life with others. Most people likely won't "get" what you're so excited about, what you're "going on about," or what you'd like to share with them. Nevertheless, you're likely to pursue and manifest your newfound meaning.

Here is an interesting thing for every one of us, including those who have commenced this process: who are traveling this journey. Our lives up to the point before beginning the journey likely accumulated certain expertise in certain directions. It's likely that we can now employ that expertise as a basis to move forward in whatever direction our meaning guides us. Even our jobs, or whatever expertise we've accumulated, can be employed or deployed to serve us as a means to an end. Therefore, we don't have to radically "throw in the towel" on our lives and become struggling martyrs. No, not at all. Rather, we can make use of what we have and can do to sustain ourselves while turning in the direction as guided by our meaning.

This can be a gradual process, or a sudden, overnight change, or a slow shift into the new direction. Each one of us has our own pace, resources, strengths and struggles.

Notwithstanding, we might go in a wholly different direction.

From time to time, some of the pathway our meaning takes us on will be scary. Imagine that we're at a point of scaling down our conventional working, and therefore our income, and therefore our expenses. This might be the next step on the path down which our meaning guides us. We might fight it; we might struggle to process or accept it. Either way, if we have the courage of our convictions, our meaning might gradually (or even suddenly) lead us into such new and even scary situations. For example, we might be on the brink of some big change, but not be quite ready due to lack of resources or lack of courage. What's important is to avoid denying, but rather accept and acknowledge our observations.

When about to make a significant change, some of us might be ready, and just go with it and take the next step irrespective of how big or scary. For others, it might be more difficult. For still others, it might be the biggest step yet. And then there is our Factor-x, which might make it very difficult for us to take a next step.

And if we let it, our Factor-x might just get us completely off the path where our meaning wants to take us. It's surely a sad day when, due to lack of courage, we don't go beyond the powers of our Factor-x, and thereby stop pursuing our meaning. But the least we can do, at those times and now, is to acknowledge our Factor-x's influence on us. It's always easier not to fight our Factor-x, but to let it come with us on the journey, like a friend rather than the enemy. Keep in mind that although our Factor-x is dead against us moving on the path of our meaning, it's still a part of us and not the enemy: not something outside us, merely a part of us holding us back because it's caught up in the quest to disprove our Factor-x. And unfortunately, it doesn't know any better. That part of us doesn't know that our Factor-x is based on a figment of our imagination.

Digressing for a moment, it's ironic that superstars, wealthy people or business giants are most likely being driven by a figment of their imagination: that is, they're on a quest to disprove their Factor-x. They have huge resources and so many skills, but they most likely lack one thing—knowledge of Factor-x's influence on their lives.

Back to the courage to get over difficult times, and the need to befriend our Factor-x and take it with us on our path wherever our meaning takes us. Based on what you've read so far, it might sound as if there are different, extraneous things making up one person. Yet these are different parts of ourselves: different emotions and components within us that make up an individual. That's exactly why we cannot move forward while kicking and screaming and fighting with any part of ourselves. On this journey, it's best to befriend each part, know it exists, acknowledge and accept each part and their contribution to your life, and then move forward, gently taking each part of you with you on your journey.

This way of describing our inner workings also sheds light on the origins of our inner conflicts. It also describes why we have inner conflicts. By seeing why and what goes on inside us, we have a chance to move beyond what holds us back to uncover our meaning, and then move forward down the path as guided by our inner meaning.

Courage to Recognize Ourselves

Having the courage to recognize ourselves is nearly impossible. We're so used to wanting to be associated, in some form or another, with society's standards and norms, that to look at what we really, really want can be very strange and difficult.

The important point is to *somehow* get a glimpse of your own value: your meaning. And for that, you'd need to look beyond what you know—beyond what exists in your frame of reference, beyond society's standards and norms, and beyond your Factor-x.

Once in the habit of recognizing yourself, your value, and your meaning, each attempt becomes easier. When starting out to recognize yourself, everything that exists in your frame of reference will kick and scream against accepting what you see. That's assuming you have the courage to look. Usually, it's just too scary to even look. Besides, there's another aspect you should probably first look at: that is, are you quiet enough within yourself to see what's going on?

So, there is a whole trainload of aspects involved in seeing and recognizing ourselves. To see ourselves is truly difficult, and there are many hurdles.

The first step is to have a reason to want to recognize ourselves. That step only comes up if we realize that we've created a life for ourselves that we don't like and possibly don't even want. Another possibility is that we get to the point where we question the meaning of the life we've created for ourselves. As mentioned before, yet another possible reason we'll stop and look at our lives is when we suffer a traumatic experience.

In short, we're most likely to stop and look at the life we've created for ourselves when we have reason to question our life. Until then, it's highly unlikely we'll see a need to do so.

Say you have the intention to stop and look at the life you've created for yourself. To quiet yourself so you can see what's going on inside of you usually isn't straightforward. Your mind might be racing so fast, perhaps because of your busy life, to slow it down is a difficult, perhaps nearly impossible task. In this case, what are you to do?

There are various ways to quiet ourselves. One is to breathe deeply and hold our breath for a moment, and then slowly exhale. Repeating this thirty times would certainly quiet us, if only slightly, especially if we concentrate on our breathing and not let our minds wander while breathing. (Later, in the section titled, "Creating an Inner Calm," you'll receive specific assistance for doing this.)

Another approach is to cast our minds to a peaceful place in nature where we can visit—if in our minds only—and look at the scenery while at the same time breathing deeply and slowly. Such calming exercises are a form of what is referred to as meditation.

Yet another approach is to apply the meditation done by David, which you'll read about in, "Meditation, Grass." This meditation achieves best results when done by a reader for the benefit of another person or a group.

Assuming we've managed to quiet our minds, when we then observe ourselves while in this quiet and most likely relaxed state, we stand a chance to observe what we're experiencing. To get here, if we've never done it before, could be considered a miracle. Our minds are usually so busy, rushing here and there and all over the place . . . and besides, even to acknowledge that the lives we created for ourselves aren't working for us takes heaps of courage.

Another aspect of this experience is to describe to ourselves what we're experiencing: not in a million words, but only one—one word we muster that describes to us, in the most powerful way, what we're experiencing. If we want to see what our lives are really about, this is an important step.

Look quietly and carefully at what you experience in that quiet moment. Don't force it—feel it. Stay in the moment. If the word eludes you, then just stop and wait and return there when ready to explore the quiet moment again.

Oh, and this isn't about thinking. Thinking won't help. In fact, all thinking will do is cause a distraction. This is about feeling, and then describing the feeling with the most apt word—describing the feeling powerfully.

Let's repeat this caution: *Thinking won't help. All thinking will do is cause a distraction.*

Now, go to a quiet spot in nature, in your minds, to explore a daydream. Look at it carefully, and in a way that you can then describe, in one powerful word, what you're experiencing. Remember, you're likely to recognize through *feeling* whether the word you'll use to describe what you're experiencing is indeed what you're all about. If you don't recognize it, and if you don't *feel* you're on track, then merely stop and return here, again and again, until you know you're on track.

If all else fails, make contact with me, via lifecanbedifferent.com under the "assisted member option," to explore whether you're on track.

———— ❧ ————

This is about uncovering yourself—something you might not ever have done before—so you're in new territory with these "firsts." The first new territory you covered was recognizing your Factor-x, and that it stands in your way to recognizing yourself.

Assuming you're able to describe your experience by describing in one word how you *feel* when you daydream, that word is most likely what your life is really about. So, feeling and describing this experience is another new territory you've broken into, by *feeling* to see what your life is really about.

Let's take it a step further. When reliving your daydreams and when quiet enough, you might recognize what you *feel*. This being the case, the experience you described in one word is likely the value of your meaning.

When living your meaning, you put your meaning into whatever you do, as opposed to looking for meaning in whatever you do.

Having gotten to this point is almost certainly a miracle. But be warned, from this point on, it will take even more courage than what it took to get here—almost certainly more courage than you've ever needed for anything else you attempted before in your life. Merely considering breaking away from society's standards and norms can be overwhelming and intimidating. You might find that merely considering going for what's important in your life as opposed to society's standards and norms is almost impossible to contemplate. So, if just considering it is so difficult, what chance do you have to actually find and live your meaning?

This is where the courage comes in: heaps and heaps of courage.

Chances are, by now you feel that surely you'll be ostracized by your family, friends, work colleagues and society in general. Yes, this is the reality. The reason is that very few people have the courage to walk down the path as guided by their own meaning. And don't think your Factor-x will let you go without putting up an enormous fight, warning you of the perils of breaking away to do your own thing and live your life outside society's standards and norms.

The irony is, while we're sticking to being dictated to by our Factor-x, it serves nobody, not even us. Furthermore, we might consider ourselves selfish if we break out, and might even think that's how other people will see us. However, while you and I and everyone else are being driven by our individual Factor-x, no one is being served: not us, not them, no one. After all, Factor-x is a figment of our imagination. Also, going on the path as guided by our meaning serves us and everyone else, so how can that be selfish? On careful inspection, it's a case of caring for ourselves that we chose to be guided by our meaning. Conversely, when we do as dictated to by our Factor-x, it's at the cost of ourselves and everyone else.

You might be thinking, *How could this be?*

When we're dictated to by our Factor-x we aren't serving anyone; its origin is a figment of our imaginations, and we're on a quest to disprove that our Factor-x exists and therefore we don't live our own lives.

Looking at it even more carefully: If there are people you care for—family, friends, spouse or partner—while you're being dictated to by your Factor-x, your caring never gets to those people. When you're guided by your meaning, however, those people receive that caring, even without you being aware of it. Your underlying attitude is different when you're driven by your Factor-x as opposed to being guided by your meaning. Therein lies the difference. When driven by your Factor-x because you're seeking meaning in your supposed caring, the people you care for feel that it isn't genuine. Just as in the following simplistic example:

Say you smoke, and you tell someone you care for that they shouldn't smoke. They feel the insincerity, and what you've told them doesn't help them. But if they see for themselves that your behavior is consistent with what you've asked—that you don't smoke—they would get the idea of not smoking.

The smoking example isn't necessarily in context, but what is in context is that those that we care for instinctively sense when we're sincere and when we're not. So if we live our lives by walking our own path as guided by our meaning, this automatically serves everyone, starting with ourselves. And that takes courage, not idle talk.

Having the Courage of Your Conviction

This is the turning point. Without conviction, nothing will change. Without courage, nothing will change. This is where it starts.

Every now and then, some times more regularly than other times, we'll find ourselves at crossroads. At these points—because life-changing decisions are difficult and our Factor-x doesn't let up easily—Factor-x will definitely create doubts about the direction we want to be moving into with our lives.

When at these crossroads, we're certainly going to doubt ourselves, and we'll conjure up many things that might happen to us because of the path we're on. Our conviction will again come under scrutiny. We might even suspect that we're only imagining things about the new direction we're taking with our lives. We'll certainly feel there might be something wrong with us, since our Factor-x will raise doubts and our preferences and journey are so very different from mainstream society.

These crossroads create upheaval in our lives. To get beyond them requires decisions, in many cases life-altering ones. They never stop; they are continuously part of our lives. These decisions lead us down paths where we're on our own, and sometimes, we get lonely. Again I'll remind you that our journeys aren't for the fainthearted, and it's no coincidence that when at a crossroads, it's sometimes difficult to make decisions. And the further we walk on our path, the greater the likelihood that we isolate ourselves further.

This is no wonder. You and I might be one of few people walking this path: the path of our meaning. Almost everyone else is being dictated to and driven by their Factor-x. So we're mostly on our own.

If you don't see the dynamics of walking your journey as a free individual or free spirit, manifesting your meaning as opposed to doing things to find meaning . . . well, it's very daunting—to the point where you might give up and revert back to being dictated to and driven by your Factor-x. As we've seen very clearly, Factor-x is merely a figment of our imagination. But this doesn't mean that Factor-x isn't there all the time, and that we aren't continuously on the quest to disprove the existence and power of our Factor-x. No, our Factor-x is indeed there all the time, and very powerful. Just look at the state humankind is in—individuals being driven by their Factor-x likely created this state.

It takes courage to get beyond these crossroads. Encountering a crossroad isn't a test for you, but moving past one can test your conviction and courage. In fact, it gets more and more difficult, until you're at the biggest crossroads with your life. Once you move beyond that, however, it's likely to get easier.

These crossroads envelop us and intimidate us to the point where it feels life-threatening. We deserve a medal for getting beyond them. And you do get something, something even more rewarding than medals, something more profound than anything else: You free yourself more and more from your Factor-x. That liberation is reward enough. You can't expect a bigger reward than manifesting your freedom away from your own Factor-x, and from the standards and norms society creates for us all—standards and norms likely created from the Factor-x of their creators. You're in fact liberating yourself from society's and our collective Factor-x. And that's a "Wow!" if nothing else.

No wonder, then, that it takes so much courage, in fact all the courage we can muster together, to get beyond each crossroads. And they keep on coming, as if to test us. Of course they aren't really testing you, even though the big ones remain daunting. They are merely there, continuously a part of your life. The more you liberate yourself from your Factor-x, the easier and less frequent these crossroads become to navigate.

Acknowledging that the life you've created for yourself isn't what you want is merely the starting point. After that, the headwinds and crossroads are continuously there until each reaches its crescendo. Only once you get beyond the little ones and grow your confidence, and then get beyond bigger ones and grow more confidence, then eventually go beyond the biggest one, does it get any easier.

Thus, until our lives get to a point where the confidence of being on our own journey as guided by our meaning gets bigger than our Factor-x, so to speak, it's one struggle after another. Some are smaller struggles, some are huge struggles, some look insurmountable, some leave us high and dry on the other side and seemingly where we can't see the road forward. There is also almost certainly no one who can assist us in this journey. After all, you and I, most likely, are in a minute minority. So our journey is most likely alone, without company, and even lonely from time to time. Yet all this time, without a doubt, we will never be without meaning. Possibly without everything else, but never without meaning.

Sometimes you might lack courage, a vital ingredient for this self-chosen journey. Without it, you can't get beyond any crossroad. When your courage wanes, all you'll have at your disposal is to recognize that your meaning isn't lacking: that your meaning is right there and has been there all along without fail. Seeing that your meaning was there all along is likely to inspire courage when the journey gets tough, or even seemingly too tough.

While on your journey as guided by your meaning, if you don't see your meaning, then it's likely you aren't on your own journey. You might instead be on a journey dictated to or driven by your Factor-x. If this is indeed the case, you will need to go back and see where you lost the path of your journey. This requires even further courage of your convictions. Without it, you won't be able to make the journey or go back to locate where you lost your path.

Walking our path, and staying on our path, knowing that we're indeed on our path takes continuous courage. Our journey requires us to continuously look and re-look at our conviction about our lives—looking at why we're doing what we're doing. Furthermore, when we're struggling, the best we can do is to stop and look at whether we're indeed looking for meaning, or living our meaning.

With the courage of your convictions and being absolutely brutally honest with yourself, and by acknowledging the influence Factor-x has on your life, you're putting yourself in the best possible position to get beyond any crossroads and face anything your Factor-x conjures up, thereby enabling you to walk your journey freely as guided by your meaning.

Standing Up and Stepping Out of Mainstream Society

The chances are very probable that when a person uncovers themselves, they would want to step out of mainstream society—not easily done, and that person's Factor-x will likely kick in and hold them back like crazy. At first, it's likely they'd want to walk their journey within society, within their current environment. Staying within mainstream society seems easier: The change wouldn't be so severe, and would be more suited to their Factor-x, which is on the quest to disprove that it exists. Stepping out of mainstream society could be construed as that something is seriously wrong with them, and this isn't at all acceptable to our Factor-x.

However and with time, as they walk their journey as guided by their meaning, they will want to step out of mainstream society to apply their trade in a way more conducive and humane than what mainstream and working conventionally provides.

Stepping out of mainstream society in itself is likely to be a scary dynamic, not for the fainthearted. Stepping out doesn't have to be scary, but scary it will be. This only becomes possible after we see and acknowledge that we desire to step out of mainstream society. By looking carefully at our individual circumstances, and with some planning and being realistic about where we're heading and how we could get there, we can gradually make the desired transition.

But, bear in mind that by having uncovered our Factor-x and our meaning, we're likely emotionally loaded. When walking our own journey, as opposed to being dictated to and driven by our Factor-x, it's unlikely that we would take care of ourselves in any lesser way. What might happen, and is likely to happen, is that due to our value system shifting continuously, the lifestyle we're used to will change—different things are likely important to us now. We'll likely take care of ourselves in a suitable way, but from a different perspective: one that's more conducive to our needs and that serves us. And as we walk our newfound path, we'll notice that pleasing our Factor-x is based on very different values, ones not necessarily conducive to our well-being, whereas taking care of ourselves as guided by our meaning is conducive to our needs and our well-being and will serve us, as well as everyone and everything else. When we serve ourselves by living our meaning, we *automatically* serve all else, and everyone else.

By standing up, and making this transition, you will likely be frowned upon by those close to you. To others it might appear as if you've "lost it," as if you're rebelling against things familiar to everyone. Support from others might not be there. Friendships might end. Other relationships might end. Almost no one will understand what you're about, because others—who haven't come to the same conclusions and realizations as you—might see you as out of kilter with everyone else. The exception will be others who've also made this self-discovery and are walking their own path based on their own meaning, as you are.

When you attempt to step out—to break out of the mold you've been in—it might be difficult at times. This is true even if you've only been in your mold for a short time. Those close to you might want to prevent you from making changes in your lives. And again, some might even break off their friendship. Or, you might want to break off friendships or even marriages or relationships. What you'll notice, as mentioned earlier, is that things have different values when you bring your meaning to what you do. Previously, when dictated to or driven by our Factor-x, almost everything had a different value. Now, those values have transitioned. We're likely to seem to be different people, even to ourselves, since such a transition does change us almost completely.

Yet we don't need to be reckless. We can make the transitioning from mainstream society as easy or as difficult as we'd like it to be. This depends on how much we let our Factor-x fight us about our desire to take charge of our lives. Your newfound self will likely lack experience in taking charge of your new journey. You're likely to lack confidence at times, or be still raw emotionally from the realizations you've made about yourself and how your life was dictated to by your Factor-x.

In short, you might feel too inexperienced to make this new journey, and might even struggle to accept the new ways as guided by your meaning. This is understandable. After all, this is likely to be a strange world you're entering; one that requires you to stand up and be counted in what you do and how you walk your journey.

Either way, as mentioned before, once we make these realizations, we're likely to want to get out of the mainstream. This, in itself, is most likely fraught with difficulty. As we enter this new world presented to us by our meaning, and as we stand up to step out of mainstream society, we're likely to encounter several crossroads. You might even be tempted to just give up, lacking the courage for some of the steps along the path. You might actually struggle and give up; or, you might struggle and see the light, so to speak, and move beyond the crossroads.

You could also take the transition calmly, gain the newly required life skills, work out a plan that suits you, take it slowly, implement your plan one small step at a time, and make a slow transition from where you are to where you would like to be. It can take as long as is needed, after all. By example, after conception, no matter what you do about it, birth happens in a specific length of time. In the same way, your planned transition can take as long as is necessary.

You can also take no action at all, and allow things to continue just as they are, to remain at a place where you don't want to be. You see the lack of meaning in your life, that you're likely just a product of your environment and your circumstances; thus, that you carry all the pain that comes from such a way of life. Yet if you are doing something about it, even in small steps, that's when your meaning is at work.

Once our meaning is at work and we stall for whatever reason, pain will again most likely set in because of our Factor-x again having taken charge. For those of us who take action, however, when we make a plan and work it, and adjust it as we get increasing courage, confidence and life skills, we can eventually stand up and step out of mainstream society's ways. It might take up to five or ten years or more, and our journey could be fun or just heartache. But once we breach the point where our confidence in our own path outweighs our Factor-x, it's likely to become easier, and even fun.

Making a plan and working it—in your case, a plan for the transition toward standing up and stepping out of the mainstream—is likely to serve you well, no matter how long it takes or how much you struggle while on the journey. It doesn't matter if you have limited life skills. It doesn't matter if you have few resources. What does matter is your intention, and that you see where you are and that you recognize that you don't like it there. When we recognize that where we are in our lives doesn't serve us, and we then make our plan and work that plan irrespective of the consequences, all that's important is that we want to make the journey because that's what we'd like to do with our lives.

Why Daydreams Come About

When we're in a position that doesn't serve us, our daydreams often act as an escape to point us in the direction of where we'd rather be—our dream and vision for the future. An escape they might be, but what can we deduce from the escape mechanism? Clearly, that we feel the need to escape, consciously or not, we aren't enjoying where we find ourselves, so the daydreams show us where or how we'd rather be.

Daydreams come in a variety of forms, and with diverse content and context. We might have daydreams related to our daily jobs, about our relationships, about our home life, about our studies, about holidays, and about so many more and different things. Do we ever look closer at our dreams and look what lies underneath them, what inspires them, what value they project to us, which feelings we're left with as a result of our daydreams? Chances are, we don't.

Isn't it time to look at our daydreams carefully to ascertain their origins?

When we find ourselves in situations that we don't like, which don't serve us, we might develop uncomfortable feelings about such situations. Because we experience such feelings, they formulate in us desires to the contrary.

These desires manifest in us in certain ways, and specifically are likely to emerge as daydreams. So over a short or long period of time, our mind, our brain, our spirit being, our soul, brings to our attention a formulation of something we'd prefer that is usually contrary to what is. These daydreams can be informative nuggets when it comes to uncovering our meaning.

So daydreams are created from certain desires. The images of the dream itself aren't necessarily what we look at when observing our daydreams. It's what lies underneath them, the desire from which the daydream images were created: that which inspired the daydream. That's where we're likely to uncover our meaning.

Daydreams are about preferences and desires, so it's important to look beyond the daydream images or pictures to uncover the underlying value.

Daydreams: Misinterpretation and Undercurrent

As mentioned, our daydreams come about from the underlying feelings and undercurrents of our experiences, and can evolve our vision, plans and aspirations. While our lives are dictated and driven by our Factor-x and we haven't yet uncovered our meaning, it's understandable that we're likely to misunderstand our daydreams—to interpret them based on our frame of reference, as created by ourselves within society's known standards and norms and from our Factor-x. We likely don't know any different, and create dreams from what we know.

That's why it's important for us to look at the underlying feelings in our daydreams.

To really understand our daydreams, it's important, first, that we stop to look at them: not at what they conjure up for us, but further, to something about our daydreams that we've most likely never looked at before.

Until being introduced to this material, you might not have had any inkling that your life is dictated to and driven by your Factor-x, and why that came about. It's also unlikely that you understood the underlying meanings of your dreams, desires, or preferences. When you daydreamed, you likely interpreted them from your existing frame of reference.

Notwithstanding, as you uncover your meaning, it soon becomes apparent how important your newfound knowledge is, and recognize that you'll see things differently all together: that you'll see things in a different light. As you get to know yourself better and look at what humankind created and is continuously creating, you're likely to see certain things created from possible misunderstandings by people of their dreams.

Every one of us is likely to possess the dynamic of being driven by our Factor-x, and as a result, live our lives with a lack of meaning. As you and I misinterpreted our daydreams, others that aren't exposed to this material also misinterpret their dreams. Looking around us once we uncover our meaning, we notice these possible misinterpreted manifestations of daydreams.

A possible example of such misinterpretations is our shopping malls. Supposedly, aside from the shopping aspect, they're a place where we get together and socialize with our community. However, when we walk from shop to shop in our shopping malls today, it's mostly in isolation. There is, in fact, very little if any community spirit in our shopping malls.

Another example. Real estate planners develop cluster, or "estate living" housing, supposedly where we would live as a community based on togetherness of some sort, perhaps similar cultures or lifestyles. However, those living in such developments mostly live in isolation from their neighbors and from the community as a whole.

In both examples, these two types of interests are almost exclusively promoted and interpreted from a profit perspective.

So it's advisable for us to look very carefully at the underlying feelings, or undercurrent of our daydreams. By doing so, we can uncover our meaning, the one that awakens our desires and we then dream about.

When you start looking at things in this way, at first things aren't so transparent. As with most things, however, with practice it becomes clearer what you're yearning for, what the basis is of your dreams. As you uncover yourself in this way, you'll of course see things around you in a very different light, or with very different eyes. Those who have commenced their journey, and whose attitudes have started shifting, are likely to recognize that our meaning is very different from the meaning we seek external to us. Our meaning is very different from what our Factor-x shows us. Our meaning is very different from what society expects from us. Our meaning is very different from society's standards and norms. As a result, we stand out as possible weirdoes. From time to time, we even see ourselves as weirdoes. Notwithstanding, we're living our meaning and now have meaningful lives, whereas before we were always seeking meaning.

This dynamic of uncovering ourselves and our meaning also results in seeing our dreams differently. We can even see how we possibly misinterpreted them before.

Just out of my teens and military service, I had just started working, still in my first year as a young adult and working a regular job for a living.

A school friend—in fact, we were school-hostel roommates—visited, and we got carried away in discussion on the balcony of the flat where I was staying. We were really just shooting the breeze and talking about everything under the sun people of that age discuss.

During the discussion, we somehow got to considering becoming farmers. For some reason, we spoke of rabbit farming. We got totally carried away and became very big farmers. During the discussion, we created the farm with very many people working on the farm. We also branched from rabbit farming to other farming. As the discussion continued, our farming venture grew and grew until it was nearly a little self-contained village.

Anyway, after this discussion, we explored all the possibilities of becoming farmers. We visited a friend who was in fact a farmer to discuss our plans. We did some research to get a better understanding of farming rabbits.

Needless to say, eventually, our enthusiasm shriveled away. And eventually, we dropped the idea and did just what we did before—continued our regular jobs and lives.

At the time, I understood the daydream as being about money and power. The money from such a large farming venture could be used to create anything that I wanted. The money would give me the power to pursue anything that the money could provide.

From the seed that was planted with that daydream, I set forth and pursued money and power. I wasn't successful at all. In fact, all my ventures came to naught. In fact, for the next approximately twenty years, I achieved nothing toward money and power. Everything I did flopped. I started several businesses that failed or didn't get off the ground.

My money and power schemes failed, and I wasn't very happy about it. The continued failures drained my energy and confidence.

Eventually I settled as a freelance contractor, which I still do for a living at the time of this writing.

This is a very broad-stroke account of the daydream and what transpired.

The point being, the dream I interpreted as *money and power* wasn't about money and power at all. It was all together a misinterpretation.

As I mentioned in the introduction, around the age of forty, my life had reached emotional rock bottom and I became a wreck, probably close to a nervous breakdown. I started looking meticulously at my life with utmost introspection, analyzing it absolutely to the bone and doing various life courses, life-awareness courses, hypnosis therapy and several other therapies, and even several visits to a psychologist. With help from a life-awareness coach with whom I became good friends, we unraveled my daydream.

What I uncovered about the daydream, the undercurrent, was a very important aspect I had missed and misinterpreted due to my Factor-x, my own frame of reference, and the standards and norms that I was exposed to up until that time of my life.

So for twenty years, I had pursued an understanding that wasn't even close to my own inner reality. And over time, as everything didn't work and as I got farther and farther away from what the dream was indeed about, the sheer disappointment and frustration of my life became too much for me. My emotional system just gave up, and I broke down into a nervous wreck.

No wonder I broke down. After having pursued something for so long and with all the failures that occurred, my life became unbearable.

As mentioned, I sought the help of a self-awareness coach, but not just any life-awareness coach. This was a very special life-awareness coach, mentioned in the book's Acknowledgements. Sergio understood life, he understood me, and we unraveled what that very important daydream was really about—we unraveled the *undercurrent* of the daydream. And I eventually understood.

In my dream, on the farm every person would be contributing what they liked doing. I developed the farm in my daydream to the extent that it was nearly the size of a small village, and the people working the farm were applying themselves to what they liked doing. The underlying theme of the farm was that people would do what they liked doing.

However, that wasn't quite it yet. There was another aspect underneath that: the core, the origin, the source, the underlying reason, the undercurrent itself of the daydream was that everyone was doing what they liked doing, and at the core of that was that they were enjoying themselves and were peaceful. The daydream equated to them being peaceful, therefore the dream was about peacefulness—*not* about money and power.

What a difference! My misinterpretation was that the daydream was about money and power. Only twenty years later did I discover that it was indeed about peacefulness. Quite a stark contrast!

As a result of this daydream and uncovering what it really meant, I now set in motion a mechanism exposing my reality to the world—one where each person has the opportunity to look at their daydreams and uncover their underlying reason—their undercurrent. Also, so each person has an opportunity to uncover their own meaning and live their lives manifesting themselves, as opposed to what they understand from their accumulated frame of reference, from the standards and norms dictated by our society, and from their quest to disprove their Factor-x.

In reflecting on this dynamic, the undercurrent of the dream was peacefulness that manifested in my daydream as people doing with their lives, on the farming community, what they liked doing. And from what they liked doing, we all lived together in peacefulness.

Therefore, I see my own meaning as that of peacefulness. I am manifesting that by way of bringing this material to interested people, so they can uncover themselves, even with the dynamic of needing brutal honesty with ourselves and the courage of our convictions.

This is, of course, a total breakaway from our frame of reference and our standards and norms as dictated by our society. And not least of all, it is a break because we can get to see our Factor-x for what it is and its impact on our lives.

Expectations: Frustration, Anger and Irritation

Now here is an animal with a different stripe. Expectations will be the death of us. Expectation spawns frustration, frustration spawns anger, and we become irritable.

Emotions Take a Beating

Every day, we create expectations for a variety of things. No matter how well-meaning our expectation, the moment the expectation isn't met, our emotions take a beating. It's as though we're barely able to resist taking a beating from unmet expectations.

We have expectations about ourselves. We have expectations of others. We have expectations of things. We have expectations of the weather. We have expectations about almost anything. And mind you, once on our path, manifesting our meaning, expectations will creep in, and we won't notice until it hits us and beats our emotions to a pulp.

What we seemingly don't ever notice is how much emotional pain we create for ourselves with our expectations.

As you and I walk our own path, we'll have the notion of not wanting to create expectations. Creating expectations is a little dynamic that has almost no resolution. Little it may seem indeed, yet its outcome is enormous and enormously painful. I can guarantee that when we expect it the least, the expectation will visit us quietly. And then, when it's nicely settled and the heat's turned up, our emotions will boil over and we won't know why we're suddenly angry, or in a foul mood, or frustrated or irritated—all because somewhere along the line, an expectation crept into the equation.

The Wild Card in a Deck of Cards

Expectation truly is like a wild card in a deck of cards. Expectations are likely created by our Factor-x, and deviously created for sure.

We can rest assured that our Factor-x decides that we're the cat's whiskers, and from such a stance, we create expectations. But think about it; we are mere mortals, but we expect some predetermined result from ourselves, others, and other things. Why should something turn out a certain way just because we want it to?

Extreme Example

This is admittedly an extreme example to show how we create expectations and the futility of doing so, but the concept depicted by the example is the same.

We arrange an outing over a weekend and suddenly the weather turns and our outing is washed out due to rain. We're suddenly up in arms, frustrated, even angry. And we're possibly irritated with the next person that comes into our space.

This is really futile. We have no say over the weather. Why would the weather respond in a certain way? The weather is just the weather, and it does what it does. In the same way, anyone or anything external to us is essentially outside our hands. Even the course of our own lives is outside our hands in a way. Let's say you walk your own path, manifesting your meaning, and say this requires that you get many people interested in what you have to offer and want to achieve—but only a few people or perhaps none show interest. Then what? Just because you decided you need this or that has no bearing on reality.

When we create expectations, are we being realistic? Things happen, people do things, and nature does what it does. Everything and everyone just does what everything and everyone does. The mere fact that we require a predetermined outcome has no bearing on reality or what the outcome is likely to be. The outcome will be whatever it'll be. We can do what we like, create any amount of havoc we desire, get as frustrated or angry as we want, or as irritable, and the reality is the reality, no matter what.

Factor-x Is Likely Undercurrent

Our expectations and our will are just not going to matter at all. Eventually, any expectation we impose on anyone or anything will backfire and create havoc with our emotions. As a result, we'll lose our inner peace, even if momentarily. The best we can do is to observe how our Factor-x is likely the undercurrent when we create or have expectations, and work with that.

Observe Expectations at Play

When things don't work out, we likely get angry to some degree. When we carefully observe our lives in general, we're likely to see another dynamic at play. In our day-to-day lives, are we possibly constantly apprehensive that something might go wrong? Another dynamic might also be at play; when something does go wrong, do you feel that something bad is going to happen to you as a result? When we observe expectations closely, we're likely to find a myriad of dynamics.

Another dynamic that might be at play when things don't work out as expected—we're likely under the impression that something has gone wrong, and that this "wrong" implies other things too. Quite possibly, when something does go wrong, then somehow—and it will serve us to look carefully—*we* are likely to have done something wrong. That being the case, *we* are likely to get into trouble, and when we get into trouble, we're right into our Factor-x, which says to us: "You see, something is wrong with you." This is something that no one wants to hear, so we fight it and get angry and frustrated and irritable when things don't go according to our expectations.

And all this time, the aforementioned dynamic has no bearing on the activity that didn't go according to an expectation. From this, can we then deduce that our emotions are indeed not living in the moment?

When we walk on our own path, this is likely to happen to us, even though we especially feel it shouldn't. Why? Since we're not driven by Factor-x, things should work out for us. But it still happens to us because we still create expectations, and expectations still don't necessarily work out. Why should things work out the way we want them to, just because we want them to?

Denying With Blame

The worst you and I can do when things don't work out according to expectations is to say, "I should have known better," or, "This isn't happening to me!" These kinds of statements take us straight into denying reality, and Factor-x loves this: It'll conjure up everything and anything just so we don't look at the reality—the facts of a situation. Because if we do look at the facts, it means we're exposing ourselves (even to ourselves), while Factor-x's job is to deny that our Factor-x exists.

So when we can blame ourselves or another, then we're okay. Then Factor-x can rest, because it succeeded in its quest to disprove that something is wrong with us. This isn't dealing with reality, which is that we had expectations. We'd serve ourselves better by instead looking at why we have expectations.

Destruction Follows Expectations

When we get angry, frustrated and irritated we don't have inner peace, and when we're in another's company, we invariably exhibit the destruction that twirls around in us. When we understand the origin of the dynamic of having expectations, we're more likely to defuse it each time, even very slowly or slightly, until eventually we don't lose ourselves, or at least don't lose ourselves so badly. Again, when we look at the origin of our expectations, we're serving ourselves.

Looking Even Closer at Expectation

When things don't work out, we get annoyed or angry. Let's look at it another way, though. Say one of your tasks at your job is to reconcile accounting books when they don't balance. You could get aggravated about it, or just reconcile the books since it's part of your job. Far better this than living on-edge like a wound-up string just ready to snap when things don't work out.

In our life experiences, there are bound to be things that don't go our way. So it's not rocket science to say that, since we know it's likely that things won't always go our way, and now we're aware of what effect Factor-x has on our emotions, then instead of being anxious or even panicky about things not working out, why not just recognize that it's part and parcel of our lives? If we do, instead of becoming aggravated, we'll just recognize the facts for what they are and go forward while staying calm and relaxed and enjoying our newfound inner peace.

Why Anger, Why Not Neutral

This brings up a question: When expectations don't work out, why do we tend to have almost-instinctive anger rather than a neutral stance? Reading this far, we know that the expectation and the anger are likely caused by our Factor-x. So now, when we observe the pattern of expectation and anger and acknowledge it, the need for expectations and the effects of expectations not working out are desensitized. What this means is that, as our understanding of ourselves grows, a neutral action is likely to instill itself, in which case we become freer and freer and can better attend to the matter at hand—that of an expectation being created and that of it not necessarily working out.

Pact to Maintain Inner Peace

Why not make a pact with ourselves to never let our Factor-x drive us, and to acknowledge that when Factor-x does kick in, we won't run with the havoc it plays on our emotions? That instead, we will stop to observe the facts, and thereby automatically defuse the situation and maintain inner peace.

When things don't work out according to expectations, no one is to blame—no one has done anything wrong, and no one is going to get into trouble. If any of these aren't so—if we feel we *are* doing something wrong or we *are* going to get into trouble—then we're likely not walking our own path, and thus not living our meaning. We're quite possibly being abused, either physically, mentally or emotionally, or doing something we don't like doing.

When walking your own path, you aren't likely to allow anyone to abuse you, even yourself. That isn't where you'd want to be, and you wouldn't be doing things you don't like doing. When walking your own path, there would thus be no need for expectations. You wouldn't be doing anything wrong or getting into trouble. As mentioned before, because you're seeing the origin of the anger and the like, you'd then defuse it and maintain inner peace. In this way, instead of propagating destruction, you could then approach the activity that didn't go your way or didn't turn out as expected and attend to the facts as they are while maintaining your inner peace.

Crutches: Observe That We're Different
With Them Than Without Them

When we rely on something or someone as a crutch, when that crutch is absent, we're likely to feel down or depressed or needy or anxious. Crutches, too, are expectations. When we're without what we consider should be present, we likely feel different and uneasy. Therefore, we lose our inner peace when we're "not ourselves" without such person or such thing. Surely, this shows a dependency. That perhaps, all along, we weren't being ourselves.

Would you not rather experience exactly the same feelings whether you're with or without something or someone? When you feel different depending on whether you're with or without something or someone, you have expectations to have that person or thing present, and that expectation dictates how you feel—it dictates your inner state.

When you see the aforementioned dynamic and attend to it by acknowledging it and moving away from it, you have the chance to uncover yourself further and to live peacefully without the expectation created by the dependency. In doing so, you free yourself of the dependency. Then you can get to a position in your life where it makes no difference if you don't have what you're dependent on for your well-being, even when dependent on a partner.

Can you truly say, for example, that your life, without ever again having a partner, would be the same as with a partner? We might think, *Surely there should be a partner in our lives!*

But observe what you might be experiencing, right now, when just considering that there will never ever again be a partner in your life. It's something most of us don't like even contemplating, because we've likely become dependent on being with a partner. If so, at least acknowledge that such an eventuality exists. Then, imagine or at least consider that you could have an absolutely normal life without ever again having a partner in your life, and consider how your life would then be.

What would it be like to be perfectly content without a partner in your life?

What would you be doing with your life?

What would you experience? Would, perhaps, another level of inner peace and inner power come to the fore?

To get to such a place would imply that you're free—that you would function normally without the dependency.

The intensity of your life would mellow, since the expectation or the dependency would likely be neutralized. This would result in you having a peaceful existence.

Expecting Special Treatment

Even when we're walking our own path and uncovering ourselves, the possibility continuously exists that our emotions could get thrown out of kilter by expectations. While walking our own path, we likely feel we deserve special treatment—hence expecting things to work out—just because we're walking our own path and thus living our own meaning—that things should work out as we want them to. Again, why should things work out for our sake, merely because we expect them to?

Let's ask again. When things don't work out, why are our initial reactions that of panic or anger or frustration or irritation? Are our expectations and the effect they have on us when things don't go according to plan likely driven by our Factor-x?

We're likely to have more inner peace once we see the dynamics of expectations for what they are and understand why they originate, and then acknowledge the dynamic that likely exists when we create expectations, and why it exists.

Doing What I Want or Like, and Doing What I Like Doing

Semantics? No, not really. Let's take a closer look at these dynamics: *Doing what I want*, or *I'll do what I like* and *doing what I like doing*.

Doing What I Want or I'll Do What I Like

These could be seen as, *No matter what, I'm doing it.* "It" is likely to include almost anything within the person's morals. In this vein, the murderer will murder. The thief will steal. For someone who has it in them to manipulate, they'll manipulate. Let's list some actions arbitrarily: make war, murder, steal, take drugs, abuse another person (verbally or physically), cheat on taxes, engage in prostitution, cheat in general, handle objects with disrespect, disregard our environment, and the like.

Is there a pattern emerging here? Could these all be related to Factor-x? Yes. Where Factor-x is in charge and because we're on a quest to disprove that Factor-x exists in us, *we'll do almost anything*.

It's also almost certain and very likely that when doing such deeds, when we take a quiet moment and reflect on them, we're likely to admit, or come clean, that *IF* we were able to, we'd prefer not to have done them. Likely, even hardened criminals and murderers say this of their inhumane deeds.

Usually, these activities don't sit well with us before doing them, while we're doing them, or even afterward—a likely sign that these originate from Factor-x.

Doing What I Like Doing

Let's look at the other dynamic, *doing what I like doing*.

Here, when we look at ourselves and observe what we do, we'll see that in most cases, we're doing what we like doing, automatically, without needing to force ourselves to like the things we do.

When do we automatically like the things we do? It's highly likely that when we walk our own path, when we manifest our meaning, we're automatically doing the things we like doing.

Rest assured there are times when you and I do things we'd rather not do, even while walking our own path. We'll find ourselves in such a position where we're likely to do certain things we'd have preferred not to do, but still do after making sure there's no other way. By example, even when walking our own path, from time to time, fortunately not often, we might get into a situation where we need to confront another person (for whatever reason). This is something we almost certainly don't like doing, but we wouldn't shy away from this, and as a result we might end up confronting another person.

Going All the Way, Not Giving Up, Knowing When to Stop

When we pursue our own path, we're bound to occasionally encounter something we'd like to pursue that just doesn't work. Since we value our own path so much, we feel that we shouldn't give up; we'll keep pursuing it, even when it turns out with the same result—that is, it just doesn't work.

Liken it to a farmer relying on rain for his crop to grow. He sows or plants year after year, and the rainfall just isn't enough to keep his crop from withering and dying. The farmer has a particular reason for wanting to farm with that type of crop. So after a while, if not enough rainfall happens, he needs to do something different. If the rainfall doesn't sustain what he'd prefer to farm, then he can move somewhere else where the rainfall is conducive to his crop. Or, the farmer stays on the farm he has and finds another crop to grow.

There is also the other side: if something isn't working, why would we still continue? Usually we'd have to stop when we've thrown everything within reason and then some at a project and it still doesn't work. But, if we haven't pursued aspects that are reasonable to pursue, it's probably too soon to stop, especially if each attempt seems to produce a different result, however slight, that seems to bring us closer to the outcome we're seeking. With each attempt, we feel that perhaps we could pursue a particular path farther.

The main thing though: Just because we're walking our own path doesn't automatically mean everything is going to work, or work out the way we expected it to. People and things have a way of doing their own thing. However, if the theme of what's working is more or less in the desired direction, even if different from what we had anticipated, then just possibly, it still serves us.

You'll likely find a variety of results from your intentions during your journey. You're also likely to observe how you mature (or that you aren't maturing) while on the journey on your path, and how you'd respond differently to things prior to commencing your journey and earlier on your journey. At different points in the journey, you're likely to experience different responses. While you're still experiencing similar responses, and especially when the responses don't serve you, you have in all likelihood not moved past certain things holding you back. Once your responses start changing, you're sure to witness your own maturing ways.

Two aspects are referred to here. At any time during, there are the *things that we do*, and *what we experience while doing whatever it is we're doing*.

It would serve us well to be aware that things aren't necessarily going to go our way. With certain things, it would serve you to stop pursuing them; with certain other things, if your results are still reasonable even though tough, it would serve you to continue pursuing them.

You might think that just because you're on your path based on your meaning, you should expect only favorable results. No way, to put the answer into common speech. There aren't any guarantees. From time to time, your journey might be just a hard slog.

Imagine a stream making its way, curling and turning this way and that way, and when confronted with a large boulder, it merely finds a way around the boulder. All the stream is interested in, on its journey, is to flow following the path of gravity. When it encounters a stumbling block, it twists and turns. It doesn't expect things to work out just because it's doing what it does (as a stream of water), or take it personally when things don't work out. It merely flows, and finds a way around obstacles it encounters.

Keep in mind that just because we're on our path doesn't mean that we have any special privileges, or that life necessarily owes us anything. You're creating; you're on new ground. It's likely not always an easy path. Look at what a mother endures when pregnant. It's the same with your creation: When we walk our own path, it's almost certainly a creation of sorts—the creation of our own unique lives, like when the mother is pregnant and when she gives birth. That process is certainly not all plain sailing. It will serve you to keep this in mind when you're walking your own path.

Why should creation be an easy, frustration-free experience? Likely, you're doing it in your stride. Likely, you're experiencing your meaning. Aside from any struggling you're encountering, you're breaking out of society's standards and norms, and your Factor-x. Up until a point, your path is likely not easy and probably not enjoyable. You might even think you're going nowhere. However, from the point when the largest hurdle is navigated, things start running smoother, and then you start enjoying the journey. Usually, only in looking back do you see that you've moved on from where you once were.

First-Choice Existence Serves Everyone

When looking at the first and second-choice existences I've referred to in several places, why is it that we can say the first-choice existence serves everyone, and automatically, as opposed to living a second-choice existence that serves no one, not even ourselves?

Second-Choice Existence

Let's start by looking at the second-choice existence: where our Factor-x is the driving force in our lives, and our lives are a quest to disprove that our Factor-x indeed exists. In a second-choice existence, the lives we then live aren't based on us being free to live and choose as our heart desires, but rather are dictated by what we thought, at some point, was fact. But as stated elsewhere, Factor-x's origin is merely a figment of our imagination. This figment of our imagination resulted in us creating our Factor-x in the first place. Because we're driven by our Factor-x, we do things not because they're things we like doing, but to disprove something—and that something is a figment of our imagination, as seen in "Factor-x and How It Comes About."

By living our lives to disprove that our Factor-x exists, we aren't being ourselves, and when we aren't being ourselves, we're undermining ourselves: Rather than living our lives naturally and creatively, we live them inwardly and in "protectionist" mode. We thus don't experience us—who we truly are—and neither does anyone else experience us, just our behavior based on our quest to disprove that our Factor-x exists.

This way of life can be compared to a fight. We're in a fight with ourselves, thus in a fight with reality. We're fighting to disprove something that doesn't exist except in our minds, and that likely originated from a figment of our imagination. This is surely a path of destruction. We're moving ourselves aside to disprove this thing referred to as Factor-x. By doing so, we're almost certainly not creating but destroying—destroying ourselves.

This self-destruction isn't limited to only us. While we're exhibiting this behavior of disproving that our Factor-x exists, we're radiating our self-destruction, and everyone around us experiences that self-destruction. Since they are likely also on a quest to disprove their Factor-x, then they're almost certainly also exhibiting that same self-destructive behavior. So it's a vicious circle where no one wins. Everyone is seemingly self-destructing—or to put it a less-harsh way, self-suffocating or self smothering.

Whatever the term, while we're on a quest to disprove that our Factor-x exists, we aren't being ourselves. When in this mode, we don't care what we do to ourselves or what we do to others. All that's important to us while Factor-x reigns is that we disprove our belief in the existence of Factor-x.

First-Choice Existence

A first-choice existence means that we live our lives as intended, free and doing the things we like doing. In a first-choice existence, we experience ourselves, and those around us experience us perhaps very differently from what we and others might be used to, but nevertheless sincerely ourselves. In this state, the behavior we exhibit is based on our integrity—naturally and automatically.

By living your life with integrity, there is no fight. You're not disproving anything. You're merely living freely and almost certainly creating an authentic existence. You radiate this creation through your actions. You aren't driven, but are merely living from inner peace while walking your own path and liking the things you do. You aren't smothering yourself; you aren't destroying yourself. On the contrary, you're living your creation. And it's highly likely that you're flourishing in the process, radiating your meaning instinctively and automatically.

By "instinctively" and "automatically," I mean this: When living a first-choice existence, we recognize ourselves first. It's automatic that we don't impose ourselves on anyone else. We can also recognize when someone who doesn't recognize themself imposes themself on us. In a first-choice existence, we don't do anything to another person that we wouldn't like done to us. Through our respect for ourselves and our integrity, we respect everyone and everything, starting with ourselves. We live our inner beauty automatically almost all of the time. (*Almost* all of the time because, from time to time, our Factor-x will be there to trip us up, and we'll momentarily want to disprove the existence of our Factor-x.)

When you're living your integrity as a first-choice existence, it isn't about lip service. It's real. Not forced, but rather an automatic and intuitive way of life. Your own path and meaning are what underpin your behavior, and you are creating, not destroying, in everything you do.

Doing Everything Else First, or First Doing That Which Is Important

If you're like most people, you likely have two approaches when doing anything: doing what's important to you first, or first doing everything else that seems to accumulate in your life. Following are the differences between the two as they relate to your new way of conducting your life:

Doing Everything Else First

You can first do the things that will give you time to do what's important to you, thus making space for you to then do what's important. This could also mean that you'd do what's important to you in the time you have left over from having done other things first.

When doing things this way, or when living our lives this way, you'll likely experience frustration. You'll become irritable and want to rush and hurry things, because after all, you'd much rather be doing something important as opposed to first doing what isn't so important at the time.

First Doing That Which Is Important

The other way is to first do what's most important to you, and then attend to other less important things. This is like saying you're not putting your life on hold while doing other, less-important things.

Herein lies the scope for some misinterpretations. How do we know what's important? What about daily chores, like washing the dishes? Does that mean because washing dishes is least important to us, it'll never get done?

The word "important" doesn't only mean big and high-profile things. Since living tidily is likely important to us, we'll do the dishes somewhere along the line, even if the unwashed dishes do pile up from time to time.

When we first do what's important, there's always time and space for other chore-like activities. Doing what's important first results in a comprehensive lifestyle, where we take care of ourselves and do the things important to us moment by moment, and knowing where that fits into our lives. When we're in a tug-of-war with what's important in that moment, we aren't quite there yet—somewhere inside that turmoil Factor-x is lurking, exerting its influence on us to obscure what's important in the moment.

When we first do what's important, we're living a life that means whatever we're doing gets our undivided attention in each and every moment. It doesn't mean we'll neglect anything, but it does mean that as time goes on and as we get to know our own preferences, those things that aren't important to us are done less and less, until eventually, they're no longer part of our lives.

It doesn't mean that we were so busy, we didn't make an appointment that we needed to make, or that we came late for an appointment. If those two things happened, that likely implies that the meeting related to the appointment wasn't important.

What we can gather by first doing what's important is that we'll live responsibly and automatically, and have time for everything and more. In any moment, we're doing what is most important to us— and the same in the next moment, and the same in the next one, and so on. It's an automatic process. So, if for whatever reason we see we won't make a meeting, for example, it'll usually be well ahead of time, and we'll inform the concerned parties well ahead of time and possibly even reschedule.

Usually, we won't have to cancel or reschedule at the last minute. And by doing what is important first, these situations where we might be late or need to reschedule won't be frequent occurrences. We're not doing things to fill the time. We're not doing things because we have nothing better to do. We're not doing things, and then later something better comes along and we cancel previous engagements under the guise that "Something important has come up." No, not at all. When we live from a standpoint of walking our own path, we're automatically responsible and sincere and do things moment by moment because the things we do are important.

In this scenario, there is always enough time for everything. Occasionally, you wouldn't be able to do what's most important, and boy, you'll know it because it will be painful. Nevertheless, even if not the most important at the time, you'll do things with your full being present, and you'll do them from the heart. This isn't always possible, but whenever possible, you'll live from the heart.

Here's an example of doing what isn't most important to us but still doing it. Say our preference is to have a self-sustaining business doing work that is related to us walking our own path. Say that business isn't yet at the point to sustain us, so we take a regular job. This is doing something that isn't the most important thing for us. However, it sustains us while we're working to get our business to a point where it *will* sustain us. Then in a way, this regular job is also doing what's important, if once removed, since it is a means to an end, just not an end in itself. When in such a situation, we might even be reporting to an unreasonable and very much Factor-x–driven person. But when seen in the light of the job being a means to an end, we might be able to better bear the situation. Or, if working the regular job for an unreasonable person gets unbearable, then if we're living a first-choice existence, we might find ourselves another regular job to sustain us.

When you find yourself in such an environment and it's unpleasant, you won't make the person or people making it unpleasant for you targets for your newfound knowledge. In other words, you wouldn't then go on a rampage to "teach them a thing or two." When we live without our Factor-x's influence, that isn't what we're likely to do. Rather, we're more likely to see where the person is coming from, it'll have less impact on us, and we'll just move on quietly doing what we're there to do. Or, as previously mentioned, if the job is unbearable, we'll just move on and get another regular job.

It's important to understand that this shift isn't about willpower, which you'll read about in "Willpower and Motivation" a bit later on. Rather, when walking your own path, you're not likely to be confrontational. On the contrary, you'd much rather experience your contentment and be peaceful and go about your business with little or no imposition on others. When unpleasantness does come your way, you're likely to look at how the unpleasantness triggered your own Factor-x to create havoc within yourself, and you won't become part of the other person's "Factor-x destruction," or yours.

When looking from these two vantage points, *doing everything else first* or *first doing that which is important*, it isn't difficult to see which is the preferred approach for us. But heed this: For us to be in a position to follow the latter approach, it's first necessary to look at *why* we're following the former approach. Once we know the answer to this, it's vital to address that *why*. Only then will we stand a chance to shift to the latter, conducive approach.

Nature and Nurture

I've mentioned the terms "nature" and "nurture." Let's take a deeper look at this dynamic, starting from expectations.

As I discussed in an earlier section, expectations are directly related to desiring a particular outcome. When the outcome isn't achieved, you or I feel the pain of disappointment and emotional turmoil.

So are all expectations related to Factor-x? Perhaps. But what about when a murder takes place or where someone is abused? We say those behaviors are in our nature. But is it? Or is that behavior nurtured? Don't we acquire that behavior through learning and being dictated to by our Factor-x? Our Factor-x is itself based on a figment of our imagination—because of the pressure we encounter when still very young, we take on as fact that something is wrong with us, even though nothing is wrong with us.

So deeds like murder and abuse are likely seated in Factor-x. And coming back to expectations and our Factor-x, when a particular outcome isn't achieved, some of us are driven over the top and perform inhumane deeds.

Such behavior isn't in our nature. We acquired it. Whether as spirit beings or as physical souls, we're only good-natured when we wouldn't wish a bad thing on ourselves or others, or for that matter, to anything. But with Factor-x, we almost don't stand a chance; all it cares about is disproving that something is wrong with us, or that our Factor-x even exists. So although we're capable of doing bad-natured things to ourselves, to others, or to things, that doesn't necessarily mean such behavior is in our nature. More likely it was nurtured, and thus acquired, and almost certainly driven by our Factor-x.

Murder and abuse, of course, are extreme examples of things we deduce to be nature, but are highly likely nurtured behavior: examples of things we learn and acquire so we can appease our Factor-x, which has only one agenda, and that's to disprove that something is wrong with us. In fact, it seems to do so at all costs, as seen from all the deeds we perform to disprove that something is wrong with us— each and every one of them destructive, even to ourselves.

In essence, we're all good-natured souls. Even so, we acquire destructive behavior in very many forms. All of these, with our Factor-x contributing, are carefully and deviously nurtured and crafted—so cunningly that we're almost certainly of the opinion that it's in our nature to be destructive. But *is* it in our nature to be destructive, thus inhumane?

Something to Do (To Keep Us Busy)
As Opposed to Walking Our Own Path

Something to Keep Us Busy

How much of our lives consist of doing things, just about anything, merely to keep ourselves busy? Something to overcome being lonely. Something to overcome being bored. Just something to do. Anything . . .

When you're keeping yourself occupied to overcome loneliness or boredom, are you fully and consciously present in the activity? Or do you come away from these activities feeling drained, or even frustrated or irritable, or even with the feeling that it likely wasn't worth it (in other words, it had no meaning)? In this situation, you might even have to conjure up some meaning or justification for why you're doing certain things.

These are sure signs that we're living second-choice existences—that our Factor-x is the driving force behind such activities. When we're doing these things, say, to overcome loneliness, are we not using the other people as mentioned before? And if it's the same for them, then aren't both parties likely using the other? This behavior, then, certainly isn't about manifesting ourselves or walking our own path.

Walking Our Own Path

When we're walking our own path, we do things in a particular way: automatically and intentionally, albeit consciously manifesting ourselves. This isn't likely about doing things to overcome loneliness or boredom, but instead about functioning like a well-oiled machine that runs in harmony with ourselves as we go about our business.

When living your own path, you're likely automatically not using or imposing on another person. To the contrary, since you're merely being yourself, you're adding to your own creation and automatically, without anyone necessarily being there, building onto yourself. If you're doing this, then whenever you expose yourself through whatever action you're undertaking, others experience you not destructively, but with harmony.

Let's look at an example. When you do things to overcome loneliness, or when you consider doing something so you don't feel lonely, what is actually happening is that the origin of your loneliness isn't being sought out. Instead, you're treating the symptom. When you've uncovered the origin of the loneliness, you have the chance to uncover yet another part of yourself, and therefore you'll be in a better position to live with yourself without the need to prop yourself up to overcome your loneliness. Eventually, when the loneliness is completely addressed, you're likely to take part in activities for your own reasons as opposed to reasons dictated to by your Factor-x.

Whenever we're taking part in activities merely to keep us busy, we're smothering ourselves. If we weren't taking part in such activities, those activities we do just to keep us busy, we'd likely be spending our lives on activities related to walking our own path.

Willpower and Motivation

Willpower and motivation are also two concepts that would probably benefit from some discussion, especially as these words relate to the theme of this book.

It seems some of us are of the opinion that we can do things with willpower. Willpower doesn't seem to yield lasting effects for us, though. When we apply willpower at some point, the thing we're "willpowering" turns up again. Perhaps in a different guise, but nevertheless, whatever we thought we had conquered or eliminated with willpower is likely to show up in our lives again.

Then there is motivation. We seem to feel we can motivate other people, or that we can be motivated by others or even by ourselves. The fact is, when motivation comes from external sources, its strongest state will likely only last while the person driving it is present, or while whatever needs motivation is being motivated. Some aftereffects will remain, however—debris of the motivation, whether enforced by willpower or motivation, so to speak, might remain for some time, or even remain forever.

What is important to observe here is that both willpower and motivation, even when employed by another on us or by ourselves on us, are used to enforce a certain "belief" on us. But what isn't addressed by the willpower or the motivation is this: Is what's being enforced necessarily something we want in our lives? In some cases, the answer is yes. Perhaps you want to stop your habit of smoking, for example—you'd prefer that smoking is no longer part of your life. So yes, in some cases, we use willpower and motivation to enforce a change, something in our lives we would like to have different. Yet in most cases, whether it's something we want in our lives or whether it's something we might not want, the fact remains: we're making the change by force if we use willpower, motivation, or both.

There is a much simpler way, and one that has lasting effects. Not *always* simple and easy, I'll admit, but mostly simple and easy—except for certain habits that we might want to break that aren't easy to break, even with this simple and easy method.

When we observe closely to whatever we're applying willpower or motivation, we're likely to see the underlying cause. And when we address the underlying cause, then we're likely to uncover ourselves even further. If we do, when we address the cause, we're far more likely to be able to make the adjustment required to move on, away from or toward whatever it is we want to achieve.

Doing it without willpower or motivation has two major differences. One is that we aren't forcing anything on ourselves. But the main difference is that we're likely to pursue only things that are important to us. Then no force is usually required, and the change happens more gradually and has lasting effect.

When you observe the origins of what you were indeed forcing on yourself with willpower and motivation, you're likely to end up realizing that it's something you don't necessarily want in your life, and that it's likely something driven by Factor-x.

Eliminating Unwanted Behavior

When we first start our journey of uncovering ourselves, we won't necessarily see each step we'd like to take with our lives. Up until the time we start our journey, our lives likely consist of a multitude of things we did that we didn't recognize as things we didn't really care for. Things we likely did because we felt we didn't have a choice. Things we likely did out of habit.

Then suddenly, we wake up to our ways. And in this maze of things we do, we now need to somehow see our way clear and know what we want with our lives. This realization, and the associated realizations, could be daunting. Due to doubts and risks and concerns about what will happen to us on our journey, which likely deviates almost totally from the direction humankind is moving in, these things might seem almost impossible to accomplish. Suddenly we turn our lives upside down, inside out and around, yet we need to see clearly which way we'd like to go. Which path we'd like to take. Which fork in the road we'd like to go down. Especially in the beginning of our newfound journey, this is likely difficult. During this time, and any time later, it would likely become quite clear to us that certain things we used to do, we just don't want to do anymore. So instead of directly taking new steps down our path, we can instead just stop doing the old things that don't interest us anymore.

To stop pursuing things we've lost interest in is taking indirect steps down our path. In so doing, we slowly but surely get closer to the things we'd like with our lives. In this way, we can uncover ourselves by eliminating previous behavior that we now see doesn't suit us, or isn't our preference anymore.

The likelihood also exists that, momentarily, we can't see our next step. There might be several reasons for this. The newness of our journey. Our journey overwhelming us. We might even be tired from having been driven for many years of our lives, so that instead of taking action and doing something, we feel like doing "no thing"—just not doing anything.

Well, we don't have to always be doing things. We can stop and do *no* thing. That is, if we're serious about our journey, and when gaps occur where we don't immediately see our next step, we can temporarily do nothing. Since we're still serious about our journey, after doing nothing for a while, the steps we'd like to take will likely become evident to us, however slowly. So we don't need to be alarmed at wanting to do nothing. Especially in the beginning of our journey, but also later on, it's expected.

By eliminating the things we have no interest in anymore, following periods of doing nothing, apart from likely gaining well-deserved rest, we'll also have more time on our hands, and with this time we can instead do things we like doing.

Convinced of Being Right: Not Seeing Reality

We have a tendency to put our minds to something, and then we lock into that something and take for fact that this something is indeed fact and reality.

Here's an example. Say we're in a relationship. Say our partner exhibits certain behavior that's difficult for us to process. We likely figure the behavior is related to some underlying reason. Each time that behavior is displayed, we build the case based on our own interpretation of why that behavior is being exhibited. That behavior elicits certain feelings in us. Over time as this cycle continues, we become convinced that we're right about our assessment of the behavior.

It might indeed be the case that our partner's behavior is based on our hunch. Or, more likely, it might be for a totally different reason than we decide. But in our minds, our partner's behavior is because of the reason we put to it as to why the behavior exists. Are we even aware of this dynamic likely playing out in our relationships and lives in general?

Let's build onto the example. In this very same relationship, because of certain aspects of our partner's behavior we find difficult to process, things aren't going as we'd like them to. We conjure up an idea that the person isn't right for us, and we'd better leave the relationship. But when we stand still for a moment and contemplate the relationship, we realize that we enjoy some aspects of the relationship. But certain aspects, albeit important ones to us, just don't seem to work for us. So now we conjure up, *It's time to go, to break off the relationship.*

The previous point is important, and therefore I'll repeat it. *Even though some things are working out, it's not the right person for us and we want to leave.* We deduced from the behavior we find difficult to process that the person we're with isn't the right person for us.

But we just can't get ourselves to leave, because we fear we won't meet another partner, one who at least has the attributes we like about our current partner. (Remember, in the example relationship, some of our experiences are pleasant, so we don't really want to lose them.)

So now we're in a pickle. We're not happy with certain things about the relationship, but happy with other things. Two factors are now at play. One: We're convinced of why our partner behaves in a certain way that makes us feel he or she isn't the partner for us. Two: We're convinced we are afraid to go. Hence, we're locked up in both these factors, and can't go or stay. And furthermore, we're convinced we're right about this.

Hummm . . . we're not free at all.

Each time we visit this dilemma, we likely run in circles. We want to go, we want to stay, we want to go because this isn't the partner for us, we're only staying because we're afraid if we go, we won't meet someone who is at least like our current partner in those aspects we like.

Oh, and no matter how we debate and argue with ourselves about this, we're convinced we are right. And we convince ourselves it's okay, we might dislike certain attributes—surely it's okay to have preferences.

Does this sound familiar?

What does this amount to, then?

We now find ourselves where we firmly believe the next thing to do is scrape together the necessary courage to leave. That is now all-important. After all, we're convinced we're right about this. Besides, we can't let ourselves down by being afraid to go. Being free, after all, is what we want for ourselves.

But what are the facts? Are we even aware there's another set of facts playing out? What could they be? Is it likely an *expectation* that lies behind this bind we find ourselves in—an *expectation* that certain things about our partner are not as we want them? And instead of addressing the expectation and because we're so sure of ourselves, we then fall into the predicament of wanting to leave and stay at the same time? And to add to the quandary, we feel that the only thing standing in our way of leaving is a lack of courage.

Those are our expectations. But again, what are the facts? Is it really about staying versus wanting to leave? About courage? About being convinced we're right? Is it about our partner being different in some aspects from what we'd have liked in a partner?

Is this, really, about expectations, not fact? And importantly, are we free to see what's going on? Are we free to take action, whatever action, irrespective of the consequences?

After all, as humans, we tend to like partners. Like a prince or knight on a white horse that'll save a damsel: like Prince (or Princess) Charming in any number of fairy tales who'll come to our rescue. Man or woman, perhaps we expect that having the partner of our dream will likely make everything okay—that when we have the *right* partner, that right partner will appease us and we'll feel good about ourselves.

The fact is, another human being can never mend the cracks within ourselves—the ones with which we created and perpetuate our Factor-x. . . . Well, maybe temporarily, or at first. Meeting the right partner supposedly tells us we're indeed okay. But here's the problem. Because we haven't acknowledged our Factor-x for what it is—a figment of our imagination that something is wrong with us—at some point, when our partner's behavior changes, suddenly our Factor-x rears its head. And *voila!* Our partner has failed us, and we build a case and become convinced this isn't the partner for us anymore. But what really happened was that our Factor-x was triggered. That's all. Furthermore, unbeknownst to us, *we want our partner's behavior toward us to remedy our Factor-x.* This is most certainly impossible. But here comes the tragedy: Because the partner didn't appease us, we hold it against him or her, and struggle to shake off that the person isn't what we wanted the person to be—the Prince or Princess Charming of our dreams. The fact that we enjoy the person—the real person—doesn't come into the equation, just the hurt inflicted by our Factor-x, and we struggle to shake off that we're convinced this isn't the partner for us.

When we're in this mode, do we even see the other person? Do they even stand a chance with us? When we're so firmly of the opinion that we know the reason for the other person's behavior and we're locked into that reasoning, they disappear from the scene all together. We likely don't see them, or experience the reality that we likely *never* saw them. Our self is miles and miles separated and away from the moment, and our experiences are skewed because we're convinced of being right.

There's yet another side to the example.

Our belief about our partner's behavior has formed an attitude within us that has a bearing on our own behavior back toward our partner, a phenomenon we likely don't realize. Quite possibly, our partner has also formed some belief about us because of our behavior. So now, we're likely locked in a vicious cycle of one partner creating a belief about their partner, and vice versa. These beliefs affect both partners, each in their own way, and is exhibited through each partner's behavior. Now, two belief systems are in the relationship instead of two people, and it has possibly been this way since meeting each other originally: And quite possibly, two lovely people are lost to themselves and to each other.

Mind you, it's likely both partners feel they're right. The end effect might be that the partners break up, and then land in a self-fulfilling, self-perpetuating cycle from partner to partner, where again, after a while, each partner is convinced and believes they're right about the other partner.

The aforementioned example is one of many. The same can be said where any belief comes into the equation. The main point is, *belief is likely never based on fact, but rather what individuals believe are facts*. Based on reality or not, such beliefs usually have an impact on us; they mold our attitude and manifest in our behavior. We become convinced of being right, and create an underlying need to be right. Our attitude doesn't even allow the facts in, and has no consideration for the facts—our attitude wants no business with the facts: reality is nowhere to be seen. We want to be, and we need to be right—we are convinced: Factor-x perpetuates and vindicates itself by being right.

Let's take the example one last step. When we want to be right, when we're convinced of being right, when we're locked into a belief, we aren't open to what is there, staring us in the face. We aren't open to looking at things differently in an attempt to see reality. The belief is anchored firmly in our attitude: Reality doesn't come into the equation at all. In fact, with beliefs, we are tightly closed. Nothing beyond our belief is allowed in or even considered.

Are we even aware of the dynamics of our beliefs, and what role belief plays when we're convinced of being right: thus, why nothing stands a chance to penetrate a belief?

To get beyond why we're convinced of being right, we need to penetrate our belief, and make the required adjustment by looking at why we have the belief, by looking at where the belief comes from—then removing the likely unrealistic belief. By doing this we can change our attitudes. Then, our changed behavior follows. By working step-by-step from where we're convinced of being right, back to where the conviction originates with our Factor-x, we have the chance to penetrate our belief, freeing ourselves, and so become free-spirited and see things for what they really are.

Convinced of being right is possibly another difficult dynamic we'll encounter on our own path. Whether careful or not, we might even slip and take an unwanted route with our lives, tripping and falling into this predicament, all because we're convinced we're right, and as a result, we don't see the reality and the facts for what they are. When we trip and stumble or go down an unwanted path, rest assured, when we're open about it with ourselves, at some point, we're likely to recognize a turning-off we took that doesn't serve or suit us. Fortunately, we can backpedal and pick up our track again.

Balance

It is likely that once you commence self-discovery by self-uncovering as mentioned in this material, you'll want to run on your path at breakneck speed. In this frenetic ensuing process to make up for what you perceive as lost time, you might even neglect yourself, your health, your finances, or your daily chores. You might even overdo things and create a lopsided life, not a balanced one. This won't do. Something will give. Rest assured there is time for everything. There is no lost time to make up. Just take an assertive pace on your new-found path while taking care of yourself—intentionally.

There might even be occasion to spend time relaxing while attending to your garden. Or spending time with your partner, just loafing, not doing anything in particular. What might not seem evident is all that has changed from before you embarked on your own life's journey, other than the reason of why you're doing the things you're now doing: You're eliminating those things you don't like doing anymore, and you're doing new things—the things you like doing. There is thus no reason why you can't follow a balanced, calm and peaceful pace. Doing so will certainly ensure that you're mostly full of energy and light of spirit.

Additional tasks might be identified. In project management, this is called *scope creep*. For example, a project you might be working on related to walking your journey might be extended, or have other unexpected further requirements. These additional tasks or timeline changes might create the anxiety of a task or project seemingly never reaching completion. Should this happen, remember that such anxiety doesn't add any value to your task or project. In fact, it creates quite the opposite effect, because anxiety can create distraction that holds us back. By being aware of this, you'll be able to maintain a balance, even while current activities, tasks or projects result in what seem like delays and thus drag out your plans. Yet keep in mind that if the supposed scope creep activities are important, you might want to attend to them instead of tossing them out. This is especially true when not ignoring them will end up requiring extra time—likely resulting in major anxiety. We're always better off when maintaining balance and making allowances for the required extra time.

There are also activities that might go wrong, requiring backpedaling or detouring to remedy. We likely continuously live anxiously, in anticipation of things that might go wrong that'll likely further drag out our plans. Such anticipation is unnerving, and requires a balanced approach: Otherwise, our emotions create havoc and we become counterproductive.

Usually, our Factor-x is what disturbs us emotionally. From reading this, I'm sure you can see that balance is vital for us to lead productive and emotionally stable lives—mature lives. As can be seen from what I share in this text about my own journey, as activities, tasks or projects within your life's vision unfold, it'll serve you to be aware of and to maintain balance.

Own Meaning and Factor-x

Proportions

It makes sense that when living from a vantage point of either our own meaning *or* Factor-x, we'll encounter occasional incidents of the other. What is the difference? It's a matter of flavor. When your life is about living your own meaning, that'll be the flavor of your daily life, moment by moment. Yet from time to time, Factor-x will rear its head. It's also not difficult to see and understand that with such a flavor, your own meaning should be the major influence in whatever you're doing.

The converse is also true. When you're living predominantly driven by your Factor-x, that's then the flavor of your life, day-by-day, moment by moment. From time to time, if in a lesser degree, your own value will surface and make itself known through some of your actions. But predominantly, your Factor-x–driven life won't serve you, or serve anyone or anything else, because it's a life built on suffocating yourself. No good will come of it, except on the odd occasions where your own meaning gets through and manifests in an action here and there.

It's merely a matter of choice standing in your way of living one *flavor* predominantly over the other.

Once your choice is made in favor of living freely, as a free spirit, and that choice of flavor is set in motion, the journey takes your life in directions where your strengths are. You'll live freely—mostly. Factor-x will want to disrupt your journey and have an impact on it. But in the main, when you're living as a free spirit who has chosen the flavor of your journey, you might have less inner conflict and turmoil. The further you travel on this journey, the more sense it will make, the easier it gets, the lighter your spirit gets, and the more your confidence grows. Your life will serve you, and will automatically serve everyone and everything else in your life.

Antithetical Energies

In the section "Inspiration: Emmanuel," I touch on the origin of my Factor-x, and in the section "Daydreams: Misinterpretation and Undercurrent," I describe uncovering my own meaning from a twenty-year-old daydream. Our Factor-x and our own meaning is the crux of the material: to introduce to readers the source of our energy. Yes, we get sustenance from the food and fluids we consume. That's what our physical body lives on, our bodily energy like the fuel used in our motorcars. But the fuel that lets us do what we do with our lives is derived from two antithetical sources: our Factor-x or our own meaning. In the first instance, we look for meaning, and in the second instance, we manifest our own meaning in whatever we do. In the first instance, Factor-x drives us and automatically creates energy toward a quest to disprove that it exists. In the second instance, where we're manifesting our own meaning because we are free, we're responsible for creating our own energy. So when free and manifesting our own meaning, and responsible for creating our own energy, we'll reserve that energy for things important to us, not for things we're not interested in.

Is Factor-x the Enemy, or What Is It?

No, Factor-x is not the enemy. Factor-x merely represents us—that is, each one who acknowledges their Factor-x—from a point in time when we were very young, possibly an age not older than around three to five years old, when we created Factor-x and got stuck in time as a survival mechanism against our environment. Our Factor-x was created from a belief that we are inferior, a belief we derived from the treatment we likely got from our supposed caregivers as described in the section "Factor-x and How It Comes About." See or imagine Factor-x as a child, a young version of yourself that is holding your hand. That child wants to protect. That child has in its mind that it and you are in some danger, and wants to protect itself and you.

Each of our Factor-x's wants to protect us from the world. But that child's mentality is that of, say, a three-year-old, wanting to protect the older person, you, by now possibly an adult, a grownup with children, or even a grandparent. That child obviously doesn't have the skills or maturity to do so, and is stuck in a figment of our imagination, not at all useful or helpful. In fact, quite the opposite. That child is, in most cases, steering us down paths we likely don't want to go down. Paths we don't even like.

It doesn't know any better. We don't know any better. So it's best we don't fight that part of ourselves and merely take it along on our journey, pointing out, accompanying and guiding it and ourselves along the way, sincerely, gently, with care and attention.

Once we see our Factor-x in this light, it might be easier to navigate our life without letting it get in our way. By accompanying that part of ourselves with care and attention, we are in a position to heal that child: to heal our Factor-x. As we heal it, it will likely grow up and accompany us with less and less interference in the sense of wanting to protect us. But keep in mind it is an immature child wanting to protect us, and that we created it at the time from a figment of our imagination.

It wants to do good. It wants to serve us. It is there for those purposes. But it doesn't have the tools. It is ineffectual. It isn't conducive. It is non-serving. Since it is a manifestation of our fear to be ourselves, it's counterproductive in its endeavors to protect and serve us. In fact, it's way off target. And for humankind, our collective Factor-x is, in essence, the creator of all the destruction we experience in and around us.

Interestingly, Factor-x is not the enemy, but it wreaks havoc as if it were.

What is required is that we expose, to us and to that part of ourselves, that Factor-x is the culmination of a figment of our imagination, and then intentionally uncover each layer of protection it has built over the years—the non-serving layers—so we and it can mature and see things the way they really are. Not the way Factor-x portrays them to us: from that child's perspective, created from that figment of our imagination. Rather, recognizing things the way they really are. By seeing Factor-x in this light, although it wreaks havoc in our lives, it's clear that it's not the enemy, but a definitive part of us that needs care and attention and guidance to grow up and to mature.

Was That Choice Indeed Free?

When making the choice to be ourselves, to uncover ourselves, to live free-spirited, we could be kidding ourselves that we're indeed at such an important point with our life. Meanwhile in reality, Factor-x might still mostly be in charge. It is just too easy to be outfoxed by Factor-x.

Here, I'll attempt to provide some insights you can look for when making a choice to see if what you're contemplating is indeed a free choice: a choice free of Factor-x's influence.

Let's start here: When making a free choice, if we could go either way, only then is it likely we're free of Factor-x's influence.

Before I elaborate, I'm not referring here to different options of something, like should it be green, red or blue, or round, square or oval.

Now, let me elaborate. Say we get to a point where we'd like to do something, to make some choice. If we can either go with it or stay without it, then we're indeed likely free.

Here is a difficulty, though. I'm also referring to choices like the one to murder. So if we can decide to murder, steal, manipulate, abuse, or so forth, while at the same time we feel just as likely not to do these deeds, like *not* commit a murder, *not* steal, and so forth, then we're indeed likely free. If we feel we must do the "something," then we're likely not free. The crux is, if we feel compelled to do something, thus we must do the "something," then we need to take a closer look, to stop for as long as it takes and see whether we could as likely do the something as not do the something. What's important is that we end up almost equally at peace with or without doing the something.

When we're not free, thus not making a choice free from Factor-x's influence, we're likely justifying to ourselves why we just *have to* do the something, or for that matter *not* do the something.

Stop and look and feel what you're experiencing. If there's turmoil . . . well, it's likely not a free choice. If the supposed free choice is filled with turmoil, must-do-it arguments, emotions running and swirling, it's highly likely that Factor-x is driving you. If your spirit is light whether you're doing the something or not doing the something, you're likely going with free choice.

Once at a mostly neutral stance of choosing to do something or not do something, we are likely free to go with our preferences: do those things we like doing. We are thus doing things from our meaning as opposed to looking for meaning in what we do.

It's not for one person to decide for another when a choice is indeed free of the influence of Factor-x. Only that person can know. You can only know when you're honest with yourself, and that takes courage.

When the choice seems selfish and likely to affect no one, or if it might affect another but you aren't doing it to intentionally affect another, then it's likely a choice free of Factor-x's influence.

An example: I vividly recall, when just starting my journey, when I saw how my Factor-x was the driving force in my life. I wanted time for myself. I couldn't cope with my life as it was. The only way I could manage time for myself was to stop working. Which I did. My wife—I was married then—wasn't working, but when required, jumped in and became the breadwinner. This gave me time to stop and take a look at my life. It was indeed selfish—or put another way, self-caring. I wasn't interested in anything else, only taking a break to look at my own life. My intentions weren't to hurt my ex-wife or to jeopardize her or my family. The fact that my decision had a major impact on her and my family is something else all together. My point is, this was one of the toughest and clearest self-caring decisions I took.

Intent

Look at intent. First, and of vital importance, is your intent to uncover yourself, to become free-spirited and free of the influence of your Factor-x *no matter what?* The emphasis here is *no matter what.* Without intent to the extent of *no matter what*, it is too difficult to get to the bottom of the moment. If your resolve isn't to this extent, when things get tough, it'll be too easy to give in to the influence of Factor-x. If your intent isn't to the extent of *no matter what*, you're not at the starting gates of your journey yet, and you probably won't free yourself. If your intent *is* to that extent, that of uncovering yourself and becoming free-spirited *no matter what*, then secondly, when stuck on your journey with a choice, what is your intent when making a choice? These two intents unlock whether a choice was or is to appease Factor-x. As can be seen, intent also has this second flavor, that of looking at why we're choosing what we're choosing. If the intent is to disprove the existence of Factor-x, then surely the choice isn't free. If the intent is selfish even, but not about appeasing Factor-x, the choice is likely free of the influence of Factor-x.

Here are some arbitrary examples where Factor-x is the driving influence, thus likely aren't free choices.

... Because I want you to be kind to me, I'll do something for you.
... Because I see you're doing things for me, I'll do things for you.
... Because I'm afraid my family will stop loving me, I'd rather not do it.
... Because I don't want to make a mistake, I'd rather not do it.
... Because I don't want to be abandoned, I'd better do it.
... Because I feel special when you treat me a certain way.
... Because if I do or have a particular something or person, then I'll be okay.
... Because I won't do it unless I know for sure it's not a mistake.
... Because I won't do it unless I'm sure I'll succeed.

Here are some arbitrary examples where choices are likely free of the influence of Factor-x.

... I'm taking time off work, even though I might end up in a cardboard box.
... I reverse previous Factor-x–driven decisions as I see them and where appropriate.
... I'm doing it whether the outcome is as I expect it.
... I'm doing it without basing the outcome on hope.
... When Factor-x wants to take charge, I'd rather sink into my emotions than run from them.
... I recognize that when I feel chirpy, it's likely because an expectation worked out.
... When I don't feel strong and lack energy, I sink into the feeling to uncover its cause as opposed to looking to do something externally to pick me up.

… I look for causes inside me, rather than externally.

… I look to see if Factor-x is the driving force when I'm wanting to do something. If so, I refrain from doing it.

… I don't blame myself or another for unwanted experiences; I look internally at whether Factor-x is driving me.

Liking What We Do

When we're free of the influence of Factor-x, we do the things we like doing, as seen elsewhere in "Doing What I Want or Like, and Doing What I Like Doing." So it's fairly easy to determine whether what we're choosing, thus what we're doing, is indeed free of the influence of Factor-x. We don't like doing things as a result of being driven by our Factor-x: You see, that's easy to grasp; it's done without free choice. When we're forced to do something, when Factor-x drives us to do those things, we're not doing them freely, so they'll be things we don't like doing. Conversely, when we like what we do, the choice is likely free and without force; we're not driven.

Free or Likely Not

In the aforementioned and as seen elsewhere in "Own Meaning and Factor-x," with Factor-x being a "tricky fox dynamic," we might or might not be (or might be partially) free of its influence.

It's fairly apparent when a choice is free from the influence of Factor-x. It's not impossible to make the distinction—unless we're unwilling to consider Factor-x as an influence. To make the distinction takes courage; it takes honesty to see the dynamics at play. Yet making the distinction makes it possible to indeed uncover ourselves, to be free-spirited, even if never shaking Factor-x completely: But we shed the influence of Factor-x more and more with each step we take while uncovering ourselves and refraining from Factor-x's influence—by stopping and looking carefully at our life as we walk our journey.

Uncovering Yourself

Because you're reading this book, it's likely you're at a point of questioning your life: questioning the meaning of your life, wanting to make sense of your life. With this material, I attempt to inspire you to stop and look at your life; show you self-help tools to see why you might be at the point of questioning your life; determine the likely dynamics of your life right now; consider what you might encounter while attempting to uncover your self and your life's path. (Note: I elaborate on the required honesty and courage for good reason.) Here is a summary of the steps you're likely to encounter as you walk your life's journey.

Realization

I talk of realizing that you're likely at a point you don't want to be in your life. This is not about a physical place. Rather, I'm referring to a place with your life where daily, perhaps even moment by moment, your experiences aren't what you'd like them to be. These unwanted experiences might be about your life in general, or something specific, like your relationships, job or family life. Correcting such unwanted experiences doesn't necessarily mean you should leave your relationship, get another job, or so on. Rather, by looking closely, you might recognize some patterns or behavior that requires adjusting. Yes, that careful look might result in you deciding to leave a situation, perhaps even if it means doing something drastic like cutting yourself off from your family. While possible, drastic actions aren't inevitable however.

The first step is merely to recognize and realize that what you've created isn't what you want with your life—that is, you're living a life of unwanted experiences.

So next, you figure it's time for change. Bravely you prepare yourself for change—for breaking out. And this is where it starts: Where Factor-x interjects and convinces you to stay put, to stay with the status quo.

Breaking Out

You'll likely not easily manage to overcome the apprehension when contemplating breaking out of your self-incarceration brought by your Factor-x and the standards and norms you've grown accustomed to. When you are at the moment you'd like to reverse a life-long previous decision—to reverse the decision when you took on your Factor-x—it will be very easy to keep running in circles.

Emptiness

As you continue along the path of your own meaning, somewhere either at the beginning or several times during your journey, you're likely to get "the empty feeling." You won't feel this intellectually, but it will still be there, in full force, wherever you're feeling the emptiness. This empty feeling might even occur when waking up from a dream. (Dreaming is described elsewhere in "Dreaming the Feeling.") Whenever it occurs, that empty feeling is a sure opportunity to recognize what you've been afraid of almost all your life. When feeling the emptiness in full force, it's no wonder that humankind is running hell-bent the other way from the raw fear of where we likely took on our Factor-x. It is indeed fortunate that Factor-x can be uncreated. But then people would need to know about it, and have the honesty and courage to see Factor-x for what it is—a figment of their imagination—and have the courage to acknowledge its existence, then move away from it, albeit one step at a time, by uncovering and manifesting themselves.

So this time, you have a choice. You can again run from it—and not address it—or merely acknowledge it and move on with your life. The latter choice allows you, in a sense, to come home by overcoming the ensuing fear of the emptiness that has plagued your life.

Nothing

One of the first apprehensions we'll encounter is that we're not going to survive financially if we follow our heart. A sure second thing is that those close to us won't be interested in us after we break out of the standards and norms and our Factor-x; as a result, we'll end up on our own, alone, ostracized. These feelings have kept us in tow for years. Likely, for as long as we can remember, they were there, guiding us to navigate a certain lifestyle. Now suddenly, we're about to make an about-turn, prepared to leave that life and pursue a life where we follow our own meaning—our heart. And this is likely just too much for us to surmount. And we'll make a strong case to stay put. We'll tell ourselves we don't have the means, or certain things in our lives, or the necessary funds, or assistance. We'll feel like we won't be able to be ourselves until certain things are present in our lives: until we put certain things in place for us to fall back on if things don't work out.

But what we'll most certainly be overlooking is that for us to be ourselves, we don't need anything. We just need to be alive and breathing. *We need absolutely nothing for us to be ourselves.* So you and I can be ourselves without anything first being in place. Nothing first needs to be set up. You can just be yourself, as you are, with whatever and however you are in the moment you make this realization. If we first needed something to be ourselves, then is that *something* anything other than saying, "If I had that shiny new car or that fancy house, then indeed I will be myself?" No sirree. *You don't need anything to be yourself.* Not now. Not then. Not ever.

When wanting to make the transition from being driven by Factor-x to being oneself, it's a matter of first being oneself, thus moving aside our Factor-x, if just for a moment, to see ourselves. Once this is done, we need to cultivate that self we had a glimpse of—no matter how fragile that self appeared—to flourish.

Intention

When contemplating breaking from Factor-x and pursuing our life's journey, we're likely to become apprehensive. Factor-x is going to fight such a move tooth and nail, as the saying goes. We're likely to feel anxious and afraid for what the unknown will bring. We're likely to get overwhelmed, and not pursue such a breakaway from our Factor-x–driven lives—life as we know it—the only life we know up to that point—that point when we're contemplating a breakout. Apart from one thing, nothing will get us past this point. Absolutely nothing else!

What is that one vital thing? Intention. Only intention will. Without intention, it's best we don't even start. Without intention, it will be impossible to contemplate, never mind actually taking the first steps before we scrape together the courage to recognize where our intention lies.

If our intention is missing, such steps are far too overwhelming. We'll conjure up every excuse in the book. We'll convince ourselves that the step isn't for us. That the theory I've presented in this material is good and well, but not practical. We'll even propose it for other people we know—whom we'll say *would* be suited to such a drastic turnabout in their lives. Without intention, we'll convince ourselves that this material is certainly not for us.

This inner debate and cycle of looking at symptoms will turn and swirl in our minds until we paint ourselves into a corner and even throw away the paintbrush, convinced that taking this new direction isn't for us. And this circular process will certainly continue, unceasing, until only one of two outcomes is possible: We stop dead in our tracks and give up, or realize that we need only one thing—and it's already inside us. And that is intention. We need an internal ingredient: intention. We need the intention to *want* to break out—an unequivocal intention that the life we have is not the life we want, and the time has come for change. And that we intend to make the change, whatever it takes.

Once at this point, when we realize we need nothing else, and that we intend to effect change, that's when it will start for us. Then, we'll have every opportunity to use whatever we have as far as skills go, possibly combined with some resources and the courage to start our own journey, one step at a time, irrespective of where it takes us.

Remember, we are not in pursuit of a destination, but on a journey—a manifestation of what we uncovered as our meaning. This is what our life is about. Nothing more! Nothing less! Our life is thus just about one thing, and that is to manifest our meaning one step at a time, moment by moment.

Journey

Okay, once at this point of being yourself, then of course there are things you're going to change in your life. All the things you used to do out of fear and of wanting to disprove that your Factor-x exists? Those things, you'll most probably drop from your life, because you just don't need them anymore. All the crutches you use, you'll drop. This is something you'll do overnight, or gradually, as and when you notice these patterns. Then, slowly, as you recognize the behavioral traits for what they are and drop them, you'll see new things emerge from inside yourself, things you'd rather pursue. Thus, you're uncovering yourself. You're not doing things to be yourself. No! You do them because you *are* yourself, and manifesting your self as opposed to being driven by your fears and Factor-x.

This journey seems easy, but alas, it's not for the fainthearted. Mostly, we're very afraid, and our Factor-x is overwhelming. With or without intention, this seemingly easy journey could be a rollercoaster ride and nightmarish. Oh, and it takes courage. But rest assured, when you reach a certain point, let's say the critical-mass point, the scale swings and it becomes easier—even as easy as described above.

Bounce

Once we shake off the driving force of Factor-x, which is instant fuel and energy for what we're doing, we'll encounter a new phenomenon. At first, you're likely to feel flat and without energy. The external driving force has now lessened and even disappeared, and what's left are your own reasons for what you're doing. You will find your own energy, your own bounce, your own enthusiasm, however. Because where Factor-x *was* the driving force—which elicited lots of energy and drive for almost anything in an attempt to disprove the existence of your Factor-x—it is no more. And, as seen previously in "Own Meaning and Factor-x," as you do what's important to you, your own energy and bounce and enthusiasm will slowly kick in and become part of your life.

But remember, during the changeover period, very little of the energy you're used to will be there. It was automatic before. Now, what you're doing is intentional and scary, at least at first. And the more power you give to the scary part, the more it will drain any energy you might muster together, and the longer you postpone freeing yourself and unleashing your own energy.

Seed-Flame

When you uncover yourself, your life's flame is likely to burn minutely, maybe even just an ember, hardly alive: but always just alive enough to start up your life's fire. Liken this flame to a tiny seed: the seed of your life, your dreams, and your own energy, like the seedling of a perfect flower just breaking the soil. To grow the flame—the seedling, the seed-flame that constitutes your life—takes caring, takes intention, and takes consciously being aware of that fragile seed-flame.

But with Factor-x just around the corner, it is as likely that every intention you have is obliterated by the strength of your Factor-x. To see and acknowledge the seed-flame takes courage. To provide nourishment for your seed-flame to grow takes courage. You're continuously up against your Factor-x, society's standards and norms, and your own reference framework. The best you can do is acknowledge how fragile your self is, how fragile your seed-flame is, and how fragile the real you is. Seeing and acknowledging the fragility of your seed-flame gives you a chance to see what you're up against so you can muster the required courage.

PART THREE

SPIRIT GUIDES

THE WHITE WOLF CALL

White Wolf, senior spirit guide. This is the main spirit guide of a group of spirit guides who are with me to provide guidance for my life and with whom I have intimate dealings. He has been with me seemingly my whole life. It seems we have rubbed off onto each other or he has rubbed off onto me. Regardless, he is awesome.

Possibly all spirit guides are awesome. I'm not sure whether spirit guides aspire to such words as "awesome," but he has certainly widened my horizons. What I like in particular is the way in which he goes about communicating with me. I can add that he's a no-nonsense soul. He provides me with guidance therapy for my own life, and with guidance related to providing a blueprint for inner peace. He also provides me with guidance for creating togetherness amongst independent individuals who have found themselves and are amongst living souls, and those who are in the spirit world. The togetherness is being created with the express purpose to create an awareness that our species can be turned from where we are headed to a path where we can live with inner peace and in harmony with ourselves, others and anything on this and any other planet.

Is It Real?

—*The White Wolf Call, Channeled by Emmanuel van der Meulen*

Relationship between White Wolf and Emmanuel

It was many years ago when I sat outside with Emmanuel in the moonlight when we discussed a plan to establish everlasting peace on

Figure 6: *Indian chief with headdress sitting with crossed legs*

Earth amongst all of humankind and also in the spirit world: where whatever is learned by humankind can be plowed back into the spirit world and vice versa.

As we sat discussing the pros and cons of very specific strategies and solutions for peace among all souls in humankind and in the spirit world, it became evident that only one solution would work, one based on reaching all souls, and one in which all souls could work together. In this solution, these souls would deploy only one technique, and that is to expose to souls that they have a second-choice existence and why that is the case. This information would be proliferated to all souls, both earthlings and those in spirit world. It would be done by methodically and meticulously exposing why souls do what they do, while at the same time showing, without any doubt, what those actions result in. The vision is to expose that a second-choice existence exists, and why it came about.

Another part of the strategy is similar to wanting to share information with parents and their children—the parent needs to be shown the information so they have the capacity to support and guide their children while practicing what they speak. This allows their children to see firsthand, from their parents as role models, how information is implemented. You cannot really only "work" with the children, or only "work" with the parents. Ideally, you would want to "work" with children and parents at the same time. This gives the information a chance to work through the cycle of parent and child, and child and parent. Otherwise, there is a blockage somewhere.

In the same way, the plan we devised for souls of earthlings and souls in the spirit world is for them to be exposed simultaneously to the existence of first and second-choice existences, and the cause of the second-choice existence. From what we saw in the spirit world and amongst earthlings alike, there is mass second-choice existence. Therefore, the plan included simultaneous exposure to both "worlds."

We discussed our plan to create peace amongst all souls, and agreed that one of us would stay in the spirit world, and the other would go to the Earth plane and walk amongst humankind to learn firsthand what it is like. It turned out, after some debate, that Emmanuel was up for it, and that he would be the one to enter Earth as a human. He was adamant that he would survive the Earth constraints, and would break through them to again be able to contact me and I to contact him. This was a pact we made many years ago.

There were other souls with ideas, and also souls who got wind of this idea. Many souls see what is happening and recognize that all is not right amongst souls. Some make plans. Whether those plans were indeed implemented, we do not know. Living so much in our own world, we were not likely to take notice of other souls and their plans. We were also aware that very many plans were already implemented, but did not seem to work.

Let me not detract from our relationship. Anyway, we forwarded this plan to our superiors, who were doubtful but agreed to let us enter the chain of souls waiting for parents so Emmanuel could take up the life of a newly conceived baby. As it turned out, we lobbied to get the best place in the chain, and notwithstanding after waiting for a very long time, the soul known today as Emmanuel got his turn. We were not selective at all. It was merely a matter of: here is the chance to take up life, and Emmanuel, with very little further thought, jumped at the opportunity. And the baby Emmanuel was born.

During his upbringing, he encountered many difficulties but somehow survived them. As I watched him, it was clear to see the wounds he was picking up, but our agreement was that I was not to interfere. Over time he got very far away, and I was sure he was lost to me. But then one day out of the blue, I recognized that he was beginning to question the Earth system and his life and how it had unfolded. He was really fully part of an earthling life, and had fallen into almost every one of the cultural patterns associated with his culture. But he definitely didn't fit in. And here was the first signal of his questioning of what it was all about.

Then, over a period of several years, the signals reached me often that he was seeking for something. I was sure he didn't know what he was searching for, but yes, he was searching. I watched him look into books written on various topics, and saw that he was visiting many different people in a search for what everything meant. I could see that he started seeing that he was onto something, but as he questioned everything, he didn't find what he was looking for.

Then he met my brother's Earth soul, and he saw for the first time what he was looking for. There were doubts, and he interrogated this Earth soul to see whether it was *truth*, whether it was what he was looking for. It seemed he found exactly what he was looking for: the meaning to his life. But as I watched, I saw he was only partly onto it. It seemed he was into an important part of it, however. It was the foundation, the difference between what he now calls Factor-x and a first-choice life.

I watched him walk and stumble, as with your babies when they learn to walk. He would get up and walk, fall down, and stay down for what looked like an eternity. Then he would get up again, all the time unraveling his situation and where he had come from and where he was going. I could see it was a real struggle for him to realign himself with his soul. And even though he thought he was getting nowhere, I could see that slowly but surely, he was getting to where he was headed. His basic tool was to look closely before taking any step, to see whether this was the step he wanted to take: a step in the direction of his first-choice life.

I followed his every move, each step of the way. My part in this partnership was to take care of him, and to determine where and how I could guide him. I would concentrate very hard on him and what I wanted him to feel regarding the direction he was headed. This was especially required when he was stuck and didn't move and was just frozen on the spot, not moving in any direction. I was merely there. I was certain he was so cut off from our arrangement, he was totally unaware of me. To observe his struggle was dreadful to see, but it was what we had arranged and agreed upon: He chose to be the one going in as an earthling to experience firsthand what it is like. This was our contribution to the well-being of humankind and the spirit world.

He fumbled and stumbled around for just over a decade, without once giving me any inclination that he was aware of what we had agreed. Then, after spending years with my brother's earthling soul, he went on his way again, still not making contact with me. As an earthling, I could see he was caught up completely as one and was lost to himself. During this period as I walked with him on his path, I learned about an earthling life, about the hardships and difficulties that exist, and also how lost he became within the constraints. I thus learned firsthand with him.

He then had an experience that introduced him to the spirit world for the first time. Even though he was seemingly very interested in the concept of a spirit world and being able to communicate with the spirit world, he was shaking in his boots. He had so many questions for the spirit world that revolved around whether the first-choice life he had stumbled onto through his daydreaming was indeed accurate. It seemed no matter how much it was confirmed to him that he was headed home, so to speak, he questioned it and himself ad nauseam.

Let me digress a bit. As an earthling, with all of his life coming to a head, he did not cope, and as earthlings call it, he had a nervous breakdown. His earthly system fell apart. He was not cut out for the earthling constraints. He was struggling and didn't want to be molded by all the constraints, and the more he accepted the constraints, the more he became unhappy and the more he was searching for the meaning of it. He seemed to be weak in his strength . . . in that not wanting to be molded got him down. He could not accept being molded by earthly constraints, and as he was accepting them, so his life became even more difficult, to the point where he could not bear it anymore and he was shattered. He could not function. A day didn't go by that he didn't panic at what had happened to him. Being a very sensitive person, he could not handle what had happened to him, and he didn't want anyone else to know what had happened to him. He could not afford to be exposed to other earthlings as not being able to "hack it" as an earthling. But he could not hide it.

His particular nervous breakdown showed distinctly whenever he panicked. Because of being a sensitive person, his body, being fragile, shows immediately when he is not at peace and confident in his ways. He was truly an earthling with a sensitive soul not coping, and it shows very easily, even today. Those souls close to him see his panic. He is not able to hide it. But he seems to manage better and better.

At the time of this writing he functions mostly normally, and from some time back, he made contact with me after visiting an earthling soul who introduced me to him. She is a soul who conveyed to him that it was important for me to let him know my name and what I looked like. Prior to this, Emmanuel went to another earthling soul who, via her spirit-world souls, channeled training-in-communication between spirit-world and earthling souls. I watched him struggle with this training. He wanted to communicate, but he was not interested in what they were teaching. He couldn't put himself through it. But I did notice that he was able to communicate. He was just scraping the surface, but he managed to channel messages from spirit souls to earthling souls.

But what he was after was to communicate directly with the spirit guide he was told was guiding his life. When he met the former earthling soul to get confirmation of some big steps he was taking in his life that he was unsure of, he got something he didn't expect. As it turned out, this earthling soul was accurate, and introduced me to him and brought to his attention what my name is and what I look like. He was still unable to communicate with me—he seemingly had a very busy life, and each time he made contact he fell asleep from sheer exhaustion as a result of his busy life. But in the main, he was still not aware of whom I was, and in fact, who was being introduced to him.

But some important points were made by this earthling soul, and Emmanuel took note. This particular earthling soul provided an audiotape, as you earthlings call it. Emmanuel listened to the tape a few times, and seemed to "fast track" and started communicating regularly with me.

We are communicating fairly regularly on most days, and some days, we communicate more than once—this being the case at the time of this writing. Emmanuel seems to struggle to see his and my soul as separate. Because we have spent his whole life together, I know him very well. So when we communicate, it seems to him that he is communicating with himself. He also feels he must be imagining me and his communication with me.

During his life, I suspect I got through to him three times with very important information regarding his life's path. Once was when he was just out of school and in discussion with his school-hostel roommate. He didn't understand what I was sharing with him, but what I was sharing never left him.

And so it was at another time when I got through to Emmanuel. In his struggle to live as an earthling, he was taking part in a life-awareness workshop, where the mood was certainly set for him to calm himself and open himself to other dimensions, as you earthlings call it. That is when a group of us stood by and, when time presented itself, we got an impression to him, which was this message:

> Emmanuel, go and do what is important to you but you must be the one doing it. Do not delegate it to others to do. Do it because it is important to you.

He got the message, our group could see he got it, but it took nearly two of your years for him to bring that message to his consciousness. I noticed that what Emmanuel used to do was to think up ideas, but then get other people to implement them. That was his way. It became absolutely important for him to do his own thing. Not just anything, not just for any reason, but for one reason: that it was something so important to him, nothing else mattered to him. Therefore, if he was not doing this one particular thing, his life was not really worth living.

As a footnote, let me add that this one thing doesn't imply one thing in total. No, more like a theme implemented through several actions and activities. See it as one thread running through a variety of things.

Then I got through to him a third time, when he was taking a break in your Kruger National Park in South Africa. He was traveling one day when I got through to him with the following.

In his quiet state, driving, lost in his own thoughts looking to spot game, he found and watched an elephant eating leaves from a small tree that seemed dead. He was in awe of how daintily the elephant managed to strip leaves from the small tree with his big, bulky trunk. When driving on after seeing this, which had obviously relaxed him (he was in an already-quiet state), I suggested to him that he and someone in the spirit world work together to expose to earthly and spirit-world souls that we are all living second-choice lives. It seemed he recognized that suggestion. He was already busy with the accompanying website, but still learning to program websites. But that suggestion got through to him, and it seemed that he became determined to learn to communicate with the spirit world.

Over time, I managed to get through to him on several more occasions, but the times mentioned above were watershed encounters.

That is how it came about that we started communicating with each other. We communicate fairly accurately. Not quite 100% yet, but we are getting there.

So we have nearly come full circle. Emmanuel is setting up the accompanying website to communicate with earthling souls, and also to communicate with spirit-world souls. In this way, he and I are back to what we discussed several decades ago and what we set out to achieve: to assist every soul in the earthling state and in the spirit-world state in uncovering their meaning.

This is our relationship and our plan. He is the one on Earth exposing to earthlings what he sees, and he and I communicate and convey what is exposed back and forth. My part of the partnership is to convey these exposures to spirit-world souls. They in turn have their earthling souls that they guide, and will then share such exposure with them. So the cycle is Emmanuel and myself. And we in turn proliferate the information to other souls in our "worlds," drawing together souls from both worlds working together, one by one as independent individuals, to create a togetherness comprising those souls willing to live their first-choice lives with integrity and without compromise, where anyone is welcome, but only if they are willing to live their first-choice lives.

In closing, this seed that began a long, long time ago, with Emmanuel and I sitting outside in the moonlight, is now nearly ready to break through Mother Earth. Very shortly, by the launch of the accompanying website, all hell will break loose on Earth and in the spirit world. No one will have any excuse anymore to live second-choice lives. To coin Emmanuel's phrase, no one will be able to say they didn't know.

Let's live our first-choice lives.

One

—The White Wolf Call, Channeled by Emmanuel van der Meulen

There is an understanding that water is what holds humans together. Here are some other ways of looking at what holds humans together.

We are one with each other through our ancestral ties. We break off in little pieces when we separate from the ancestral body. Each piece is a soul unto its own. A soul is nothing more or nothing less than life.

So see the ancestral body as a pool of souls. There is one pool of souls for humans and another pool of souls for each other thing. But here we'll stay with the pool of souls for humans. So humans are part of their own like body.) See this body as a collection of all of human experiences over time. And by the way, this time is longer than we care to imagine. It goes back longer than anyone has ever attempted to measure.

So the body of life for humans is a pool of life. Each time someone is born . . . and listen carefully . . . we are born as humans who walk the Earth, humans who walk other "Earth planes," and humans who walk in spirit. So humans are not only born into the Earth plane, humans are born on many other Earth planes unknown to earthlings. That is yet another piece elsewhere.

When we are born as souls—born only in spirit—it merely means that we don't have the Earth-walking experience. Rather, we are as much a part of the pool of humans as those walking on Earth or elsewhere.

If you're thinking, *Why would humans be born in spirit only?*, this is the stage before it is required for an earthling or humans elsewhere to receive life. Meaning, a soul exists in the spirit world, born from the pool of humans, awaiting a turn to take up life of, say, an earthling conceived by two parents.

So there are souls waiting in the wings, to coin an Earth phrase. But not all souls decide to take up life of such a conception. You see, when we are truly free and have freedom of choice, we can choose to become one with conception, or just remain as souls only and not be part of taking up life as an earthling.

Some souls, like me, decide to observe the pool of humans and those born from it like earthlings, and then make a contribution toward the well-being of the pool of humans from the perspective of being a soul. Thus, we contribute merely from observation, and of course our experiences as part of the pool of humans. Then there is also the possibility of "working" as a pair or team—to have a combined and planned experience from a soul-only perspective and earthling experience combined, but where this experience commences with a particular purpose in mind. I elaborate on this in another piece titled, "Is It Real?" In this piece, Emmanuel and I set out for a particular purpose, fairly elaborate: to combine the soul-and-Earth experience, with guidance from the soul to the earthling, up to the point of reaching into humankind's experience on Earth and then breaking through all the barriers built by individuals on Earth: to reunite as part of the same team or pair, and then build on both the soul experience—in the spirit world—and the Earth experience, thereby getting insight from both these perspectives and getting guidance and gaining wisdom so the pool of humans is grown and developed a minute part at a time, each time closer to maturing itself.

The purpose for this elaborate plan is to explore the possibility of working together in this way, and then building on the concept that we are free, but don't know that to be free depends on us: that is, each individual soul. Yes, even souls in the spirit world. Souls in general don't see that they are free. A more accurate way of putting it is, they are free to take up the choice to be free. This sounds like it is difficult to grasp. Yet it is more fascinating than difficult. Put another way, each soul is free to take up their choice to be free. So we are not born free but we can be free, but only if we exercise the choice to be free. And when free, it is up to us to make with our lives whatever we desire.

In mine and Emmanuel's case, we decided to bring this working-together amongst souls to the pool of humans, as well as bring the message as conveyed in this material to all souls. Then, the few or many souls who see our message might take up their freedom and possibly work with us to spread this to all other souls. Through this working-together as independent, individual souls, and with some momentum developing, the pool of humans would develop its maturity in its wisdom.

Over time, this may have a major impact on the way souls, both on Earth and in the spirit world and on other "Earth planes," will behave and experience each other. There will most probably be greater harmony amongst souls. There will most probably be camaraderie amongst more and more souls, and we will create a world for ourselves, so to speak, where everyone benefits, not only those who can fit into the system.

For today, there are many souls who don't cope in the existing system, and are merely tossed out to rot and to fend for themselves. This behavior doesn't suit anyone. When you look carefully at the dynamics, you'll notice that those that make it "have," and those that don't make it "don't have." So it seems that those that "make it" do so at the expense of other souls. Why not, instead, devise a system where each soul gains each time and every time? Those souls who don't cope might be exceptionally skilled in areas we don't think of, or areas still unknown to us. But because the pressure is too much for them, they buckle.

The question I want to leave with each reader is, when these souls buckle, do those who don't buckle stay unaffected, or are we all affected when someone buckles even if we don't know about them or have never even met them?

If we are all part of the pool of humans, and one soul is not coping with the current system, then is the soul of humans not hurting? And if we recognized that we are as one, then if a minuscule part of us isn't coping, aren't we all thus hurting? When one day we see that connectedness, and realize that we are indeed part of one another, then would it not be in our best interests to stop and overhaul the system: to make it so everyone can be part of a great life or a great soul, or a great pool of humans . . . to ensure that human life is in a shape where we all live together in harmony and when someone hurts, we address the cause of why that soul is hurting?

Is this not what we would want if we were to see the connectedness?

I would take it so far as to say, even if there is no connectedness, why would we not want to address our system and make it so every soul wins? That no soul is ever lost and left behind, but rather, that we accommodate each soul in the system and we live as one.

But unfortunately, we cannot merely decide we want to devise such a system and then go away and devise it. Luckily, that would never work. Perhaps it would work for a while, but never on a sustained basis. Why is that? Because until we address *why* our system is the way it is—not being supportive to each and every soul, in that some souls "have" at the cost of other souls that "don't have"—we can never correct it, but can only dream of correcting it. Thus, and fortunately, we have to start at the cause—look at *why* our system is the way it is, and then address it at that level. If we don't, then our plan would merely be a quick fix—a treating of the symptoms. And before we knew it, we would be back to where it is now, where we don't have a system conducive to all souls thriving. So there is only one absolute remedy, and that is to look at *why* the pool of humans is the way it is. Only then do we stand a chance to correct it with sustained results.

LIFE CAN BE DIFFERENT: CONCEPTION

Globe

—*The White Wolf Call, Channeled by Emmanuel van der Meulen*

Globe—what earthlings mean, generally speaking, a planet. As is well known by earthlings, there are also other planets besides Earth. You see them. You know of them. And certain people on your planet have already seen even farther than the originally discovered planets making up your solar system. It is also known by your people in the study of the universe that there are other solar systems like your own. The question is, is there life on the other planets of your solar system, and is there life on other planets in other solar systems?

We say yes, there is life on other planets. It is not only your planet that has life. People or souls on other planets are similar to your people. But yet again they are very different, and it is the composition of those planets and solar systems that makes people on other planets different from planet to planet. That is the only reason they are different, and they don't only look different. Their composition and what they are exposed to, "the elements," as you say on Earth, make them look different and have different behaviors.

I just said that they are similar, and yet I also said they are different. Similar, in the sense that they represent the equivalent of your species, humankind, on their planets. Each planet that has a species comparable to your earthling species has a different composition, and therefore, those species comparable to humankind are different. What is similar is the distinction of the "humankind" species from the rest of the species on such planets: Like humans are different from animals and plants on your planet. The "humankind" species on the various planets all have the capacity to think for themselves and have the option to be free to choose their own destiny in terms of breaking out of the mold of a basic culture. Take your plants and animals. They are more or less set in their ways, and more or less continuously do the same things over and over.

As with humankind on your planet, where that comparable species exists on other planets, they have another attribute—the ability to go beyond the basic pattern. You can develop your own pattern.

200

You can do things that, say, animals and plants can't do. In that sense, there are species on other planets that can do different things: establish different patterns. They can live beyond the basic pattern of the species. These are also the species that have the option to be free and break out of the pattern of what the species prescribes—and sadly, most every soul in that species merely follows and hardly questions.

Yours is the species with questioning ability, the species that can alter its patterns. Your patterns are vast in number and diversity. In that sense, species on other planets with your capabilities exist. So life, in more or less your form, exists on other planets in other solar systems.

Those species are at a different evolvement stage from yours on the Earth plane. They are, at varying degrees, less or more evolved. Those that are less evolved have not yet come out of the dark ages, as you refer to it. Or like the middle ages you talk of. So humankind on Planet Earth has come through stages, or ages, in a similar way that species similar to humankind on other planets have come through ages of their own evolution. As a result of the composition of those planets, life is different, and those species want different things and they evolve differently.

This evolvement refers to these species' emotional and intellectual natures, not the physical, albeit they are also different physically. Their needs and what they encounter daily are interpreted differently, so they respond differently to what they encounter. Yours and their evolvement is more or less similar, in that you and they adopt and adapt to the environment, albeit differently. The differences in daily lives and encounters of yours and theirs lie in the composition of yours and their planets and environmental conditions. Like for example, your planet has what you call an atmosphere. All planets do not. All those environmental conditions and differences in composition play a role in the needs, requirements and preferences of those species, as with yours.

On every planet where life exists in a form similar to your humankind—a species possible of thinking freely and evolving—those species apply themselves differently to their needs and environment. As a result, their evolution is at different stages from your own.

As an example, on your planet, different people apply themselves differently when faced with addressing something before them. In the same way, those species apply themselves differently. Their outlook and what they are attempting to achieve with their lives are also different. On your planet at this stage, it is about surviving. That is the theme. You could have it differently, where it is not only about surviving, but about providing a different quality of life to each individual. But at this time, your species is still only thinking about surviving and not breaking out of the mold as dictated to all along during the lifespan of your species. You have not managed yet to break out of it. You are still at a point where surviving and being dependent is the order of the day.

There are further steps to take, those of independence and those of a quality of life for everyone, where individuals manifest themselves, not according to the existing patterns of the species, but differently, where they become themselves in their own right, truly independent and living individually, not within the constraints of fear but within the boundless possibilities of life itself, thus being free to manifest unhampered by the existing patterns. When living this way, independently and unhampered by the fictitious constraints that still exist, each person in your species will benefit, and will become free to manifest their true self. Your world would be a different place, without your fear of living that keeps you boxed in and within the pattern: the very same pattern that frustrates you to the extent that you take it out on each other and even yourselves.

There is just no harmony in the pattern that your species is in at this time. Once beyond it, and with the true independence of each person and independent of the fear of breaking out, your species would develop a pattern that serves everyone, starting with each individual and building it out to other species and also other things, and your planet would have a state of harmony.

In the same way, the species similar to humankind on other planets are, in varying degrees, at different states of their freedom: some this side of freedom, still very much caught up in their survival, some on the other side of freedom, very much alive and living their lives to the fullest. If physically looking and sounding very different from your species, these souls, in essence, are sitting with similar day-to-day things and looking for ways to cope and to survive and in some cases live to the fullest. And of course, where that has already taken place within their species and the freedom has set in, they have a very different outlook. They are, in fact, almost to a soul, living in harmony with themselves and with other species on their planet. And they are a caring bunch. They care for themselves to the extent that they automatically care for every other soul as much as for themselves.

The results of their independence and their freedom in themselves is that they create patterns that serve everyone and everything, without fail. They have a harmony, a lightness of spirit; their souls are free and they think for themselves, not dictated to by anyone. This results in a blissful harmony, and they have reached a state within themselves that you call heaven. Albeit that "heaven" is not where they go to as stated by some people of your species; it is their heaven just where they are. Their souls and their spirit guides have a close relationship with each other. They live in harmony and in close communication.

There are also those planets where the souls are caught up in their darkness, where they struggle for survival and are even further behind, as your saying goes, than even your planet.

The task at hand is a great one: to uplift the spirit of the "humankind" species of all the planets, that we might all experience natural life and be free of the self-imposed constraints that are so very deeply entrenched into our pool of spirit.

As it stands, the task is to expose and awaken every soul so they may see for themselves their self-incarcerated state, and also how they have self-perpetuating patterns to entrench their state farther and farther.

Luckily for us all, there are some souls who see, and some that have awakened, and some that are making it their life's work to expose to the "humankind" species and the pool of spirits that we can have it very differently.

Fortunately, it is not yet all wasted and a forgone conclusion: We can break out of our own captivity and free ourselves of the inhibiting constraints—we do stand a chance to evolve past this point, toward freedom. This is not the kind of freedom where someone else is keeping us captive; this is not the kind of freedom where we are keeping ourselves captive; this is the kind of freedom we take up for ourselves. It is the kind of freedom available to everyone to be taken up, and is being born on all the planets where it is not yet a part of general life: where souls are not yet generally living their natural lives.

Kite

—The White Wolf Call, Channeled by Emmanuel van der Meulen

As a young boy, Emmanuel flew his kite in a park. He had much confidence with the process of flying his kite. A lot of that confidence is coming back into his life now. At the time of flying his kite, his confidence as a child was natural and taken for granted.

As we grow up, our confidence might change. We grow our confidence or we lose our confidence. Once lost, it is a painful process of getting our confidence back again.

Anyway, Emmanuel lost his confidence, and then, once he saw the cause of losing his confidence, he was able to slowly, painstakingly slowly, rebuild his confidence, this time not taking his confidence for granted.

How does Emmanuel's kite flying and confidence relate to all souls not born into the physical plane?

It does not.

Here is how it began.

I, White Wolf, was born as a soul. As a soul, I have the choice to be part of the physical dimension, and I can also decide not to become part of the physical dimension. I chose not to become a part of the physical dimension. I felt I did not need that phase. I felt that phase was limiting to what I wanted to achieve. From a young age I, as a soul, recognized that my capabilities were as a thinker. I could think logically, and through that talent of mine, I was able to look at things differently. As a result, I just never took up my role to take up the life of a physical being.

When Emmanuel and I debated and pondered and made plans to "work" on Earth, it was both his and my choice to take up life in the physical form and live on Earth. And as mentioned previously, it was he who finally took up the choice and came to Earth. So I stayed behind, knowing my inclination as a thinker was best suited to stay behind and work abstractly at the problem of what we saw happening on the Earth plane and in the spirit world. It actually suited me down to the ground, as you say on Earth. Emmanuel, being a researcher and liking hands-on exposure, suited the task of manifesting physically. So in a way, we both got what we preferred, and of course that is the best recipe for success and enjoyment. When we, anyone, everyone, do the things we like doing, it seems more or less effortless, and that is exactly how it happened.

So I, White Wolf, have never ever lived on Earth. I never walked the Earth plane. I have always been a soul only.

Now to the question of why do I, then, expose myself to Emmanuel as an Indian chief and why the name White Wolf.

Here is what I decided. During the time when we were debating and looking at what we had at our disposal and what it was we intended to do, the thought occurred to me that for Emmanuel to recognize me, it was important that I choose something that existed on the Earth plane that was already familiar to him. It would just be that much easier that I take on a form of familiarity as opposed to appearing in soul form, which is not really something visible to Earth souls. So I scratched my head, so to speak, and observed Emmanuel on the Earth plane, and noticed that he was intrigued by the behavior of Red Indians. Not the kind of behavior that gets portrayed in your movies, where Red Indians are supposedly savages, but the part about where they live by certain ethics and that they have the wise chief who guides them and sits in council with other elders in the tribe as the central figure in the tribe: the wise one, the one who guides the tribe. I also noticed that Emmanuel was drawn to their way of life, where they migrated and lived off the land and did not overextend the land: They migrated before that happened. Then there are the wild ones in the tribe, and it fascinated Emmanuel how they were guided by the wise ones.

Based on this, I chose to present myself as an Indian chief, a wise man who could provide guidance to Emmanuel.

As it now stands, the image of the Indian chief is not really required anymore. My point is made, my connection is made, and we are an established partnership. The guise doesn't matter anymore. It served its purpose. However, I do see Emmanuel still pondering on the chief, and speculating about what such a chief's life is like and what they do outside the role of being chief and providing guidance. So perhaps it still serves a purpose for Emmanuel.

The beginning of this piece sets out with Emmanuel flying his kite. It has absolutely no bearing on this piece other than that I noticed Emmanuel wasn't quiet enough when we started channeling, and that was my way of getting his mind quiet and focused. It worked. It thus served that purpose. It was a means to quiet Emmanuel to the point where I got his attention, and then I was able to convey more easily because his mind was on the point being communicated.

As we are channeling, I notice him pondering on whether this piece should include the kite information and whether it serves a broader purpose. Being a visible example of how spirit guides guide their physical souls, I suggested it stayed in this piece, as a reminder to him and also as an example to readers of the interaction of spirit guides and their physical counterparts.

Orange

—*The White Wolf Call, Channeled by Emmanuel van der Meulen*

These are the funniest ways to start a topic: of course Emmanuel's thoughts.

When we commence any channeling as you call it, best to start with a point of focus. Focusing on something, in this case focusing on an orange, draws the attention of the person channeling, and it is then easier to communicate.

To the question of protection: that is, protection when in meditation to make contact with spirit guides. David refers to spirit guides and protection. [Emmanuel's note: as seen in the later piece titled,

"Meditation, Grass"] What is meant by protection, and how does it work, and why is it necessary, and how will it work with readers who are unaccustomed and inexperienced and don't know about protection?

Let me shed some light.

Whenever your people contact our people, protection is required. Bear in mind, in amongst your people there are ones with undesired behavior; amongst our people there are also ones with undesired behavior. In both cases, these are souls that are caught up in darkness and don't bring forth lightness, but evil and darkness, because they seek power and the like. They have not yet tasted their own inner power and inner peace, because if they had, they would not seek it external to them. Such ones with such undesired behavior might want to interfere. For that eventuality, we set up a system whereby these souls with dark behavior are prevented from interfering with any communication between light souls in your Earth plane and in the spirit world, as people in your world call our world. This is to protect souls as they interact and communicate between our worlds. It also prevents anyone who is not supposed to be part of such an event from "gate-crashing" and causing a disturbance. Gate-crashing, as it is termed in your world, is an apt description of uninvited souls with undesired behavior interfering with these events.

So our people have guides whose sole role is to protect, and we refer to them as gatekeepers, or gatekeeper guides. Whenever we are called to participate in your world, it is best for your people to instill the gatekeeper guide to protect the gathering. In this way, it is safe for us to communicate; the participants can concentrate on matters at hand and also know that specialists are attending to keep it safe for us all.

As an aside, protection is also required so that uninvited parties, those with no direct interest in the gathering, don't impose on the space created by your people and our people. Again, it is to make it safe for matters at hand to be communicated.

In some instances, it is also required that a gatekeeper guide brings in assistance. Where protecting the gathering at hand is big and unwieldy for one gatekeeper guide, they bring in others to assist.

It is their area of expertise. They are a breed unto their own. They work together and are a quiet bunch.

Gatekeepers have other strengths too. As Emmanuel has experienced when he asks for protection from his gatekeeper, John, at that point of asking for protection, if he is not quiet and fully at peace—if he is struggling emotionally with something in his life at that point—John's other attributes and strengths come to the fore. John notices Emmanuel's mood, and Emmanuel immediately senses that things are not right with him, that his mind and emotions are caught up elsewhere. Emmanuel also notices when he feels heavy from struggling emotionally. So, a gatekeeper with such other attributes, or strengths, can also facilitate in making it safe for those asking for protection to notice where they themselves are at emotionally. In this way, there is the chance for the emotional playing field to be leveled—for the emotions to be acknowledged—before commencing communication.

So protection is a wide function, performed by souls on our side who have extensive experience in such matters, and they oversee the safety of a gathering.

Now, what happens when a gathering is initiated by meditation where the person on your side of the world is not familiar with protection and so forth? What then? Is there a chance for souls with unwanted dark behavior to interfere with the proceedings? Well, as stated in David's meditation, senior guides are called upon to assist and arrange for protection.

But what if a senior guide is a soul with dark behavior? Let me spell it out this way. When people, souls, guides and senior guides who are in the dark, participating in such a meditation merely because they have dark intentions with the meditation, no one really knows the outcome, but they would likely not worsen their state because of reading the meditation.

On the other side of the coin: People reading such a meditation are likely not the kind with only dark behavior. They will have already started opening their hearts, and from the instant anyone opens their heart, whether soul in humankind or soul in the spirit world, from that moment on, from that very instant, souls of light are given space. In fact, in that very instant, this opening of the heart is in fact achieved by the light souls managing to wriggle free in the soul's heart. As a result of that wriggling, the soul is at a space and time in their lives that if they were governed by some dark behavior or governed by dark behavior only, for the first time, light would seep into their lives. That "opening up" is in fact achieved by a light spirit guide being there and being let in, as you say, into the life of the soul with the dark behavior. Therefore, the light spirit guide has already gotten the gatekeeper guide there with them, so the necessary protection can take place and be in place.

A thought comes to mind: This is like in your movies, when the doctors are performing some operation on a patient. Everyone necessary to be there is already there when the operation begins, from before the operation commenced.

Oh, and if you're wondering, Emmanuel really watches lots of movies. It is his favorite pastime, especially movies that relate to humanness and life. He doesn't enjoy and cannot watch heartless violence, and unrealistic or horror movies.

Anyway, back to the operation. Everyone needed is there, and is prepared. In the same way, when souls with dark behavior, whether on your Earth plane or in our spirit world, soften their hearts, it is because there is a team of souls already there "operating" on the souls to make it happen. Everyone needed is already there, and is immediately part of it and enables it to happen. So in a sense, protection is already in place.

However, one very important aspect is that everything works with freedom of choice. Or, a more apt way of saying it, everything works by souls being free to choose.

Now, when a soul with dark behavior is softening their heart, and a team of spirit guides is there, nudging the softening process and standing by to be let in, so to speak, none of it is done without the soul, any soul, choosing the softening process, no matter what. The law of the universe, when it comes to light souls and souls with dark behavior, is that once any soul moves across the line into the light, from that moment on, once a soul lives naturally, souls don't interfere with force. Rather, it is all about making what is on offer available, and then waiting for the other soul to accept what is being made available.

An example comes to mind. When Emmanuel walks into a super-market, no one there forces anything on him. The store makes things available, and then if he sees what he needs, and likes it and can afford it, he then buys it. In the same way, light souls make things available, and those that are exposed to what is being made available and like it can choose to go with what is being made available. When still in the dark, souls tend to force things on themselves and other souls.

There are many examples of souls that are in the dark who force themselves on themselves and others. Such souls stay in the dark while they are driven by their Factor-x. Souls in your Earth plane and here in our spirit world stay in the dark while still driven by their Factor-x.

Coming back to souls with dark behavior who open their hearts, in this very same way, light souls make available their wares, and then, when a soul with dark behavior takes up what is on offer, the whole "protection team" is there to participate in the *breakthrough*.

Coming back to the meditation, where souls unfamiliar with this process take part in the meditation and through the meditation communicate with spirit guides. As can be seen from the aforementioned elaboration of souls in the dark and the souls in the light making their wares available to be accepted or not, and the "operating team" standing by whenever any soul or even group of souls takes part in the meditation as described by David, when a soul gets to the point of opening up their hearts to observe what is there, everything required to let the event happen safely is already in place. Everything to do with the event is already safe—every soul required is already there and functioning in their areas of specialty, and the space is already safe. Therefore, protection is in place, arranged by the senior spirit guide present. Those participating are in safe hands, and the space is in protected mode, so to speak. So the proceedings are a safe haven, as you say.

There is a point that I mentioned that needs elaboration.

Mention is made of souls in the spirit world with dark behavior. And it is implied through this piece that they, too, have light souls in the background guiding their existence. Yes, this is the case. Light souls and souls in the dark are in abundance. All souls, whether in the dark or the light, have souls guiding them, and light souls are right there with souls in the dark. This is not very difficult to grasp when looked at from the following vantage point: Each and every one of us, that is, souls of humankind and souls of the spirit world, are in essence light souls. But we have created such a system that souls stay in the dark forever, and only very few souls have seen the light. Nonetheless, inside every soul there is the essence of a soul of light.

Now you may ask, but how does that work when a soul is in the dark, but in essence, it is a soul of light? While they are in the dark, they surely sow destruction. So why will souls in the dark have a soul in the light standing by with a team of specialists to protect and guide them?

Simple! Let's look at it this way. Each soul, in essence, is a light soul. Each soul that is in the dark at the time of taking part in the meditation constitutes a pair of souls—an Earth soul and a spirit-world soul. For each humankind soul (in light or in the dark), there is also a spirit-world soul (in light or in the dark). However, the light souls in the essence of both the souls, whether in light or in the dark, are present continuously. Each soul is, in essence, a light soul.

Hold onto that.

Each dark soul is thus a light soul, but in the dark.

Hold onto that too.

Now, here is the important thing: Each soul in the dark is in the dark because of their Factor-x. Therefore, the moment anyone opens their heart, that soul is letting in the light soul.

Hold onto that as well.

And where is the origin of the light souls? Right there. The light soul is the essence of the soul in the dark, now softening their heart and allowing in the light.

Hold onto that.

Now, where is the light coming from? Right there. It has been there all along, as the essence of the soul in the dark now coming into the light, let in by the soul in the dark softening their heart.

Hold onto that.

And thus, the light enters the heart of the soul with the dark behavior, displacing some of the darkness.

What if the Earth soul with the dark behavior opens their heart? Then their essence, their light soul, comes through, even if only slightly, and the specialist team is on standby.

This aspect requires elaboration. What if the spirit guide of the Earth soul in the dark is not at the same time opening their heart and letting light come into their heart?

Well now, exactly what now? Is this a tricky situation or what? Indeed tricky.

So now, we see that each soul has a spirit-guide soul, which has a spirit-guide soul, which has a spirit-guide soul, which has a spirit-guide soul. And this goes on infinitely.

The same question can be asked: What if any one of those souls in that chain of souls with their spirit guides, anywhere along the chain, doesn't, in the same moment, soften their heart to let in the light soul in their essence? Can anyone address this eventuality? Gee, this seems impossible to address. And what if this can't be addressed?

Well, let's see if it is possible to address this eventuality without leaving any unanswered questions. Here goes.

All these points I asked that you hold onto previously—therein lies the solution to what might look like a riddle.

Each soul is, in essence, light. A light soul stays in the dark while it is driven by its Factor-x. Each soul thus has two proponents: the light one that is its essence, and the dark one that has come about as a result of Factor-x. Thus, each soul has another soul right behind it, guiding it. And that soul is again in the exact same situation.

Or is it in the exact same situation?

Are you ready for it? The answer is, in fact, quite simple. Each spirit-guide soul is, in fact, the soul in essence guiding the manifestation of each individual soul. When a soul is in the dark, it is struggling with itself, dark and light struggling with itself. The Factor-x–laden soul is split. Once the split is removed, thus once Factor-x is removed or moved to the back, the spirit guide that has guided the earthling soul is in fact the soul of that manifestation. So what seems like a hierarchy of souls is, in fact, one and the same soul for each soul.

Therefore, Emmanuel's soul referred to as White Wolf is in fact none other than the soul manifesting Emmanuel. And what Emmanuel feels is his soul is merely the soul he experiences as a result of his Factor-x exerting its control on him. The other spirit guides that he experiences, namely David and John and Joan, are in fact aspects of himself that he is experiencing.

There is the part of him that protects him: John.

There is the part of him that brings the lightness of his spirit to the fore: David.

There is the part of him that expedites his daily life: Joan.

There is the part of him that brings the whole lot together: White Wolf, which is me.

So in the moment when any one of us softens our heart, in that moment, we let aspects of our own light soul come into being. Put another way, we allow part of us to come to the fore, to manifest.

So now, what about the mystery? Is Emmanuel made up of several souls? Am I, the spirit guide referred to as White Wolf, different from Emmanuel's soul? No, this is all one soul.

We can state it this way by example. Emmanuel is healing himself of the split in himself that was created by him taking on his Factor-x. Then, as the reverse of this takes place over time by him questioning his meaning, he lets in the light parts of his soul each time he breaks down a barrier that was placed there by his Factor-x. As he was doing this, there were other aspects of his soul that he started recognizing, and as earthling souls do, he put names to things. And so each aspect of his soul was grouped and given a name, and over time, he has let those aspects into his life. Do we exist separately of him? In a way we do. We are so far in the background, we sometimes feel as if we are different souls. But no, we are not.

As Emmanuel lets all aspects of himself in—by removing the barriers he placed in his life as created by his Factor-x—he is letting in more and more aspects of his soul, and thus manifesting himself more and more.

Now, what does this have to do with the other pieces written by him and that he is channeling from us? We'll just have to wait and see what materializes from this piece and its revelation.

Back to the protection issue, where this piece started, and what is described here and how the puzzle fits together. The last question asked—how each individual is being exposed, and how we let in the light, and then what if the guides' souls don't also soften their heart at the same time as the earthling softens their heart—seems to be answered and addressed. It is clear that there is only one soul, and when a part of it softens, it is in essence allowing in a further part of the very same soul, not a different soul.

Therein lies the absolute safety and protection of all participating souls. There is no more to say on this topic. For now, all is said.

JOHN: GATEKEEPER & PROTECTOR

Sumo Wrestler

Figure 7: *John, the gatekeeper, appears to me as a Sumo wrestler and provides protection when we (White Wolf & Co. and I) communicate*

When John takes up his gatekeeper position of protector, I see him as a Sumo wrestler. The moment I ask for protection, I feel every aspect of myself in context. I sense my mood, whether it is light or heavy. It usually lightens my mood for having seen my heaviness.

When I make contact with him, my body tingles. It feels as if he climbs into my body, taking up my body space. Imagine if you will a Sumo wrestler climbing inside the body of a regular-sized man.

My contact with him as protector seems to have another dimension—that is, he levels the playing field and prepares me for communication by indicating to me where I stand emotionally. It seems that my contact with him creates the "right mood" for communication.

John declined when I asked whether he wanted to add any message to the book. As gatekeeper, however, he seems to lay the groundwork for communication. He also ensures that only those that are required to be present for the communication are there, thereby making the communication safe.

This is my relationship with John. It seems he's always ready and up for the task, seemingly getting nothing in return, just being himself and thereby showing his inner beauty.

What Joan Sees

Strict Teacher

Figure 8: Joan, the teacher, appears to me as a no-nonsense teacher who provides me with planning and expediting guidance

Flowers and Leaves

—What Joan Sees, Channeled by Emmanuel van der Meulen

We are gathered here today, as you earthlings like saying when addressing a congregation, so it is befitting that I also open this piece in the same way.

Emmanuel is getting one shock after another, and yet he comes back for more. He has endurance if nothing else.

But that is not what this is about.

Flowers and leaves that surround you on Planet Earth are there in full swing, and they beautify your surroundings. Our world is different. We see the flowers in spirit form, where they are in full bloom without any blemish from the environment. They display themselves to the fullest. They show everything they can be. The conditions for them are conducive to showing their every detail and their every beauty. On your plane, they are only part of what they can be. They cannot necessarily look after themselves. They depend on their surroundings to take care of them.

In the wild, flowers are what the surroundings allow them to be. Yet they excel. There are places on your Earth where flowers are a wonderment to humans, for with so little and such harsh conditions, they still show themselves in beautiful ways. They have little choice other than what is bestowed to them by their caregivers, be it their immediate surroundings in the wild or when planted by humans and then cared for. Some humans are very good with plants, and when humans are their caregivers, flowers can then show of themselves better than when just left to their own devices, which are very few.

Plants and flowers in general can only do with their "lives" what their surroundings allow them to. If the surroundings have very little nourishment or their surroundings are harsh, or both, they will only show what they can, and even then, it is usually only beauty.

Leaves are part of their survival system. They take in some of their nourishment from their leaves, especially sunlight.

When we take this over to the human species, then we see that humans do not live by this code. Humans live by another code.

Humans have very many faculties. They can alter their surroundings. They can migrate to where they can nourish themselves. They too need some sunlight. Well, not as much as plants, but some sunlight helps them along on their path of well-being.

But what do humans do? They take and take and take. They hardly give of themselves. Emmanuel makes this observation and says he actually meets very few people, in fact hardly any people, who have the courage to show of themselves. When they do show of themselves, it is only to show themselves in comparison to everyone or something else. They do not just show of themselves. Emmanuel is such a person. He is someone who likes to show of himself.

But alas, your system that you have devised does not serve such an outlook. It serves only an outlook where individuals show of themselves in relation to something. Usually wanting to be mentioned, or wanting some honor, or wanting to be better than or wanting to outperform another. Very little of just showing what you are, just for the sake of being yourself. Showing of yourself without wanting any further recognition or wanting any prize or wanting to overcome any perceived deficiency. Showing of yourself just to be yourself for whom and what you are. Just for that sake—for nothing more and nothing less.

For anyone who has followed this material up to this point, I suppose it is nothing new as to why earthlings do such things. Why they are not just showing of themselves, just for the sake of being oneself. I suppose some can say why. I suppose most readers at this point who have followed the material would be in a position to say why.

Factor-x. That is why. In an earthling's quest to disprove their Factor-x, their own intuitiveness and their own instinct is lost. All that remains is the survival instinct of disproving Factor-x.

I dare you, come on, just let your mind go and see where it leads you. See where you end up in your imagination if this was the case and your lives consisted of just you, without needing to prove anything to anyone, least of all to yourself.

I dare you. Can you let your guard down for just a moment to see your own beauty just for the sake of being you? Not wanting to prove or disprove anything? What might you see? Well, we see that part of your lives. We see you when you are just being yourself. We see that beauty.

In that world, the one that we see, you are all just functioning naturally, to use an earthling phrase—where your skills and experience are rendered for the love of it. We see, when you live naturally, then instead of hurting each other, even yourselves, you live in a way that serves everyone. No one is left out of the equation. Everyone shares equally in everything that is available. Emmanuel's Earthfriend, Sergio, coined that phrase. It is a beautiful phrase. It is sad that mostly humans do not see the beauty in it. The current system of survival and being on a quest to disprove the existence of Factor-x does not allow that space to exist. That space where we see everyone as one. That space where whatever exists is there for everyone to share in—not in measured portions based on some form of infighting. No, a space where everything that exists is unconditionally available for everyone to share in.

Well, "unconditionally" is not quite the way to put it, because it can only be seen as "unconditionally" once an individual gets over their Factor-x. Not before that moment. And after that moment, everything changes. And that moment is not when an individual thinks they see it. It is when they know they see it.

Once an individual overcomes that moment, when they live beyond their Factor-x, then that individual sees that once we get beyond our Factor-x, everything that exists is unconditionally available to everyone.

Alas, go in peace. Find yourself in the maze of your quest to disprove your Factor-x so everyone will see your beauty, just for the sake of you being yourself—not for other reasons.

How David Works

Male Flying Fairy—Jovial

Figure 9: *David appears to me as a flying male fairy who provides me with lightness of being and expediting guidance*

Meditation, Grass

—How David Works, Channeled by Emmanuel van der Meulen

We will be playing on a wide-open expanse of lawn. The grass is green and well groomed and soft, and there is so much of it that we can play and play and there is no reason why any of us will bump into each other while playing. We'll run around and with our arms pretend that we are airplanes or birds, and with our arms stretched as wide as we can get them we'll run around and around and around until we feel we are flying.

There are people everywhere. We are in a big park-like area with trees and lots of lawn and children playing and grown people enjoying being outside and being in amongst the children running around. Others are just walking around leisurely, taking in the surroundings and the trees and those around them. It is a scene of lots of laughter. There are some who are in deep thought and some just taking it all in.

A butterfly is flapping its tiny wings in the summery-day sky, flying jaggedly, not in a straight line, and not going anywhere in particular, just flying as if swaying in quick strokes from left to right and back again and even in circles. A boy is flying his kite close by his family. They are picnicking in the clear, open sunlight, enjoying the sun on their faces.

Luckily, the sun is not so hot. No one out today will scorch in it. The people out today are of all shapes and sizes, and are wearing colorful clothing and accessories. It is not every day that the sun shines so pleasantly. In amongst the shady and cloudy and rainy days, there are the absolute-scorcher days, when it is so hot that just being outside for more than a few minutes brings on blisters. Today is different, one of the milder days. Not too hot, not too cold, but with a sun that brings with it joy and fun and just enough heat for everyone to enjoy and maybe even to burn us slightly, ever so gently, just enough to burn those with fair skin a slight red, and those with less-fair skin color an almost-instant tanned color. Those with dark skins, where sun color is not noticeable, are merely enjoying the warmth brought by the sun.

In the park-like area there are trees scattered sparsely and clustered together here and there. People are playing or are just together in ones and twos and in smaller groups and also larger groups. It is a typical day outside to frolic and just relax. And we are here to relax amongst this jovial bunch of people. We'll relax while taking in their playing, and their calming and relaxed demeanors. It is our turn to stop the noise in our heads . . . the turmoil of our daily lives . . . the rush we are caught up in. We are just so busy with our lives that we do not have a moment of silence. Not silence as in, nothing is making any noise. No, silence inside ourselves, so we can see what we are thinking about. Silence so we can look at our thoughts and observe where they are taking us. See whether they take us into situations where we'd rather not be. Very many of these thoughts are not about being quiet and relaxed but about being anxious—anxious about what we are busy with . . . anxious about what we have and don't have. There is just not quiet and peace in our lives. And here in this park-like setting where people are quietly going about their leisure and having a fun and relaxing day in the sun, we have an opportunity to slow down our thoughts—slow down our racing minds, maybe just long enough to see that we actually yearn for quiet.

It is our chance to sit quietly or lie down quietly or stroll quietly and feel the quiet sink into our bodies, with sunrays warming our faces and whatever else on which it gets its rays. We can just be quiet and take it all in and let go of the things in our daily lives that keep us so busy. We can get a glimpse of the hectic lives we lead.

Quietly, slowly, we slow our minds down from a frantic race of solving some problem we have. Something that is not going the way we'd like it to go. We feel fidgety and notice a small yellow ball on the ground. We pick it up and roll it in our hands, and squeeze it, and throw it in the air, and the ball relaxes us while we engage it.

We are becoming quiet now.

Some of us do not get quiet easily, becoming quiet being quite a struggle. But we can come back to this piece as many times as we like and just read it, each time slower and slower, until we manage to slow our minds enough to enjoy it. This is as easy as it'll be. No rush, no further reason to become frantic. There is no right way and no wrong way. There are just each of our own ways and only one important thing, and that is to slow ourselves down—slow enough and slowed-down long enough to feel what it feels like to be quiet, not rushed or frantic or panicking or driven by whatever is in our lives that drives us. That is all that is important.

In this quiet state, seeing that we are relaxing now and reaching a level of peacefulness, do we recognize that our breathing has slowed? That our heart rate is calming? Do we observe any aches and pains in our bodies? Maybe there are none, and maybe there is more than one ache or pain. Just observe, and feel where the pain is. Just observe whether we have any anxiety. Just for a moment though. Observe and feel what the origin is of the anxiety or the pain—again, just for a moment. And remember, there might not be any anxiety or aches or pains, and there is no right or wrong—there is just whatever we observe in ourselves, even that maybe we observe nothing. We do not need to do anything about it, just observe.

Are we quiet enough to realize how busy our tongues are in our mouths? Are our tongues wriggling this way and that way? Are we unable to relax just enough for our tongues to also be quiet in our mouths?

Maybe our tongues are quiet. Maybe we have a twitch? Maybe we observe another symptom?

There is no right and no wrong. Even if we do not quiet ourselves enough to observe these things, or anything, there is no right and no wrong, even if we are just calm and do not notice anything while calm. None of us is the same. Some will have similar observations, and others will have different observations. All that is important is to quiet ourselves so we are able to observe ourselves.

That is all—observe ourselves.

As we take our focus off ourselves and focus on the people wandering around in the park-like area . . . walking on the groomed grass . . . children running and playing and not being able to sit for a moment, playing till exhaustion sets in . . . and we observe the peacefulness and quiet of the people sharing the park-like area with us . . . we feel a part of them from a distance as we observe the temperature on our bodies and how the sun is splashing on everyone. We feel another level of calm set in. We are relaxing and enjoying this day out—with everyone. Calming ourselves might even be unusual for some of us, and possibly very usual for others. The main thing that is important is that we are able to quiet ourselves, even if just a little, and take it in. Take in ourselves and take in those around us. Observe everyone out today in the sunlight. Observe by contrast our possible lack of being quiet in our usual day-to-day lives.

That said, we are now focusing on ourselves in relation to our everyday lives. What is important is that we are possibly, for the first time, doing very different things from what we usually do in our everyday lives. Observe whether we like it or not. It might even be scary to be quiet. We might be considering that we might want this quiet each and every day, and that our busy lives do not cater to it. We might even feel that we could never live this quietly in our day-to-day lives. Be that as it may, what is important is to taste a quiet moment and observe ourselves and feel whether we like it or not.

If we do not like it, that is okay. But it is strange that we observe quiet and peacefulness and say that we do not like it. It is okay, but questionable, and we might just want to stop for a moment to observe why indeed we do not like this quietness and peacefulness when visiting the park-like area to experience everyone else here and how quiet they are within themselves even though busy with their own activities. Notice on their faces there are no frowns, no strokes of anger. Everyone is merely enjoying their day out, quietly and peacefully. Today they have left behind what usually drives them to have frowns on their faces, to have strokes of anger over their faces. And just for today, we can enjoy that same quiet and peacefulness.

What is important is that we experience the quiet, even if just for a moment or a few moments. If we manage to experience it and observe the contrast with our everyday lives, we stand a chance to desire the quiet again and again.

It is the quiet that we are after. Observe the contrast between this quiet and our hectic everyday lives. It is the contrast we are likely to observe that is important.

And now, let's quiet ourselves even more. Take a slow, deep breath and hold it for a while, and exhale slowly, very slowly. We might feel as if we are ready to fall asleep. We might feel as if we are drifting outside ourselves—as if separate from ourselves. We're quiet, and possibly even feel we are not a part of ourselves. We're just mingling in a trancelike state. We feel as if we do not care about anything anymore. We're uninterested in fighting anything anymore. We feel like staying in this state for a few moments longer. We are taking this opportunity to relax and be quiet and feel numb and unconcerned. We spare a thought for those around us in the park-like area . . . we hardly notice them . . . they are there, but not vividly anymore. We are more or less in a sleeplike state. We are very quiet and very relaxed. We notice that what we experienced previously—the rush, the anger, the anxiety—these are so far removed from us at this point, we cannot imagine that it was so profound and so vivid just moments ago. Oh, and it does not feel like moments ago, more like hours ago, more like days ago. It feels so different now that the calm has at last set in, and we may even feel like falling asleep.

But hold it there. Do not sleep. But if you do fall asleep, that is fine. If you can stay awake, do so. Those that fall asleep take in some more rest in your day-to-day lives. Then eventually, when quieting yourself, you would stop falling asleep.

So we're not asleep yet, and we are observing our own quiet state and the peacefulness of it.

Now, when in this deep quiet, and calmness and peacefulness, let's look up ever so slowly. What do we see? Don't look to see anything, just look and see if anything appears there for you to see. No matter that you might think you are imagining it, just go with what you see.

We're just stopping for a moment to mention that, at this point, it is important to ask for protection from those that guide our lives: those in the spirit world who have been with us our whole lives to guide us and protect us. We ask that each guide of everyone present reading this and taking part here today is protected. We ask that the senior spirit guides present assist with the protection and bring in whoever is required to make this event—this special meditation event—safe for everyone present. That each person here and each spirit guide present is protected, so the forthcoming event can proceed in safety.

Before we get back to looking up and observing what we see: This might be a very strange experience for those of us who have never done it before, and your frames of reference and standards and norms might at this very moment be kicking and screaming to stop and not to go where we are going. That is okay, just observe what is transpiring in you, the way you are fighting and kicking and screaming against this event. Do not fight it, accept it. Accept that your standards and norms are fighting this tooth and nail. You are welcome to calmly return and awaken out of this meditation, and calmly and slowly get back to where you were sitting, or lying, or walking, or whatever position you were at when commencing with us. Just slowly and calmly go there feeling refreshed and wide-awake. A last request to those of us departing now: It would serve you to take in the material and see where you are headed with your life, and remember that at any time, you are welcome to return here and take this journey with us and see where it takes us. Go in peace.

Those of us staying, take a deep breath, hold it and slowly, very slowly exhale. Calmly look up, but don't look to see anything, just observe what you see. Might it be that you see or sense your spirit guides? And when saying "Look and see," in most cases your eyes are closed. So it is not about seeing with your eyes and not about looking with your eyes, but sensing and seeing with your mind's eye. Is it maybe that we see our spirit guides—maybe very faintly, but nevertheless seeing them there when looking up with our mind's eye?

The spirit guides are there—we request them to reach out to us. Each spirit guide is requested to reach out to the Earth-soul they guide. The spirit guides are with us all our lives, and guide us, and want to get through to us to give us guidance in accordance with how such guidance works.

Some of us might see our guides. Some of us might recognize that we see them. Some of us might feel we are imagining things. Nevertheless, we do have a chance to see or sense their presence and it might even be a familiar experience. It might also be our first experience of this kind. It might even be a scary experience. Merely acknowledge it as such. If too scary to continue, you are welcome to calmly return and awaken out of this meditation, and calmly and slowly get back to where you were sitting, or lying, or walking, or whatever position you were in when commencing with us. Just slowly and calmly go there feeling refreshed and wide-awake.

A last request to those of us parting now: You have come far with us on this journey. It would serve you to take a breather while absorbing more of the material, see where you are headed with your life, and remember that at any time, you are welcome to return here to take this journey with us and see where it takes us. Go in peace.

Those of us that are staying, take a deep breath, hold it, and slowly, very slowly exhale. Let us mingle with our guides, just quietly looking up and feeling the calm on our faces while we are looking at them and mingling with them.

Enjoy the experience of mingling with our spirit guides, and know that we are safe with them. Even before now, they have been there all along, most probably knowing our every experience as between a parent and child. A caring parent is always there, whether the child knows it or not. The parent guides the child whether the child is conscious of it or not. The parent also gets to know the child well and learns from the child. The caring parent is never far away from the child, and is always aware of what is going on, even when the parent is in another room or out somewhere. In the same way, our spirit guides are there and they know our every move and are fully aware of us, just like a caring parent, whether we are conscious of them or not.

Let's mingle some more, taking in our spirit guides' relationship with us. We may not necessarily see them all this time, it might even be an effort to see them all the time while mingling, and we might not be aware of them, but they are certainly aware of us and care for us deeply and guide us, even though we might not be aware of them. They nudge us all the time with guidance, and mostly we are too cut off from them to know it, to sense it or to take it in. Nonetheless, they are there all the time, guiding and caring and nudging. Are we ever going to become aware of them to the extent that we would consciously let them into our lives?

Note the emphasis here is on caring parents. As with a caring parent and a child, even though the child is oblivious of the parent and the parent's intentions, does the child ever let the parent in? Does the child ever connect to form a true and everlasting bond with a caring parent? Is the child usually oblivious of their parent and their parent's intentions? Are children ever rebellious toward their parents?

Like with a caring parent-and-child relationship, we are guided by our spirit guides, and are we ever going to let them in and connect with them and develop a bond with them?

We have probably mingled enough for this outing. We probably have gotten enough food for thought. We have probably seen enough for now and experienced enough for now. It is time to return. For now, we can say good-bye to our guides. Good-bye, guides. Thank you for being here and exposing yourselves to us, go in peace.

To the guides providing protection for the proceedings: Thank you for making it safe for us.

To the senior spirit guides present that took charge of arranging the protection and oversaw the proceedings: Thank you for arranging the protection and for overseeing the event.

To every spirit guide present for this special event: Thank you.

To everyone present, a last "Thank you and good-bye and go in peace."

To every person taking part in this meditation event, let us now go back slowly to where we started. Can we see the people in the park-like area? Is the sun still out in a mild-mannered way without harming anyone with its strong rays? Are the children who were playing and running around . . . the other people who were lazing around on picnic blankets . . . those who were walking around . . . all taking a nap? Are they mostly quietly sleeping somewhere? As we get back, we see them awakening and starting to stir. They are awakening because while we were away, they became very quiet and took a nap. Now, everyone is stirring as they are awakening. Some people and some children did not sleep; they were just lazing around or talking quietly so as not to disturb anyone.

And we are back, quiet and fully rested and wide-awake and refreshed, and when we are ready we can open our eyes.

Hello everyone, welcome back.

Nuts

—How David Works, Channeled by Emmanuel van der Meulen

Walnuts—that is the theme here. So, where to start? What to say about walnuts, where do they fit into the scheme of things? What is the context?

Walnuts are a nut of the edible kind. A walnut looks a lot like the human brain in its form and shape and detail. But that is where the similarity ends.

Let's look at dissimilarity from another perspective. When we are doing something—it does not matter what—we each have our way of doing things. Each reader, and for that matter anyone, has their own unique way of doing things.

We can tackle tasks with passion, with haste, with ease, with difficulty . . . being relaxed about it, and doing a task peacefully, with harmony, from anger, from anxiety. And yes, we can extend this list of "from what perspective we tackle doing things" much further. Any task, no specific task, just any old task.

But now, and here it comes: Whenever we tackle doing anything, would we prefer to tackle it feeling great and bringing ourselves to what we're doing, or to be absent when doing a task—as in, letting our Factor-x drive us? Rest assured, when anyone performs a task after having shaken the grips of Factor-x, therefore just getting on and enjoying almost every task and doing it in the way we do it when we are present and manifesting ourselves, that is indeed the preferred way to do things. When the converse is present, thus where Factor-x drives us, it almost certainly is not fun and not enjoyable.

But before I continue, there are some tasks that are not so much fun, and certainly not so enjoyable. Especially when one is involved with large tasks that just go on and on. At several points during the duration of a large task, it just gets a bit much, and it requires us to focus and refocus again. There are very few people who are indeed able to tackle long-running tasks, say, longer than a year, or even three or five or seven years. Those tasks require continuous focusing and refocusing. Ask Emmanuel. He has tackled some of these long-running tasks. They just seem never-ending.

Then there are the other tasks, which just need doing. They are the tasks where we might get ourselves into a situation where it requires confronting another person. That is usually not fun and not easy to do and not enjoyable.

We now have out of the way the following points related to the topic of from what perspective we tackle doing things. First, doing something and enjoying it because we are manifesting ourselves. Second, in some instances some tasks are just not fun all of the time and require focusing and refocusing repeatedly. Third, having to confront another person is hardly ever fun.

But now let's get to the nuts and bolts of getting on with serious tasks that we'd like to tackle but, say, we do not have the resources or the know-how or the vision to tackle. How and where would a person start?

Well, the first step is to look at why we want to tackle the task. If the *why* is not to appease our Factor-x, we are on track.

Another place to go is to take the next step. Which is the next step? There are just so many steps. If we slow down and relax ourselves and quiet ourselves, then it'll come to us. We usually have the next step there at hand, but usually, our Factor-x prevents us from seeing it.

Take careful note of the previous sentence. That statement is vital and worth repeating: *Factor-x is likely what prevents us from seeing our next step.*

Oh, but there is also another thing that might be in our way to see the next step. We might just be in a place we've not been before, and therefore, the next step has not emerged yet. Then why not just stop and continue with something totally unrelated? Any chore will do, as will any type of relaxing—just taking a break or resting will do. Before long, the next step is likely to emerge. Maybe that next step is not the favorite or the easiest or the most popular one, and possibly is something totally different. And as you say as earthlings, it might require that you take the bull by the horns.

Hey, please, not physically but merely as a figure of speech! Well, let's dissect that. Taking the bull by the horns is surely a scary and possibly even a dangerous thing to do, something that might even cause discomfort. So there it is. You might even find that the next step causes discomfort to just think of it, never mind taking the step.

When such a step is required, a step that looks as if it would cause discomfort, well, then, that is what is required. Steering away from such a step because it is scary or might cause discomfort does not necessarily mean it'll turn out to be something that'll cause discomfort. But yet again, it might cause discomfort. And when we take that step, usually we'll notice that it leaves a feeling of strength, a feeling of contentment, a feeling of peacefulness, even though that step might have started out in a way that felt threatening.

And then there is another step, the one that we *can* see. The one that we know is the one we'd like to take. The one step we are petrified of. Why? Because when taking it, we cannot see how we'd ever manage. Because it is the one where we feel that if we were to take that step, nothing else will be available to us, nothing left to hold onto. When such a step is taken, we might feel naked, and petrified of what is likely to happen to us—that by taking it, it would hang us out to dry and we would have absolutely no recourse, no matter what the consequences of taking the step. That perception is likely Factor-x kicking and screaming.

Well, now, well now. Does taking our next step frighten us? If so—and if all previous steps are in place and checked, and what we're likely to do is in line with something we'd really like to do, and we see what is preventing us from taking such a difficult or scary step, and we see that by taking the step we might end up with nothing and no one in our lives—then that is probably one of the big ones, one of the big, scary steps. Irrespective, without that step, we'll probably not regain our life. Whenever we are facing a seemingly big step, one where we feel that we're hanging ourselves out to dry, that indicates that is the step we need to take. So, when petrified to take a step, and you've ensured that the previously mentioned steps and checks and balances are in place, then just take the step.

If the step takes us down a dead end and it becomes apparent that it does not serve us, irrespective of what transpires, it would certainly not have been in our interest and it was likely driven by Factor-x. And some checks and balances might not have been in place. The origin of the step might have eluded us—the origin was likely Factor-x.

Oh, and initially, it might just be that we *think* we are not surviving the step, or that we are now in such new and strange territory, it just feels that we are not going to survive the step. Backpedaling might be an option. Like getting out of an abusive relationship, the getting-out part feels so overwhelming, and we feel we might have made a mistake because now suddenly our life has peace, but our next step seems even more difficult. And now that we are out of the abusive relationship, we're all alone. Now we wonder how would we take care of ourselves being on our own, and what'll we do when we get lonely. Best is to backpedal and get back into the abusive relationship.

No sirree, definitely not! That'll not serve anyone either. Take the bull by the horns again and go with it. Instead, take the next step.

Taking a next step might mean that a different or "downsized" lifestyle is required. But so what, if we are at peace and living very differently from what we were used to? Measure the step by our inner state: scared but at peace. If that is the case, why not just go with it a little more, a little further? Take the next step again and again and again—some larger ones and some smaller ones.

And now, for the very last hurdle! Sometimes we might find a situation where the easiest step just takes us back to the previous situation, the one that did not work. Because when we look at taking an easier step and dissect it, we'll notice the minute that panic sets in from taking a step, we tend to take a familiar step whether it totally suits us or not. We would possibly even take a step backward.

Emmanuel found that as a pattern. Whenever he got onto rocky, difficult ground and panic set in, he would immediately want to backpedal and again do things he did previously. And we would not need to be rocket scientists, as your earthling saying goes, to figure out that backpedaling does not help. It merely delays the inevitable—that some step needs to be taken, and that a backpedaling step will not serve us, whether immediately or shortly after or even much later after taking a next step.

So just be aware of each of these eventualities. Take heed that we might encounter even more such eventualities. We might even create some eventualities of our own. The main thing is be aware, put ourselves in charge, and do not give away our destiny into the hands of what would not serve us. Take heed of the checks and balances however. It is healthy to stop every now and then to observe whether we are on track, or whether the circumstances are just creating a life for us that make it *seem* it is meaningful.

Be aware, stop and look and take heed, and look at the checks and balances, and let's instead take steps at our own pace. And let our spirit guides into our lives. They are sure to be of excellent and awesome assistance and guidance.

Back to the walnut! Like the walnut is very different from another nut, say an almond, each of us, souls in humankind and souls in the spirit world, are unique and different. For instance, imagine if, in the process of growing, a walnut is forming itself and just being itself and for some reason it is influenced, hypothetically speaking, by over-hearing an almond speaking of how it forms itself. And now the walnut attempts that same "formula" as the almond to form itself. Surely it is not difficult to see that the walnut will not end up quite like an almond, and that it might even damage itself in the process. The walnut might even find out that forming itself like an almond is just not possible. As with the walnut, what works for one soul does not necessarily work for another soul.

In the same way a walnut would not serve itself to be an almond, we would not serve ourselves by attempting to be someone else. Rather, we would be fulfilling ourselves by just sticking to being ourselves. Look and observe and see our own next steps, which might be very different from Emmanuel's or anyone else's.

Oh, and another thing. It can be fun and it will be fun, but only after the difficult and scary steps are taken. Especially once we have broken free in the main from our Factor-x's influences on our lives. So the more naturally we live, the easier it'll be, and the more fun we'll encounter. At times, we might feel we're not having fun and might never again have any fun, but it'll come when we least expect it. Be aware of the level of fun in our lives. And at some point, our fun is likely to start. In Emmanuel's case, the fun started years and years after commencing his steps.

Afterword: Life *Can* Be Different

As you read when you first picked up this book, my intent is to "jolt" souls in both humankind and the spirit world to come together to improve the lot of all. This jolt has no guarantee of any effect, of course. Humankind and the spirit world might not be ready for such an extreme exposure of what we're creating, or of being shown that it's up to each one of us to stop and observe our ways with brutal honesty, and then have the courage of our convictions to uncover ourselves and walk our own path, thereby manifesting our meaning and thus living naturally.

Yet to everyone who reads this book and website, I'll state my intentions: it is worth any amount of effort and risk to do so. Should we manifest our meaning, our inner beauty will replace and displace, albeit one person at a time and even if it takes over a million years, the self-destruction we're living today, as independent individuals and as a species, as souls within humankind and the spirit world.

Humankind and spirit-world souls can only accomplish such a togetherness through consciously exposing what is driving the self-destruction while at the same time uncovering each individual soul.

This book is that seed, the conception of what is driving the self-destruction, simply exposed for anyone to understand, and it attempts to assist anyone willing to break out of the cycle of self-destruction. Breaking out of the cycle comes when individuals uncover themselves and then manifest what they have uncovered as independent, individual souls.

Emmanuel van der Meulen
October 2007

PART FOUR

APPENDICES

Appendix A

Reliving the Moment to Uncover Its Importance

Let's make ourselves quiet. And if you do not already have a technique to quiet yourself with, then maybe you can by taking a few deep breaths and then slowly releasing them (up to thirty times, but you can stop when you feel relaxed). Then let a moment that you want to look at into your mind. Do not look for it, do not think about it—let it in by being relaxed and not getting anxious if it doesn't come to you.

Once we have a particular moment, it is important to slow the moment down into fractions of the moment. Think of the moment as a movie reel made up of many frames. With life's moments, there are very many such frames in each moment. In fact, as we get to regularly dissecting moments, we'll see that the frames could be slowed even further, and further frames will emerge from any particular frame, which can again be dissected further into more frames. Get the picture?

It is probably unfamiliar territory, but any particular moment could quite possibly consist of hundreds, or thousands, or even millions of frames. We are complex beings. Our makeup is thought, emotion, desires, perceptions and so forth. In each moment, these dynamics meld together to bring our experiences.

So to reiterate, slow down the moment so it can be dissected. Our way of reliving a moment is to quiet ourselves and not to think about the moment, but to *feel* the moment. We could relive a moment in a few seconds, even while doing something else; it's only necessary to become quiet and to feel it. The quieter we are, the more the moment will reveal to us. But the emphasis is on feeling the moment, then putting the moment into words, thus describing in words what we feel in the moment.

We could also walk for days to relive and capture the importance of a moment. We could even walk for months, and even longer, to relive a moment. When the moment is important to us, it shouldn't matter how long it takes us to get to the bottom of such an important moment. It's important, though, to get there.

That importance might be something so big for us, the truth of the moment holds us back from seeing it. All we can do is acknowledge this fact, and not fight or deny it. And it's best that we don't make just anything fit because we are keen to get there. When we lose it or don't get it, nothing stops us from returning to dissecting the moment at a later stage: maybe even days, weeks, months or years later.

As we develop our skills for looking at moments to reveal their underlying value, we might return to a "stubborn" one later. If we miss out on it all together, thus not getting the underlying value of a particular moment or even never returning to such a moment at some later stage to determine its underlying value, some other, unrelated moment is sure to trigger what resulted in a particular or similar previous moment—a moment for which we want to ascertain its underlying value. While we are serious about uncovering ourselves from a particular moment, nothing is ever lost. At some point, possibly when we least expect it, all will be revealed for a particular moment.

. Oh, and by the way, we could look at any moment, not only recent moments, but those as far back as when we were a toddler, or a baby, or even all the way back to after conception, while still in our mother's womb.

When observing the moment, you'll find noise—other things that keep popping into your mind. Look carefully; most of them are distractions. What you'll also notice: We tend to instinctively engage with what comes up in the moment. Our minds get involved in what's there in the moment, we engage the findings in the moment, and this stops the flow, like a blockage in a water pipe. As a result, the *flow* of moments stop and we don't get any further. Sort of like the rest of the movie stops if the movie projector is interfered with.

What is critically important and also extremely difficult is to refrain all together from getting entangled in the things that come up in the moment. All that is required is to observe, observe, observe.

We need to train ourselves to disengage and observe and to feel the moment. We don't want to stop the *flow*. We don't want to cause a blockage in the water pipe. We don't want to stop the "movie of the moment" until we've *seen* the whole movie. We stop it by engaging rather than observing the moment. Oh, and disagreeing with what is revealed in the moment results in the flow stopping immediately. It's about observing the moment and nothing more, definitely not engaging in the revelations of the moment.

Coming back to the importance of the moment, you might be asking how you'll know that you got to the importance of the moment. The interesting thing is, until you know you've captured the importance of the moment, all you'll know for sure is that you haven't yet captured it. Or, to put it another way, guessing or thinking about it won't get you to it. We aren't able to force anything to fit into being it. But when we get to the importance of the moment, we'll know we got it. And the more we stop and look at the importance of any particular moment, the more distinctly we'll recognize the importance of the moment. We'll know we've got the importance when we feel it. It is about observing and feeling what transpired in the moment, and then knowing we got to the moment's importance.

The harder we try to find the importance of the moment, the less the importance of the moment will come to us. It can be likened to when we grab at water in a stream: we'll probably not get any. But when we gently place our cupped hand in the water, it will fill up instantly. That's what is necessary.

Now, if the importance of the moment eludes us, but we're still interested in getting it, we'll just let it go. We'll notice that by letting go, thus getting away from it by removing the urgency of finding the importance of the moment by relaxing or by doing something else, it'll most probably come to us in the quiet of whatever else we are busy with at another time. Just be aware. It might just creep up on you when you least expect it.

Mainly because this dynamic requires that we are calm, relaxed and quiet inside, we should definitely not be anxious—even though we might want to get to the importance of the moment urgently, it'll only come when we are calm, relaxed and quiet. (If you need

LIFE CAN BE DIFFERENT: CONCEPTION

assistance to do this, you'll find it in the following section titled, "Creating an Inner Calm.")

When referring to the importance of the moment, it's not necessarily something of life-and-death importance, but of course it could be. It might even be something small, usually not insignificant, but it could be small. We could see these moments and their importance as nuggets. They usually are like gold nuggets, in that when we're looking to relive a moment, we'll notice that, in amongst all the other stuff (emotions, desires, anxiety, pain and frustration) there's something of importance just waiting to be uncovered: like finding gold nuggets when mining. (And here, there is no importance placed on gold nuggets; it is merely meant in a metaphorical sense.)

In the moment, the importance of it might be the reason behind making some choice, say, opposed to what we'd rather have chosen. Or the reason why suddenly we aren't feeling well—feeling angry, or frustrated or the like. When stopping and retracing our steps and finding the moment from when we suddenly started feeling "off," then when reliving that moment, it's possible to uncover exactly what resulted in throwing us off and causing us to not feel well. This can be discovered from any moment, no matter how long ago.

We can use this technique, or dynamic, to get to the bottom of a daydream: to find its importance. In fact, it's available to us for exploring any moment for any reason.

Say that we got angry and want to see why. Say we realize we feel euphoric and we want to see why. Say we feel anxious and we want to see why. This is definitely a great mechanism to also uncover the underlying source of our daydreams.

Creating an Inner Calm

When our minds race and we can't think straight and we're generally not calm, we can easily obtain that calm through a combination of breathing and focusing our minds on calming images, especially those of nature. For instance, you can take your mind to where you are on your own, somewhere on a mountain, or at a river, or at a

244

stream, or at a waterfall. Breathing calmly and casting our minds to such a quiet place brings about an inner calm.

By calming yourself, you're able to regain composure and take your mind away from rushing around in a hectic lifestyle.

When your mind is calm, you're able to see things more clearly.

An example: Sometimes when asleep, we awaken with a solution to some problem we might have been toying with. It is in the calm of our sleep that we create the solution.

We can also calm our minds when awake.

With this as some background, calm your mind while awake. Start by breathing deeply and steadying your breathing, and then visiting a quiet spot in nature.

Here we go.

- Take a deep breath, but inhale slowly and once inhaled, hold it there for two to three counts and exhale, slowly all the way.
- Now, push the last bit of air from your lungs and once exhaled, hold it there for two to three counts. And again, breathe in deeply and slowly to steady your breathing.
- Once inhaled, inhale the breath a little more, stretching your lungs and then holding it there for a count or two.
- Exhale slowly, again pushing the last bit of air from your lungs, then hold your breath after pushing out the last bit of air.
- Now slowly breathe in, filling your lungs to the point of stretching and expanding, and then hold the air for a moment or two.
- Exhale slowly. You might feel like coughing or become dizzy. This might be because you haven't taken such deep breaths for a while. It's okay to cough or become dizzy. In fact, there's no right way of doing this and no wrong way either. You do it whichever way suits you.
- Keep to the rhythm of breathing in slowly and stretching your lungs to get a little more air into them. Hold it again for a moment or two, then exhale slowly and again gently push out the last bit of air, and then hold your breath for a moment or two once fully exhaled.

- Repeat this at least thirty times, preferably sitting up. Sitting might be better because you might fall asleep if you lie down when calming yourself, especially if you are tired or exhausted from other activities. In that case, you should instead do these calming exercises to rest. Once rested, you can again continue doing them to calm your mind as opposed to doing them to sleep.
- Next, focus on going to a quiet spot in nature while doing the breathing exercise. Observe whatever place in nature comes to mind. It doesn't matter which spot. Don't go looking for a spot; let the spot come to you.
- Once you see a spot in your mind, look at what you see. Look carefully and observe what the spot looks like. Don't force your looking, just let your mind see what's there. Take it all in.
- If you don't see anything, just be quiet and relax and enjoy the calm. When you do this "quieting" or meditation exercise again later, you might experience a spot in your mind's eye somewhere in nature where it is quiet and calm and peaceful and relaxing.
- If you do see a spot, take in what's there, without forcing anything. Just enjoy the moment and let the quiet of your visit fill you and grow in you.
- While you're there and taking it all in and observing your surroundings and yourself, stay there in this inner calm for a little while longer. You might become so calm and relaxed, you fall asleep. That's fine; that's the calm of the moment. Let it fill you, even to the extent that you fall asleep.

You can calm yourself or meditate often to train your usually frantic and restless mind to also experience calm and peacefulness. You can meditate as often as once a day, several times a day, or once a week or several times a week, or once a month or several times a month. It doesn't matter how often you meditate, as long as you meditate. There might come a time where you meditate very often. And there might come another time where you don't meditate for months. You can meditate as and when it suits you. But if you don't meditate at all, you will lose touch with the inner calm you experience when you are in the habit of meditating regularly.

You might want to play calming music while meditating. You can do this as often as you like. The important thing is that you meditate, always starting with the breathing and looking at whichever quiet spot in nature comes into your mind. The spot itself isn't what is important. Oh, it might be. But the quiet spot has more to do with you focusing your mind away from the racing and frantic states we get ourselves into.

Your mind will grow accustomed to this calm, and when you aren't calm, this is a good way of calming yourself—you can meditate as often as you like to calm yourself.

The important thing is to give your mind and emotions and physical body a rest, and the more you do it, the more you'll like it. The calm and peaceful experience is also a very good indication of how busy your mind and emotions get. The contrast becomes apparent when you meditate. And until meditating here now, it's even possible that this is the first time in a very long time, or possibly ever, that you calmed yourself.

The calm and peacefulness we gain from meditation is an indication of the state we'd prefer our mind and emotions and body to experience. It is also an indication of the state we usually find ourselves in: You'll notice it from the contrast between when you're quiet and when you're not.

So go on; let's create an inner calm regularly.

Uncovering Our Meaning

Let's take a look at our daydreams.

But first . . .

Say you and I and others have all the money and any other resources in the world. What would we like to do with our lives?

Say we don't need to work anymore. Say we have everything that our heart desires. Or, say we have nothing that our heart desires.

Imagine Having Whatever Money Can Buy

Then let's imagine having whatever money can buy, then.

Let's say we have everything already, or nothing. Say we are down and out.

Let's imagine you have nothing, but you have everything at your disposal. Particularly, you have all the money you would ever need at your disposal. And say that everything you can imagine is possible for you to achieve, and because you have the money to achieve whatever you want, you could also obtain any resources you require.

Oh, and like the others, you have so much money, it'll never dry up. Whatever we use is immediately replaced.

So the groundwork is set. You have wherever your life is at when reading this, and in addition, all the money in the world at your disposal. What would you do?

You could go and buy the house of your dreams. Once that is done, you could buy the car of your dreams. Once that is done, you might take the holiday you've been daydreaming about. And since you don't have to worry about going back to work, you can take an extended holiday.

You might have other dreams also—for example, that you meet the partner of your dreams.

You might already have some of what I'm mentioning here. If so, you can just skip over that point, or get or do an alternative.

There might be other aspects. Say you're distant from people close to your heart. You might now be in a position to rekindle that relationship with a friend, a partner, a family member, even your children.

The point being, you now have all the time in the world and you can come and go and do as you please. And furthermore, you could get the things you've always only dreamed of.

You might even go and look for a child you've lost contact with. You might even go and look up a parent you've been estranged from. Or look up a family member you've been meaning to find.

You now have all the money and resources, and yes, let's say you now also have all the courage you usually lack.

So you could now go and find those people, buy these things, do the things you've always wanted to do.

You might not even know what you'd like to do. You might have had such a deprived life up to now, you don't even know what your daydreams are, or what they are about, or how you would attain what your daydreams are about.

But as you go for your daydreams, one small step at a time, the courage and confidence would grow and grow until, after very many little successes, you'd feel like you can do just about anything. And besides, you have all the money in the world and all the resources.

You might even go on a binge of drinking and drugging, since you can now afford anything and everything and as much of anything and everything as you might desire.

You might even "buy" friends or create a flamboyant lifestyle since you have all the money you could ever need or want. You might even get yourself an entourage to go with you wherever you go. You might even get yourself bodyguards and the like. You might even want to get your cars armored.

Imagine that you have everything at your disposal and your whole life ahead of you. And, if you're older, you might still have some years to go with which you can do whatever your heart desires with the rest of your life. You can do things you like, you can do things you don't like, you can do whatever you want and you have enough money to buy your way out of whatever trouble you might get into along the way.

You might even buy an island. You might get fashion models for partners. Remember, you have all the resources and you can't deplete anything ever.

This imagining has no end to it, it's not a joke, and the money will never dry up. The more you use the money, the more the money is replaced.

Whatever you can imagine, that is what you can have.

So the scene is set. You might even get a village and get whomever you want to live there in the village with you. You don't have to work. You don't have to ever give money a second thought. Your slightest wish or daydream or command is what happens.

You might buy an oceangoing liner, just for your pleasure, and invite anyone you want to join you, and you might then cruise to anywhere in the world. You might go even further and build your own space vehicle, and travel in space wherever the technology can take you. There is absolutely nothing you can't have or can't achieve, and this will never stop. And the more you do, the more ideas you'll get, and the more you'd be able to do.

And by the way, because of your stature and status, you even have a following, so you'll never be without admirers and friends.

You could have movies made based on whatever theme you can conjure up. You can have musicians make music for you of whatever music you like.

If you like something and someone else has it, you can merely make them an offer they can't refuse. If someone doesn't want to play ball, you can get a team of legal experts to find a way to get what you want and drive the hardball to a point where they'll give up what they have so you can get what you want from them.

If a country doesn't want to play ball, you could get another country with the necessary armament to declare war on the country that is playing hardball.

There is nothing that you can't get. You have all the money and all the resources. You can even fly to your destinations with your own planes that are custom-designed to suit you and your own style. You can hire the best and most professional people to do for you whatever you might want done or might desire.

By now, the scene is nearly set to the fullest. Is your imagination running wild yet? Have you gotten what you wanted? Is there anything left that you can still think of that you'd want?

Oh, you might, at last, with all the resources at your disposal, have any partner you desire and have as much sex as your heart desires. You might even live any and every sexual fantasy that you've always dreamed of, because it's now in your power to find exactly the person or persons to live your sexual fantasies with.

You might now have the power that you always wanted, and with this power you can do the things you've always wanted to do before you had all this power. And besides, if anything bothers you or gets in your way, it's merely a matter of getting a solution to overcome whatever bothers you or gets in your way.

Is the scene almost completely set yet? Not yet.

Imagine some more, and do or have whatever else comes to mind. Have it. Do it. Nothing is too big or too small. Live every moment with the understanding of having and doing whatever your heart desires. No matter at what cost.

The scene is set. If it is not yet set for the others, then run with whatever comes up: No matter what, just go and have and do, and don't mind those that have already got to the point where the scene is set. We'll wait here for those who still have things to do and who have desires not yet fulfilled.

Thus, the scene is set for some and not yet set for others. And this is where we'll all wait for those still imagining and desiring and fulfilling those desires.

Oh, there is a last-minute desire that just reared its head. Okay, okay, go off and explore that desire, and don't let anything stand in your way. This is indeed the case where we *can have* and *can do* whatever we want. Everyone will oblige us, and if someone won't oblige us, we have the means to make those not wanting to be part of our world play ball with us.

Okay. Now it seems the scene is fully set, and here is where we'll wait for anyone still out in their world doing whatever they want to come and join us. We'll just wait here for however long it takes.

A last-minute desire that you just remembered popped up. It's about where you take a trip, in your car or on your motorbike, around the country. Oh, and yes, you'd like to write that book you've thought of several times. Well, now is the chance for you to do it. Do it. Take that trip and write that book, and remember, it doesn't matter how long it takes. But it is important that you take the trip . . . or write the book . . . rather than just thinking about it. Go on, take the trip or write the book.

Something Missing

At this time, everyone is done with the imagining exercise and busy settling down.

We now go into another direction. This time, we're going somewhere else all together.

As you undertook these imaginary activities, what did you experience? It's likely that you were exhilarated, even anxious. It might have felt unbelievable. But in the main, when the dust settled on all these imaginary activities and when your emotions returned to normal and when you calmed yourself, and when looking back, what is it that you experienced during and after doing the imaginary activities?

Oh, by the way, keep in mind you undertook these activities in your imagination, and now we all might even be years and years older, even if just in our imagination.

Might it be you experienced that something was missing when doing the imaginary activities? Did the activity provide satisfaction? Were you content? Did the satisfaction only last a bit longer than the activity? Is it possible that the satisfaction died out, even before you were finished with the activity?

And it doesn't only need to be satisfaction that you experienced. With any uplifting feeling you experienced, any euphoric sensations you experienced while living the imaginary activities, is it likely that you feel as if something was missing?

Whatever you experienced, was the experience lasting? Was the experience enjoyable? Are those imaginary activities things that you'd want to experience again and again? Or, is it likely that now you've done the activities, albeit in your imagination, and experienced their upliftment, that you're at a point where you've had enough? Certainly, there would be some things you'd like to experience again, possibly many more times.

Again, when looking at the imaginary activities and recalling what you experienced, could you conclude that something might have been missing? If so, do you dare look at what might have been missing?

Let's work on some assumptions. Everyone might not have felt that something was missing. Some of us might still be yearning for some imaginary things we never got around to, or imaginary things we'd like to repeat again. Some of us might not have such imaginations where we could feel and experience sensations from these activities. And some of us might not have experienced much, or maybe experienced nothing, or experienced just a little bit. Or we possibly thought that the imagining exercise was just silly. To any one of us who didn't experience much, or who thought the imagining exercise silly, it's likely that this imaginary world is possibly not for all of us. It's also possible that we might not be ready for this material yet—or might never be ready.

However, for those of us still reading, and having felt and experienced something more than a little from the imagining exercise, let us continue.

Let's look a little deeper into what might have been missing.

During these imaginary activities, we were "living" certain activities we might have daydreamed about. They were born in our daydreams, and we manifested them in our imagination. We can almost be certain these activities were devised from us thinking that if we had the things or did the things we imagined, we would be rid of whatever need the dreaming was based on. Or, that we would be satisfied in ourselves for having gotten or done those things.

Unfortunately, things don't likely work that way. Whatever shortcomings we might have on which the daydreams or desires are based—not physical shortcomings but emotional ones—they're likely based on our interpretation of the daydream, an interpretation that was likely created from our Factor-x.

So, getting or doing these things, as per the imagining exercise, isn't likely to do it for us. At the end of the imaginary activities, when the dust settles, even if over months or years of pursuing a dream, we are likely left with the same emptiness, or still feeling that something is missing. We are unlikely to be able to address what is missing, or to fill that possible emptiness with anything. This isn't because the activities were imagined.

Extent of What Is Missing

The problem is, there is no hole to be filled. Nothing is missing. There is no deficiency to be attended to. There is no emptiness that needs filling.

We daydream about things, and we interpret those things as things we'd like to do, and we *believe* that when we do those things, we'll feel fulfilled. We thus feel that whatever is missing will be attained. But the daydreams are likely interpreted from our perspective created by our standards and norms and our Factor-x.

Oh, the need to fulfill ourselves is there, and the daydream is created from a need, but nothing we have or do will fulfill or remove the feeling that something is missing. That is, while we're looking external to ourselves. With our frame of reference and our Factor-x looming, we're likely to interpret desires and needs to be fulfilled externally. Thus, we're likely looking externally.

When we start uncovering what the missing feeling is about, and we look internally, we stand a chance to uncover the origin of the missing feeling. As a result, we can address the missing feeling.

Anything else we do while looking externally is merely treating the symptom. When we stop and look internally, however, that's when we're on a track to address the cause. When we address the cause of the feeling that something is missing, that's likely the only way we can get away from either the feeling that something is missing, or the ensuing feeling of emptiness.

Our Meaning Is Missing

So now, the scene is completely set for us to look at what is missing.

Our meaning is almost certainly what's missing when we want or do things to appease us.

When we've uncovered our meaning, we'll be manifesting ourselves, and whatever we might need or want will be things that are part of us manifesting ourselves, as opposed to us wanting or doing things to address something that might feel missing—to fill a hole in our lives.

Oh, and now the scene is really set to look at uncovering our meaning. We are now ready to build the case for uncovering our meaning, slowly, very slowly, one step at a time, from here on in.

When you refer back to your daydreams on which previous imaginary activities were based, it's important to uncover what lies underneath the dream: the undercurrent that inspired the daydream. We almost certainly always misinterpret our daydreams. We interpret them from our current frame of reference: from our Factor-x. We interpret them from things currently in and around our lives: From the current standards and norms of our society: from our Factor-x.

Those things in and around our lives and our society are all likely based on us and society seeking to fill the hole of what we think is missing in our lives. So we aren't aware that other aspects of our lives exist. Our society is also unaware that other aspects exist. Our society is made up of individuals like ourselves. Our society is not something "out there" (as the cliché goes). We are part of our society. Our society is part of us. We feed our society, and our society feeds us. So if a vital flaw indeed exists—that we feel something missing in our lives and attempt to fill it with external stimuli—then that same flaw is perpetuated from our society to us, and back again to society. The cycle locks us in, and we have no say in and over our lives while we don't see the flaw in our lives and in our society. And this is handed down to us, as seen in the section titled, "Factor-x and How It Comes About."

So when we look for guidance from our role models—parents, teachers, professors, bosses, government, ministers, churches, religious leaders, as seen in "Forms of Crutches"—they are likely unable to give us the guidance for us to uncover ourselves. They too are caught up in the cycle of looking externally for something to fill an emptiness inside them—an emptiness that can't be filled, because it doesn't exist in the way that filling it will take it away.

So what are you to do? It seems there is nothing you can do that will fill the emptiness, or that will address the feeling that something is missing. It seems you can't look at our society for guidance either. It seems we are all doomed.

This isn't so. We aren't doomed, and we're indeed fortunate when we get to the stage of seeing what exactly is happening in our lives and around us.

LIFE CAN BE DIFFERENT: CONCEPTION

Misinterpreting Our Daydreams

There's only one thing left for you and I to do, and that is look at why the emptiness exists. Why the feeling exists that something is missing from our lives. Why the feeling exists that our lives seemingly don't have meaning.

We can start by looking at our daydreams.

Our daydreams have an undercurrent on which they are based. We can look at that undercurrent to see what our daydreams are really about. By moving your existing standards and norms to one side, you can get a glimpse of yourself without your frame of reference or the standards and norms imprinted on you by your society and by your Factor-x.

"Daydreams: Misinterpretation and Undercurrent" elaborates on this with an example of misinterpreting a daydream from the perspective of society's standards and norms and Factor-x, rather than from the perspective of the undercurrent of the dream. It also expounds on uncovering the undercurrent of the same daydream. This is not as easy as it sounds, though. Your standards and norms, your frame of reference, and your Factor-x will kick and scream and not let you move it aside. So you'd need to quiet yourself, as seen in "Creating an Inner Calm," and then observe and be brave and collect all the courage you can muster to be more honest than you've ever been with yourself to acknowledge what you see and experience—to observe and acknowledge what you uncover.

This, again, is easier said than done. As mentioned, everything in us will kick and scream and resist us moving aside our standards and norms and our Factor-x. Remember, to move aside your frame of reference, your standards and norms, and your Factor-x goes against the grain of everything in your life as you know it. A way you can get past your standards and norms and Factor-x is to not become entangled in what you uncover, and to at least acknowledge what you uncover—to flow with whatever you unearth about yourself, irrespective of how "weak the signal strength" of what you uncover. Later, you can assess what you encountered, and let the signal strength of what you uncover from your inner self grow so you can grow.

Be forewarned that every time we question or fight what we see and uncover, the flow of what our inner self exposes to us stops in its tracks. The movie stops, in other words. The best we can do is to acknowledge what we uncover . . . just let it be, let it flow, and observe without interfering by engaging in what is exposed, but taking absolute care to see and acknowledge and take in what is being exposed to us by our inner selves. In this way, by letting your inner self inform you and letting the information flow, you stand a chance to observe the undercurrent of your dreams.

But be aware that allowing this uncovering to just happen isn't easy, especially at first. You might just acknowledge and accept what you uncover about yourself. You're just as likely to shoo it out as you would a stray animal wandering into your campsite.

Dissecting Your Daydreams

If you observe what you experience while you observe your daydreams, and slow down your daydreams and your experiences (as seen in "Reliving the Moment to Uncover Its Importance"), like with the frames that make up a movie, you can look at each frame one at a time to feel what you feel, thereby feeling what is exposed by the experience of your daydreams—from its undercurrent exposed from your inner self. And if you don't quite feel anything, then you can slow the movie even further. In between each frame in the movie of your daydream are more frames. And in between those frames are even more frames, and so on.

Our minds contain such frames as those making up a movie, frames by the millions. Once we get the knack of dissecting those frames, like looking at movie frames one at a time, we can slow the daydream or any experience to the point where we can make sense of their undercurrent. In this case, you want to determine the undercurrent of each of your daydreams to see them for what they are—without any interpretation, without thinking, just feeling. This needs an open mind . . . open beyond our frame of reference . . . open beyond our standards and norms . . . open beyond our Factor-x.

Understanding Your Daydreams

As opposed to accepting what we uncover about ourselves, when we uncover the undercurrent of our daydreams, we are likely to find these aspects.

The first is this: From the undercurrent of the daydream you now presumably see, you just don't accept what you uncover about yourself. *It just can't be,* you think, or *It's unbelievable.*

The second is this: What are you to make of it; what are you to do about it?

The third is this: You don't believe you can do anything with or about it. *After all,* you think, *who am I? I'm just too insignificant.*

And fourth: Where would you get . . . the know-how . . . the finances . . . the resources to manifest yourself?

These are usual and understandable apprehensions. Up to this point in your life, you likely had a very different outlook and understanding of yourself. Now suddenly, you're exposed to a different outlook and a different meaning. Very definitely a scary prospect. But not only scary. Up to now and for some time to come, your Factor-x is likely dominant in your life. Now you're faced with something new to you: something so different, and something that requires you to look past what you likely know, past the standards and norms of society, and past your Factor-x. Not for the fainthearted.

Nevertheless, by acknowledging what you uncovered, and with patience and getting to understand yourself, over time it might become easier and easier to see what you're about. You might possibly even develop the courage to go for what you want with your life.

Oh, and then there is Factor-x. With such an overbearing drive from our Factor-x, it's virtually impossible to acknowledge, never mind accept that we could set out to achieve with our lives what we uncover as the undercurrent of our daydreams. As mentioned, we might think to ourselves, *After all, who am I?* And then, with what our society's standards and norms and our frame of reference and our Factor-x dictate to us, we're likely to go diametrically opposite in our views and understanding.

Appendix A

Your Own Meaning and Direction

With whatever you encounter as the undercurrent of your dreams, you're likely to go into a different direction with your life. This would almost certainly require finances and resources you might not have. Again, what are you to do?

It's actually very simple. We take small steps. One small step at a time. We take steps cutting out the things in our lives that we don't want there, adjusting our lives so that our "Yes" is indeed yes, and our "No" is indeed no. Again, if we have the courage, we'll take those steps.

If we lack the courage, we'll stay where we are and look for ways to justify to ourselves why we can't and shouldn't take those steps. And that would be that.

For those of us with the courage of our convictions, who can move forward and can take the steps, irrespective of how scary the step seems, we will encounter several crossroads. As we get beyond the crossroads, as we get to know ourselves better and our confidence grows, we'll find that some steps are easier to take, and others extremely difficult. And rest assured when the steps are difficult, it's usually because of some debris from your Factor-x that is making it too scary for you to move forward.

And then, there are steps you'll take that won't work out. In those cases, you'll need to backpedal and find your path again, as if on a journey and getting lost along the way. Yet when you look carefully and backtrack your steps, you're likely to see where you lost the pathway. Forward or backward, no step taken is wasted, and all of them add to your experiences.

On the point of finances and resources: These are very scary prospects indeed. And you might feel like you have lived for so many years now, and likely feel that was time wasted, and now want to rush. And as many people say of themselves, they are too impatient and want it now.

Unfortunately, it doesn't work like that. You'll soon see that nothing along your natural path, the path of your meaning, can be rushed. It has a timing and rhythm of its own. You can only take the

LIFE CAN BE DIFFERENT: CONCEPTION

steps for which you have resources, financial or otherwise. No matter what you do or want or expect, you can't do more than you have resources for.

However, you *can* make a plan to get from where you are to where you want to go. Here, you might feel that where you'd like to go with your life might take forever: a month, a year, two years or even five or ten years. Again, it might even look as if it'll take forever.

That doesn't matter; your path is your path. Your resources are your resources. It is merely a matter of realizing where you want to go. Acknowledging that it's your own path, and about your own meaning, you're likely to notice every now and then that you would check and recheck your journey, and even reorganize your plan. And as your confidence grows and as you gain experience in your *new* life, you'll notice that you'll even add things to your plan, or take things away and reorganize your plan and shorten your plan, and then lengthen your plan, and vice versa.

Notwithstanding any of this, it is your plan, it's your way of life, and you will get to the destination whenever you get there. And the getting there, thus the journey, is all part of your newly found life—your life based on your meaning.

Be aware, observe. You might notice that you have your life on hold during the journey, and are holding your breath, so to speak, until you get there. Be warned, that doesn't work. Live the journey. The journey is all part and parcel of your path based on your meaning. If you're not living the journey, you're off-track and not enjoying your journey. As a result, you'll experience frustration and more, as seen in the section titled, "Expectations: Frustration, Anger and Irritation."

So you uncovered the undercurrent of your dream and now you want to implement that, but it turns out to be a massive project and you don't have the necessary resources to manifest yourself. What are you to do? As mentioned, take one small step at a time. Plan and re-plan, remembering that each step we take is the manifestation of ourselves—the undercurrent of our daydreams.

Some of us, reading these points about uncovering our meaning, will not be able to manifest ourselves. Others will. And some of us will go with manifesting themselves, and others won't. Using marketing terms, some of us would be leaders and others followers. The leaders will uncover their meaning and go with it—manifest themselves. The followers will uncover their meaning and not go for it—not manifest themselves. The latter group will wait for the leader-types to go for it, and when the leaders establish unconventional organizations that the followers can join—where the followers would be in a position to manifest themselves as independent individuals—they will then join and manifest themselves.

And here, "leader" doesn't necessarily mean one person leading someone else. No. It merely means taking a lead by uncovering our meaning and going for it and manifesting ourselves. Like when something new comes onto the market. The leader-type people would see the value of this piece or service or product and go for it. Others would only go with it later on, more or less when everyone else is doing it.

If you are unable to uncover the undercurrent of your daydreams, make contact with me via the accompanying website, lifecanbe different.com, under the "assisted member option," to explore finding such undercurrent.

Dreaming the Feeling

It seems that dreaming is a topic with many theories as to why we dream and what the dreams mean. This discussion is about my own experiences, and how it works for me, a simplistic overview of my dreaming. Yet I'd be very surprised if dreaming doesn't work this same way for you.

I have two types of dreams. One is a dream related to something I encountered during the day that upset me, such as a scary scene in a true-life dramatic movie. That upsetting feeling plays out in a later dream. In fact, when watching or experiencing such an event, I sometimes know this will likely come out in a dream of sorts. Those dreams usually aren't the ones of value. It is the other type of dream I find more valuable.

Let me start with these questions. When waking up from a dream, we usually have some sensation, a feeling of sorts. We might ask ourselves, *Is the feeling I have when waking up from a dream the result of the dream?* In other words, did the dream create the feeling? Or: *Is the feeling the reason why I had the dream?* In other words, did the dream portray an underlying feeling I've been walking around with for some time: maybe for an hour, a day, a week or even weeks? For me, the latter scenario is where I gain most from my dreams, in that they portray underlying feelings I've been walking around with, either aware of or unaware of my feelings. When I don't clearly see the underlying feelings, my dream will come along and make a "movie" as a visual aid so I can more clearly see what it is I've been walking around with.

When I wake up from a dream, I sense the feeling and I recall the *dream-movie*. I attempt to put words to the feeling, without fighting it, and merely acknowledge and accept the feeling. Once I have the words for the feeling—not elaborate, but short and simple, or even one powerful word to describe the feeling—I then relate that description to the dream-movie: *without* forcing the words to fit. If the words don't fit, I revisit the feeling to find accurate words. The combined description of the feeling and the *movie* depicted by the dream portrays to me what I'm not sensing in my day-to-day life.

Then there are recurring dreams; they are valuable aids. The scripts underlying these dreams are set from a pattern. Some underlying feeling is continuously not being addressed. The dream will likely reoccur until one of two things happens: the underlying feeling is incidentally altered due to changing circumstances, or the underlying feeling is intentionally addressed.

Here is an example of a dream and its related words. From time to time, I have a dream that seemingly reoccurs even though I address the underlying cause each time. It is obvious to me that I have the same dream for different reasons, and it depicts a similar feeling at different times. In the dream, I am looking for something I don't find, an elusive *something*. In each dream, I look for something different. But each time, when I get close to finding it, what I'm supposed to be looking for changes, and then I need to find *something else*. Each time, I awaken feeling lost. Thus, different things at different times while on my life's journey create a feeling in me that

I'm lost. When I awaken from this dream, then find the words and relate them to the dream, I recognize that the thing I'm attending to at the time creates in me a feeling of being lost. I use this as an opportunity to look at what I'm attending to, and acknowledge that I'm lost and don't know which way to turn or which option to take. Recognizing and acknowledging that I'm feeling lost assists me in finding direction.

Dreaming the feeling is an invaluable self-uncovering aid.

APPENDIX B

Reincarnation and Karma

Now here is a topic that we should look at very carefully, because when some behaviors and experiences can't be clarified or explained, the consensus amongst certain people is that we must have lived previously, or that we have lived several lives.

This phenomenon is supposedly for us to learn from each life, supposedly because, in our lives, we make mistakes or we do things to other people that aren't nice. So when we live these lives, we'll get in return, in some form or another, that which we handed out, and in that sense learn from our mistakes or learn life's lessons to make better people of us.

And all this time, we don't know where we are and we don't know where we're headed and we float around from life to life without any measure of where we are, what we've done and where we're going, or what we still need to learn.

And when anything is unclear or difficult to understand, it's put down to that we have to learn something from it, because supposedly it has connections to a previous lifetime. We can liken this to a ship with some cargo to deliver, floating around on the seas, faring this way and then that way, and the captain stating to his men and them firmly believing that eventually they will get somewhere to deliver the cargo onboard.

There is also the notion amongst these believers or followers that subscribe to this phenomenon that we can regress into previous lifetimes to see and relive some experiences.

It seems so dramatic, and so much like that we're lost and have no say in our lives and our destiny, and that we'll merely be shaken in our barrel of life until some destination is reached. And that the destination is determined by what we've learned and what we still have to learn and how many "bad" things we've done, which then in turn results that we might have to live certain lives again to learn some more lessons.

The way this is portrayed and thought out is more or less indicative of someone else being in charge of our lives, that we have very little say in the matter, and that we are to blindly follow and learn those lessons.

Whereas, when we look very carefully at this phenomenon, it strips us of our ability to be ourselves and to uncover our own path, and then live that path. Again, another ploy devised by our standards and norms to disempower individuals and place the power over our lives in the hands of some unknown force in charge.

When we consider the previous lives and regression into those lives that the followers of this phenomena claim to have experienced, is it likely that somehow they get in touch with spirits in the spirit world, through whom they then experience these phenomena? As you read in the section titled, "Is It Real?," the spirit-world souls are also in need of guidance, and might be guiding Earth-souls through their own best intentions, but from their own misinterpretations of what they're experiencing.

About the Website

Interested souls that arrive at the accompanying website, lifecanbedifferent.com, who want to pursue what is offered have three options.

Visitor Option

With the *visitor option*, certain information, including newsletters, is available free of charge to the visitor, subject to and in accordance with the site's terms and conditions. The information is self-contained, so can be used to uncover your meaning and then to live that meaning. All that is required is a command of the English language, willingness to become familiar with each author's individual writing style, and great courage: enough to be brutally honest with yourself. If the visitor is brutally honest, then their role within this option can be seen as that of the DIY ("do it yourself") person who can help themselves from material that is totally free of any charge.

Member Option

The *member option* includes the visitor section plus access to further information, including different newsletters, that elaborates on both the visitor section's topics and new topics. The member section will expand over time and further expose how much we have created that serves no purpose other than to hold us back and stifle the harmony that might otherwise have existed, within ourselves and amongst humankind (souls that are alive) and in the spirit world (souls not in physical form).

Members may join by paying a subscription fee, and there are several options to suit each member's subscription and payment preferences. Membership is subject to and in accordance with the site's prevailing terms and conditions.

Assisted Member Option

The *assisted member option* is available to visitors and existing members. A visitor or member becomes an assisted member by obtaining a "support subscription" for a period the visitor or member themselves determine.

The assisted member option is in addition to the visitor and member options (where applicable) and provides further information, including different newsletters. In addition, with this option, individual personal support is available, with the website's one-on-one forum the preferred method of communication for its recordkeeping and time-flexibility capabilities. The assisted member section will be extended over time to provide topics to support assisted members with uncovering their Factor-x and uncovering their own meaning.

The assisted membership is subject to and in accordance with the prevailing terms and conditions. Flexible payment options allow the visitor or member to easily determine and extend the period of assistance.

The assisted member option subscription is independent of the member subscription period. The assisted member subscription can run simultaneously with and in addition to any member subscription where applicable.

The assisted member option is personal and individual one-on-one support, and is therefore available to a limited number of people at any particular time. A booking facility exists whereby requests can be made on a first-come, first-served basis to subscribe to assisted membership.

Notes

Subscriptions do not have to be renewed and can even be cancelled. The remainder of the subscription fee is terminated immediately upon cancellation. Where a subscription was paid in advance, the remainder pro-rated portion will be credited with immediate effect. However, the member should allow up to fourteen days for the cancellation procedure to be concluded.

Should a visitor or member require a further option or options but cannot afford the subscription, they can apply for free assistance by making contact with the author via the accompanying website life canbedifferent.com. All applications for free assistance will get urgent and sincere attention and be answered within a reasonable time.

Books and eBooks

From time to time, certain material will be extracted from the website, made available in book and eBook formats, and sold on the website as well as in other popular Internet and/or brick-and-mortar bookstores.

Additional Website Authors

Over time, I'll invite Sergio Salotto to share his guidance on the accompanying website, and then you can meet him and/or his work. White Wolf has asked me whether he can also provide information on the website, so you'll definitely see his work and be exposed to his guidance. Other spirit guides in White Wolf & Co. have asked if they can also provide information on the website, so you'll also get to meet them and get exposure to their guidance.

Updates

All material contained in this book is also available at no charge on the accompanying website, lifecanbedifferent.com. No future editions of the book are planned at this time. Pending any possible future editions of the book, additions and alterations will be made on the website. Such updates can be easily identified by the date reflecting such changed material. So, for those interested in additional and altered material, please navigate to the website from time to time.

BIBLIOGRAPHY

I do not subscribe to references made in the following books and movie regarding religion and God. I merely acknowledge the roles the books and movie played in the process of uncovering myself.

Books

I'm not necessarily recommending these books, and specifically, I add that they didn't go all the way to guide me to where I am and what I wanted. Their authors go part of the way only, and in that context, I mention them here:

First was *The Road Less Traveled* by Scott M. Peck. This book gave me the softening blows. Prior to reading this book, I was stuck in my own thinking. This primer made it possible for me to consider that there might be more to what life was about than what I thought.

Another book that gave me good insight as to what might have happened to me is *The Primal Scream* by Arthur Janov. Yet, as mentioned before, the author stopped just short of taking the last few steps. Still, an excellent description of how I got onto the path I didn't really like.

Movie

I'm not necessarily recommending the following movie, and specifically, Mother Theresa seemed very much an entrenched believer and follower of God and her religion. In her view, she was convinced that she was doing God's work and working his plan. At the end of the movie, she is portrayed as saying that people will be judged for what they do for and against the poor. My view is that whatever we do should definitely not hinge on such threats, but rather what comes from our hearts. However, important points are portrayed in this movie that are related to sections in this book.

LIFE CAN BE DIFFERENT: CONCEPTION

Mother Teresa: In the Name of God's Poor (1997)

In this movie, Mother Theresa gives up everything, at one point even her own food, to assist the poorest of the poor while they lay dying. Several parts of the movie acknowledged my own path, and in particular an instance of what not to do—such as failing to take care of ourselves and giving our food away, because if we are undernourished, we won't be in a position to continue with our work. (But this is true for other situations as well, not only related to food and care of our physical selves, as seen in another section in this book, "Standing Up and Stepping Out of Mainstream Society.")

From Mother Theresa's world-known achievements, it is evident what one person can do with their life. The particular context isn't what's important here; rather, what *is* important is what one person can achieve, and, as seen in another section in this book, "Responsibility: Do We Recognize Our Responsibility?", where the groundwork for this case is laid.

Another important point is also made near the end of the movie, in a discussion between Mother Theresa and the journalist regarding her efforts as a mere treatment of the symptoms of poverty. In this scene, the journalist asks her (loosely quoted), "What about treating the cause of where the poorest of the poor come from?" This question relates to another section in this book, "Treating Symptoms and Addressing the Cause."

EXTENDED TABLE OF CONTENTS

www.ingramcontent.com/pod-product-compliance
Lightning Source LLC
Chambersburg PA
CBHW052032090426
42739CB00010B/1873